LAW AND
SOCIAL CHANGE:
Civil Rights Laws
and Their Consequences

POLICY IMPACT
AND POLITICAL CHANGE
IN AMERICA
KENNETH M. DOLBEARE, Consulting Editor

Designed as brief supplements for American Government and other undergraduate political science courses, books in this series confront crucial issues of public policy in the United States. The primary goal of the series is to demonstrate the utility of analytical concepts of political science for understanding the most pressing social and political problems of our time. Some books will be addressed to the question of how adequate present policies are to cope with current problems, and others will deal with questions of political change. Each book will be published in both soft- and cloth-cover editions.

HAYES: **POWER STRUCTURE AND URBAN POLICY: Who Rules in Oakland?**

RODGERS and BULLOCK: **LAW AND SOCIAL CHANGE: Civil Rights Laws and Their Consequences**

SHARKANSKY: **THE MALIGNED STATES: Policy Accomplishments, Problems, and Opportunities**

LAW AND SOCIAL CHANGE: Civil Rights Laws and Their Consequences

HARRELL R. RODGERS, JR.

Department of Political Science
University of Missouri–St. Louis

CHARLES S. BULLOCK, III

Department of Political Science
University of Georgia

McGraw-Hill Book Company

New York   St. Louis   San Francisco   Düsseldorf   Johannesburg
Kuala Lumpur   London   Mexico   Montreal   New Delhi   Panama
Rio de Janeiro   Singapore   Sydney   Toronto

This book was set in Press Roman by Creative Book Services,
division of McGregor & Werner, Incorporated,
and printed and bound by The Murray Printing Company.
The designer was Barbara Ellwood.
The editor was Robert P. Rainier.
Ted Agrillo supervised production.

LAW AND SOCIAL CHANGE:
Civil Rights Laws and Their Consequences

Library of Congress Catalog Card Number 72-163303

8910   MUMU   8987654321

ISBN 07-053378-4

To

Beth B., Becky B., Pat W., Jeff W., Mark T., Martin W.
in faith that their's will be a wiser and more just world.

The price of the liberation of the white people is the liberation of the blacks—the total liberation, in the cities, in the towns, before the law, and in the mind.　　　　　　　　　　　　　　　JAMES BALDWIN

If law can teach, can inculcate, can widen and deepen the citizen's humanity, then knowledge of how law works is and indispensable step in using legislation to produce better citizens. Moreover, making the knowledge of its effects available to all, instead of leaving insight into it the monopoly of a few, protects against the misuses of law.

WILLIAM K. MUIR, JR.

CONTENTS

ACKNOWLEDGMENTS

Like most books, this one has benefited from the assistance of a large number of people. The data the research is based on was frequently supplied by public officials. Congressman Robert Stephens, the late Senator Richard Russell, and Senators Walter Mondale and David Gambrell have all been especially helpful. Mr. Charles Bullock, Jr., of the U.S. Bureau of Labor Statistics provided a great deal of unpublished information and provided insightful comments on the employment chapter. Various officials of the United States Commission on Civil Rights, the Southern Regional Council, particularly Dr. Charles Rooks, the Department of Justice, the Department of Health, Education, and Welfare, and the Department of Housing and Urban Development came to our aid on more than one occasion. We thank all of these individuals and wish to make it clear that they are in no way responsible for the manner in which we have used or interpreted the information.

Professor Kenneth Dolbeare performed his job as series editor with such dedication, intensity, and skill that we were tempted to blame him for any deficiencies in the final product. Only gratitude dissuades us. Professor Ira Sharkansky and our colleague Michael Cohen read the entire manuscript and helped us beyond measure. Our colleague Robert Clute read the first and eighth chapters and contributed substantially to their improvement.

Our research assistants Jack Ethredge, Robert Neilson, and especially

James Whitford performed some of the more tedious tasks associated with the book with good humor and accuracy. To take nothing away from those mentioned above, we suspect that those who have labored hardest for us are the various typists who have transformed scribbled sheets into legible pages of type. We are sorry to report that more than one secretary found the job more than she could handle, but those who persevered were Miss Barbara Gilbert, Mrs. Teresa Epps, Mrs. Bonney Langley, and our wives Judy Rodgers and Fran Bullock, who have always been willing to rush in when departmental services or resources failed. We, to say nothing of our wives, were particularly appreciative of a grant by the Department of Political Science which allowed us to hire Mrs. Langley to type the final draft. Research and some of the writing of the text were expedited by summer research grants made to us by the Department of Political Science for the summer of 1970.

What follows is a highly value-laden book written by two native Southerners who believe that although there have been some notable successes in civil rights, basically too little has been done. We hope that by laying bare (as best we can in a short book intended for introductory students) the factors associated with successes and failures in civil rights we can stimulate in some small way progress toward the goal of racial equality.

HARRELL R. RODGERS, Jr.
CHARLES S. BULLOCK, III

CHAPTER ONE

Introduction

In 1969 Tom Clark graduated from high school—an all-black school. In the 12 years of his education he never had white classmates or a white teacher. Yet 3 years before Tom entered the first grade the United States Supreme Court ruled that enforced racial segregation in public schools is a denial of the equal protection of the laws guaranteed by the Fourteenth Admendment. Tom's case is not an isolated one. In the fall of 1969 there were 3,326 racially isolated schools in the nation. Even more distressing is the fact that in many large cities—New York, Chicago, and Philadelphia, among others—racial isolation is becoming more, not less, severe.

Eldon Tullock, a high school graduate, wanted to become a skilled worker in the construction industry, in which he could have earned close to $4.00 per hour. After three years of unsuccessfully seeking entrance into a union apprentice program, which is a prerequisite to employment, Eldon was still working as a busboy earning $1.10 per hour. In 1969 a mere 0.8 percent of the jobs in the higher-paid mechanical trades were held by blacks. The income Eldon was earning was insufficient to support himself, his wife Suzanne, and an infant daughter. The marriage ended when Eldon, humiliated by his inability to provide for the needs of his family, falsely accused Suzanne of infidelity. On this pretext Eldon moved out of his mother-in-law's apartment. Suzanne and the baby went on welfare. The police are looking for Eldon—he found a new way to make a living.

Dr. Charles Richardson is a member of the black elite in America. He is among the 2 percent of all doctors and dentists in America who are black. Dr. Richardson, a graduate of Meharry Medical School, has a successful practice despite the fact that he has substantially more charity cases than the city's white doctors have. He has property holdings and a diversified portfolio of securities. Although he is in the upper-middle-income bracket and he has an attractive home, it is located near a ghetto. Three times Dr. Richardson has sought to move into integrated neighborhoods where his children could attend biracial schools. The nicer homes in his city have, however, been unavailable to him because of his race. Three times he has had to settle for housing at the periphery of the ghetto. Invariably, within a few years of his buying a new home the surrounding area has become all black.

The vignettes above depict situations which should no longer occur. That they exist indicates some of the failings of civil rights endeavors. This is not to deny that there have been changes. During the decade of the sixties we witnessed a number of efforts to destroy racial barriers. By legislative fiat, judicial decree, and Executive order, those laws and practices were attacked which prevented blacks from voting, from attaining good jobs, good housing, and equal accommodations, and from attending integrated schools.

These topics have been matters of Federal concern for at least two decades. Voting rights and public accommodations are areas in which Federal activity has a century-long heritage. The Federal commitment to achieve racial equality was first made by the Radical Republicans during Reconstruction. Their pledge did not prove binding. By 1900 the gains made in the wake of the Civil War had been largely undone in the South. It was not until the middle of the twentieth century that Federal policy makers again became receptive to black demands.

The reemergence of Federal concern for racial equality was heralded by several decisions of the United States Supreme Court a quarter of a century ago.[1] The fifties saw increased activity by the judiciary as well as the first civil rights act passed by Congress since Federal troops were withdrawn from the South. In the two historic *Brown* v. *Board of*

Education cases,[2] Southern school boards were ordered to integrate schools "with all deliberate speed." This decree marks the beginning of contemporary Federal civil rights policy.

Since the *Brown* decision the Supreme Court has played a less important role in extending Federal protections into new areas. The Court has continued to provide much of the moral leadership and has processed literally hundreds of complaints involving discrimination. These decisions have not usually brought additional rights under the shield of Federal protection, but have been rearguard actions to enforce rights established by Congress and the executive in the face of obstructions.

In the sixties Congress and the executive branch have led the way, very gingerly, into virgin territory. New laws were enacted by Congress in response to demands that the scope of federally protected civil rights be expanded. During the decade legislation moved beyond regulating governmental behavior and sought to end some types of discrimination practiced by private citizens. As Thomas R. Dye observes:

> This was a more positive concept of civil rights. It involved not merely restrictions on government, but a positive obligation of government to act forcefully to end discrimination in public accommodations, employment, housing, and all other sectors of private life.[3]

In 1960 Congress passed a weak civil rights act designed primarily to protect the right of blacks to vote. In 1964, despite a Southern filibuster, Congress passed the most comprehensive civil rights legislation since Reconstruction. The 1964 act contained provisions designed, among other things, to help insure the right of blacks to vote, to have equal access to public accommodations (restaurants, hotels, motels, etc.), to have equal job opportunities, and to attend integrated schools, and authorized the Department of Justice to initiate and be a party to suits to protect these rights. The following year Congress passed the Voting Rights Act, which curtailed local discretion in voter registration in the Deep South. Three years later in the wake of Martin Luther King's assassination Congress ratified the Open Housing Act. This legislation built upon an earlier Executive order issued by President Kennedy barring racial discrimination in publicly owned or financed housing.

Despite these efforts, the condition of many black Americans has not improved substantially. Millions of black students are still in segregated schools. Discrimination in employment is still the rule; unemployment remains considerably higher for blacks than whites; and blacks still do four times their proportionate share of household and unskilled labor. Almost four times as many black families as white subsist in poverty; and most blacks live in segregated neighborhoods.

These disturbing facts raise a central question: Why have governmental efforts not been more successful? Why, for example, did it take 10 years after the *Brown* decision before 2.5 percent of black children in the Deep South attended previously all-white schools? A number of answers might initially be suggested. Federal efforts may have been too meager, or Federal priorities may have lain in other areas. Or, noncompliance and disregard for law may be responsible for thwarting good intentions. But these answers only raise new questions, which are among those we seek to answer. Why have Federal efforts not been stronger? Why has success been given a higher priority in some areas of civil rights than in others? Why has noncompliance with the law been usually high?

The purpose of this book, then, is not simply to recount the actions taken by the Federal government to end racial discrimination. Granted, we do detail the provisions of various laws, court interpretations, and Executive orders. Our goal, however, is something more than description. We use governmental edicts as a standard against which to measure movement in the direction of desegregation and equal opportunity. We attempt to delineate the effects of particular laws on the realization of specific policy goals (e.g., integrated schools), and we also attempt to determine what factors produce these effects. The actions the government takes to achieve racial equality may be thought of as policy outputs. The effect, or result, of policy outputs can be thought of as political outcomes. Our central purpose, then, is to compare the degree to which political outcomes have approximated policy outputs and to analyze why goals have or have not been achieved.[4]

This analysis will lead to an examination of three central questions.

1. How much change has occurred in five policy areas?
2. What factors account for change or its absence?
3. What are the consequences of change or the absence thereof?

In attempting to identify the factors which account for change in each policy area, we shall analyze such potential factors as the commitment of various branches of the Federal government to racial equality, the strengths and weaknesses of specific civil rights laws and court decisions, the enforcement efforts of government agencies, and public acceptance and compliance with civil rights laws. The presentation will not always be balanced because of differences in the amount of progress achieved, in the availability of data, and in the standards used to measure progress in the various areas of civil rights. Where little change has taken place, emphasis will be centered on why the law has been ineffectual.

The next five chapters are arranged so that we move from matters in which political outcomes most closely parallel outputs, to those areas in which the gap between the law and reality is greatest. Chapters Two and Three deal with those two areas, political rights and public accommodations, in which change appears to be the most substantial. Chapters Four and Five focus on areas in which progress has usually been in the form of tokenism. School desegregation and equal employment fall into this category. In Chapter Six we look at open housing, a goal for which achievements are so sparse that even a minimal level of tokenism has yet to be attained.

After comparing the responses to public policy with the policy itself in chapters Two through Six, Chapter Seven will be devoted to explaining why the Federal government has been inconsistent in exerting pressure for equality in the five goal areas. For example, an attempt will be made to explain why freedom of choice has been tolerated in some areas but not in others. We shall also consider why potent Federal enforcement agencies have been created to oversee compliance in some areas but not in others. Chapter Eight ties together our findings and a number of suppositions about the role and success of law in affecting political outcomes and suggests a theory for understanding legal compliance. The final chapter, Chapter Nine, reflects on the broader implications of Federal activities in civil rights, in terms of the progress achieved and the lack thereof, for maintaining public support[5] and stability in the American political system.

CIVIL RIGHTS CHANGE IN THE SOUTH

As an aid to reading the following chapters we suggest a simple scheme for characterizing change in civil rights in the South. This scheme shows six basic stages (outlined in Table 1-1) suggesting that progress against overt resistance in civil rights during the sixties often followed a predictable pattern. Briefly, the pattern has been for blacks to initially assail the inequities of the system through various kinds of nonviolent protests. These have been met by a white backlash, in response to which the Federal government has taken a few tentative steps to bring about equality. Federal intervention has produced little more than token change because commitment has been insufficient to prevent circumvention by noncompliant whites. When the initial Federal law has failed to satisfy demands for change, continued protest has often led to even more rigorously drawn statutes and court orders until some progress is made in securing black rights. In other words, we note a process of mounting demands extracting incremental changes. Early government actions have often been largely symbolic, with actual changes coming only after subsequent judicial or legislative action. We shall now spell out each phase of the transition in some detail.

Civil rights protest, nationwide and in innumerable towns and cities, began contemporaneously with indigenous challenges to the white-controlled status quo. While the later protests have enjoyed at least the tacit support of Federal policy, early ones had at best the support of the Supreme Court, often vaguely defined. Relying upon such slender reeds, outraged citizens, black and white, confronted laws, folkways, and the very culture of the South. Typically the initial civil rights protests in a community have been nonviolent. Marches and demonstrations to awaken citizens of both races to the injustices of the system, accompanied by rallies to inspire a will to resist degradation and to persevere for change, have signaled that racism was to be under siege.

TABLE 1-1   Stages of civil rights change

Stage	Characteristics
1	Nonviolent confrontations challenging apartheid rules
2	Violent white backlash
3	Initiation of protective Federal policy resulting in tokenism
4	Efforts by state and local policy makers in the South to avoid Federal directives
5	Increasingly explicit Federal standards and raised level of enforcement
6	More equal treatment achieved by blacks

Economic boycotts have been another form of peaceful resistance to discrimination.

It is noteworthy that while nationwide black protest has escalated beyond Martin Luther King's exhortations of nonviolence, on the local scene initial challenges to discrimination continue to be peaceful. During 1970 blacks who for the first time were emboldened to present their grievances used the time-tested rallies and marches to publicize their complaints.[6]

Just as blacks inaugurate protests today using the same strategies as in the fifties, so too is white reaction often the same in communities newly experiencing racial tension. Time and again initial black protests have been met by unyielding whites who have acted forcefully to forestall black attempts at equality.[7] By the 1950s, however, Southern transgressions were no longer ignored by national leaders. The omnipresent eye of the television news camera did much to jar national awareness. Northern opinion leaders in the past, while deploring fire and faggot as a particularly unsavory Southern folk custom, had remained aloof. In the fifties and sixties scenes of fellow humans being beaten by police and mauled by dogs prompted religious leaders, labor union officials, and politicians to demand a Federal response to Southern lawlessness.

With substantial support and pressure outside of the South, Congress and the courts took at least symbolic steps[8] to combat discrimination. Early Federal involvement produced changes in voting, public accommodations, and de jure school desegregation in the Border states and in sections of the South having few blacks.

In much of the South, however, progress was curtailed severely because of the near universality with which state, local, and even a few Federal officials have circumvented Federal directives. Obstinacy usually triumphed over loosely drawn Federal laws and court orders. The paramount example of the futility of the vague early edicts must be the "with all deliberate speed" standard for implementing court-ordered school desegregation. Instead of acceding to Federal orders, voting registrars, school boards, and private citizens throughout the Black Belt dug in their heels, unfurled the Confederate battle flag, and screamed "Never!" Policy makers from governors on down devoted their energies to concocting strategies with which to avoid compliance instead of seeking to calm and reassure a troubled citizenry. Techniques of discrimination were refined as criteria less blatant than race were introduced to foil Federal efforts. The ingenuity of the Deep South in carrying out its opposition so muted early civil rights decisions that integration was confined to scattered instances of tokenism.

The commitment of Federal authorities to insure equality has developed with the kind of hesitancy that is a sign of an ambivalent attitude. Years elapsed as timid attempts were made to get Southerners to show that deep down inside they wanted to do the right thing for blacks. During this time all too many Southerners demonstrated what they felt deep down inside as paternalism turned to viciousness. As protests mounted in the face of Southern obstinacy, Federal intervention gradually increased and the leeway available in interpreting Federal edicts was minimized.

Increasingly detailed statutes and court decisions in several areas have made explicit which practices will no longer be tolerated. The unwillingness of Southern policy makers to abstract the intent of individual court decisions and apply the meaning of the law to their own situations has resulted in a transfer of the situs of some civil rights battles from courtrooms to administrative offices. The transfer has expedited implementation of integration as the slow, costly case-by-case attack has been replaced by broad legislative standards capable of being administratively applied throughout the nation with a minimum of delay and expense. Federal agencies responsible for overseeing racial practices in some aspects of civil rights have been created.

While most sections of even the Deep South have experienced some reduction of discrimination, there remain enclaves in which the most overt kinds of racism persist. There are areas, generally rural, in which blacks encounter difficulties when trying to register to vote, in which they are denied any but menial jobs as a matter of course, and in which they are shunned everywhere, from barbershops to doctors' offices. In communities like these, blacks often have not yet challenged the restraints about them. When they do become restive, they may follow much the same process as that mapped above.

CHANGE IN CIVIL RIGHTS OUTSIDE THE SOUTH

In the North civil rights protests have been directed against a narrower range of inequities than in the South. Outside Southern and some

Border states, denials of the suffrage and access to public accommodations have been rare. Consequently, civil rights efforts in the North have been primarily directed against discrimination in employment and housing, de facto school segregation, and a matter not dealt with in this book, police treatment.

In the North as in the South, the initial actions in a community have often been sparked by religious and civil rights leaders. Early strategy has usually called for peaceful marches, sit-ins, and so on. Depending upon the locale or the antagonist, the response to peaceful protests may vary from indifference to verbal as well as physical attacks. To threaten the insularity of low-income whites' schools or communities or the security of their jobs often provokes violent reactions, North or South. Challenges to Northern white landlords or employers may be either ignored or responded to by public officials if a law has been violated.

While Southern protests have typically been intended to prod some agency of the Federal government into becoming an ally of the blacks, elsewhere protests may seek to provoke the involvement of state or local officials in addition to, or in place of Federal officials. Involvement of public officials may prove useful in arriving at compromises even in the face of hostility from certain groups within a Northern city, such as hyphenated Americans who oppose black efforts on behalf of fair housing laws. Whether it is because blacks can obtain some degree of satisfaction from state or local elites, or whether it is because of a decision to dispatch the available Federal manpower and money to the South, protests in the North (short of riots) have been less likely to produce Federal intervention.

While Northern blacks have been more successful than their Southern brothers in eliciting some positive local or state response, real change has often remained elusive. Grievances have often been smothered by referral to blue ribbon committees. In other instances forthright commitments have been given to remedy conditions which remain uncorrected years later, changes inaugurated have proved insufficient to satisfy rising black demands and expectations, and instead have fed greater discontent.[9]

Black protests in the North differ from Southern ones in that their grievances have different foci. In the South the evils are often more blatant, consisting of overt refusals, often bulwarked by law, to give equal treatment to blacks. Discrimination in the North has been more refined, less overt, and consequently more difficult to dislodge. Culprits here have less often been easily identifiable as racist and instead have been actors, public and private, who have applied nonracist criteria to achieve segregation.

With the earlier statutes and court orders being directed against Southern style discrimination, especially abridgment of the suffrage and de jure segregation, inequities in the North continued untouched for several years. Discrimination in the North came under attack only with the second wave of civil rights laws, those beginning in 1964. De facto segregation in Northern schools was not prosecuted by the Department of Justice until 1968 and is presently tolerated by the Nixon administration. Tools with which to combat discrimination in employment and housing are still being forged, and according to a recent Federal report, are deficient.[10]

Also, the goals which have eluded Northern blacks may be ones on which there is less widespread agreement a right that exists. Thus more people would probably support an attempt to punish those who interfere with the suffrage than would favor punishing a landlord who refused to rent his property to a black family. For these and other reasons, the aspects of discrimination which have come under fire in the North have been pursued less diligently than have some of the practices tackled in the South.

TYPES OF DISCRIMINATION

As previously alluded to, discriminatory techniques have been refined to keep pace with innovations designed to facilitate integration. Since discrimination in various guises will be an almost constant accompaniment to our discussion, we shall briefly delineate four major types.

The easiest discrimination to challenge has been differential treatment authorized by law or by public officials. State or local statutes requiring blacks to attend segregated schools or prohibiting integrated seating in restaurants illustrate state-imposed discrimination. Bigotry that is sanctioned by law or by agents of the state constitutes state action that has long been held violative of the equal protection clause of the Fourteenth Amendment. This, one of the world's great monuments to human rights and dignity, forbids a state to "deny to any person within its jurisdiction the equal protection of the laws." This constitutional peg has supported numerous attempts to equalize voting and education opportunities and access to public-owned facilities.

The equal protection clause has also been of service in rooting out discrimination accomplished through arbitrary behavior by public officials. The gap caused by overturning laws requiring discrimination has often been plugged by public servants who continue to use racial criteria in performing their duties. The best examples of this second type of discrimination are drawn from the voting rights struggle. Until recently local election boards had virtually unlimited discretion in judging the competency of prospective voters. Literally hundreds of thousands of blacks have been kept from voting by arbitrary enforcement of the preconditions of voting, as is discussed in detail in Chapter Two. Unequal application of literacy and good character tests, which on their face are color blind, has been held incompatible with the equal protection clause.

The third type of discrimination is that practiced by private citizens. Discrimination by public officials, while constituting the bulk of the problem in voting rights and education, was of only marginal concern in some other aspects of civil rights. So long as private citizens were permitted to discriminate in employment, housing, and in extending public accommodations, black Americans did not enjoy equal treatment. Private discrimination remained immune to Federal law after unequal treatment in the public realm had come under attack. Progressively, however, the leeway in which a person can indulge his personal bigotries has been limited. Specifically, to eliminate such private discrimination Federal laws have been promulgated forbidding the use of race as a criterion in employment, real estate transactions, or public accommodations. Complaint processing offices were established in each area, and separate enforcement agencies have been created to police employment practices.

The last category of discrimination is comprised of intimidation in the variety of hideous forms it assumes. While the first three types of discrimination were carried out within the framework of laws, albeit a form of law sometimes distorted almost beyond recognition, not even the perpetrators of intimidation were so callous as to maintain the legality of their behavior. Those who have burned crosses, set dynamite charges, beaten and shot civil rights workers, or threatened others with bodily harm have justified their actions to themselves, but not within the context of acceptable political behavior. Klansmen and others of their ilk defend their free use of violence as essential to protect their way of life.

When the practitioners of violence are public officials, such as law enforcement officers who beat black prisoners in their custody, they have sometimes been punished either for denying the plaintiffs their rights without due process of law or for interfering with their civil rights. If the intimidators are private citizens they can be made to answer for their acts on a charge alleging interference with the plaintiff's civil rights or less frequently on a state-prosecuted criminal charge. While state remedies have been available to blacks subjected to intimidation, they have rarely found satisfaction at that level. Typically perpetrators of violence have been punished by Federal courts applying Federal law on charges carrying lesser penalties.

In addition to physical intimidation, economic coercion constitutes another variety of intimidation. Blacks daring to seek to vote or to enroll their children in white schools have had the white sources of capital cut off in some rural towns: loans have been called in, tenancy contracts have not been renewed, and credit has been terminated. Restive blacks have been driven from their homes and forced to migrate to the already overcrowded cities. The Supreme Court has held economic intimidation to be unconstitutional.[11]

Remedies now exist for all four types of discrimination. It is the evaluation of the effectiveness of these corrective measures which constitutes the bulk of this book.

NOTES

1. During the forties the Supreme Court outlawed the white primary, the last major obstacle to black political participation which had been incorporated into the laws of most Southern states. Smith v. Allwright, 321 U.S. 649 (1944). The Supreme Court also declared unconstitutional the inclusion of restrictive covenants in sales contracts—Shelley v Kraemer, 334 U.S. 1 (1944)—and some types of segregation in institutions of higher education.
2. Brown v. Board of Education, 347 U.S. 483 (1954); Brown v. Board of Education, 349 U.S. 294 (1955).
3. Thomas R. Dye, ed., American Public Policy, Columbus, Ohio: Merrill, 1969, p. 47.
4. See Austin Ranney, "The Study of Policy Content: A Framework for Choice," in Ranney, ed., Political Science and Public Policy, Chicago: Markham, 1968, pp. 6-9.

5. Supports are attitudes and behavior that buttress the political system and add to its stability. There are two types of support, specific and diffuse. Specific support is generated by the gratification of specific individual demands, such as when wanted goods and services are provided. Diffuse support is a reservoir of good will that an individual has toward a political system. Diffuse support enables the political system to survive during periods when outputs do not satisfy demands. See David Easton, *A Systems Analysis of Political Life,* New York: Knopf, 1965.

6. For a discussion of the use of protest in attempting to mobilize support and effect policy change, see Michael Lipsky, "Protest as a Political Resource," *American Political Science Review,* 62, December 1968, pp. 1144-1158.

7. The violent reaction of some whites to integration can be explained but not excused. To some, defense of the institution of segregation becomes a holy war. In the South many resisted integration because to give in would betray one's ancestors who had died fighting for the lost cause of the Confederacy. In addition to the Scarlett O'Hara fantasies there are guilt pangs. Also, fears of black rule that are traceable to the Reconstruction era's "black and tan" legislatures, and the memory of slave revolts led whites to believe that segregation must be preserved.

   The lower-class white (often called redneck) has traditionally been the staunchest opponent of black equality. See Albert D. Kirwan, *Revolt of the Rednecks,* New York: Harper Torchbooks, 1961. We shall not attempt to determine conclusively why the lower class has been the most prejudiced but shall mention several often-suggested reasons. Status anxiety may account for many of the apprehensions of poor whites. The desire not to be at the bottom of the social scale is universal. As long as blacks were kept segregated, the poorest, most shiftless whites had a group whom they could deprecate. Moreover, blacks constituted a gioup whom all society would readily recognize as being inferior to any white. Among the more sophisticated there may even be a recognition that equal treatment of blacks would lead to competition for jobs. It has also been suggested that racial antipathies have been promoted by the upper class as part of a divide and conquer strategy. By perpetuating the hobgoblin of racism, the likelihood of an alliance of the poor of both races was attenuated. Sowing racial fears and hatreds has reduced the likelihood of challenges to the political as well as the economic elite.

8. An excellent treatise on the role of symbols in the political sphere is Murray Edelman, *The Symbolic Uses of Politics,* Urbana: University of Illinois, 1967.

9. Harold L. Wolman and Norman C. Thomas, "Black Interests, Black Groups, and Black Influence in the Federal Policy Process: The Cases of Housing and Education," *Journal of Politics,* 32, November 1970, pp. 895-896.

10. U.S. Commission on Civil Rights, *Federal Civil Rights Enforcement Effort,* Washington: GPO, 1970.

11. U.S. Commission on Civil Rights, *Voting, 1961,* Washington: GPO, 1961, pp. 36-37.

CHAPTER TWO

Voting:

Perseverance Pays Off

An item of great importance in modern political life is the right to choose one's rulers via the ballot. While the requirements for voting in the United States have varied during its existence, a basic premise upon which our government rests is that all who meet the criteria are entitled—indeed have a duty as citizens—to use the franchise. The assumption has been that through the ballot the tyrant can be checked, the scoundrel can be barred from public life, and the will of the public can be enacted into law. Conscientious officeholders are expected to legislate in response to the policy demands of the majority. While modern empirical research has raised some questions about the accuracy of these assumptions, they remain important myths of democracy.[1]

This model which sees decision makers as delegates functioning on behalf of their constituents helps account for the vigor with which many have assailed abridgments of the suffrage. The belief was that once blacks could vote freely, discrimination in other aspects of life would disappear as competing politicians courted their votes. As expressed by a former United States Attorney General:

> The right to vote ... occupies a key position because it provides a means of protecting other rights. When minority groups exercise their franchise more effectively, it almost invariably follows that they achieve a greater measure of other fundamental freedoms.[2]

In his valedictory former Voter Education Project Director Vernon E. Jordan concluded that "[b]lack political power . . . will be 'our most effective weapon.' "[3]

Another aspect of the franchise which has made it the foremost goal of civil rights is its symbolic value. Even in countries such as the Soviet Union in which the ballot is a useless frill according to our standards, pains are taken to assure a large turnout. In our country the right to vote is the only aspect of political maturity accompanying legal coming of age. For many whites, registration is something one does without much thought upon reaching the prescribed age. For Southern blacks it has often been attempted only after extensive mental preparation for the indignities and even physical beatings which this political interest may evoke from whites. Consequently, while 49 percent of the South's whites registered within a year after coming of age, only 5 percent of the blacks took the step this soon. The significance of registration for blacks is further pointed up by the following comparison. A third of all registered blacks, contrasted with 13 percent of the whites, saw in the registration act a symbol of becoming a man and acquiring a new mantle of dignity.[4] In a culture in which a black's name was "boy" until his hair turned gray, whereupon he became "uncle," the right to vote has become a symbol of equality and dignity. As Stokely Carmichael has written, the vote "gives one a sense of being. . . . The black person begins to live. He begins to create his own existence when he [refuses to bow] to someone who contains him."[5]

It is not entirely surprising that the suffrage, with its symbolic significance and assumed potential for power, has been extended grudgingly. Whites have accepted, as have the blacks, the thesis that black suffrage will lead to changes in policy outputs, social structure, and in the self-perceptions and attitudes of blacks. And even though no state is now predominately black—although scores of counties are— many Southern whites, haunted by stories of the rule of blacks and carpetbaggers during Reconstruction, have a phobia about political dominance by blacks. Many have feared that large-scale black voting would cause the dissolution of the hallowed Southern way of life. W. J. Cash goes so far as to see in this fear of black political dominance the white bugaboo of miscegenation, and abhorrence for sexual relations between black males and white females.[6]

In this chapter we shall discuss techniques of disfranchisement and the extent to which such practices have been corrected by Federal policy. After showing the increase in black registration in the South, we shall consider the effects of additional black voters in terms of candidate selection and policy outputs. We shall also speculate on what factors seem to explain increased registration.

DISFRANCHISEMENT

The right to vote without regard to race, creed, color, or previous condition of servitude supposedly became law in 1870 with ratification of the Fifteenth Amendment. Instead of ending the struggle, it merely signaled a high-water mark of black political participation. The Federal edict, backed by Federal troops, was honored. Former slaves voted and sought public office, being elected to the gamut of posts from local official to United States senator. Even following the troop withdrawal, blacks continued to vote in large numbers, playing roles in the politics of Southern states. As late as 1890 (14 years after Reconstruction), there were 71,000 more black voters than white voters registered in Mississippi. Blacks sat in several Southern state legislatures until the 1890s. A North Carolina district continued to send a black congressman to Washington until 1901.[7]

It was during the 1890s and early 1900s that Southern and Border states eroded the guarantees of the Fifteenth Amendment. Black disfranchisement was an outgrowth of the Populist movement. The Populist challenge constituted the single interlude between Reconstruction and Barry Goldwater's candidacy when anything approaching bipartisan competition existed in the South. Competition raised the possibility that blacks through bloc voting would exercise the balance of power. To forestall this possibility a number of laws were passed disfranchising black voters. The effectiveness of the Jim Crow laws in creating a white electorate was almost flawless. For example, in Louisiana there were 130,334 registered black voters in 1896; eight years later only 1,342 remained on the rolls.[8] Civil rights efforts of the last two decades have in part been directed at undoing these statutes.

The techniques used to abridge black voting rights have been diverse. Of the four types of discrimination outlined in Chapter One, all except private discrimination have been used. Except for some comments about the white primary and the poll tax, we shall, however, be primarily concerned with arbitrary practices by voting registrars, and intimidation.

By the time the current era of civil rights legislation began, most state statutes barring blacks from voting had been found unconstitutional. Laws giving preference to illiterate whites[9] and banning blacks from the Democratic primaries had been overturned. The white primary laws limited participants in the Democratic primary to whites under the rationale that a political party, like a fraternity, is a private organization and therefore can restrict its membership for arbitrary reasons. After a 24-year legal battle, the Supreme Court, noting that in the one-party South primaries were the only meaningful elections, ruled that participation in them could not be made a contingency of race.[10]

Except in some cities, however, elimination of the white primary did not result in widespread black political participation. By 1947, three years after the white primary was outlawed, only 600,000 of the 5,000,000 voting age blacks in the South were registered voters. Several reasons were behind the continued low levels of black registration and voting. Part of the explanation lay in the political culture of the South where voting even by whites has consistently been lower than elsewhere in the nation. The lapse of time before any newly franchised group acquires norms supporting voting must also be considered. However, an item of far more consequence in keeping black participation low was the granite-like resistance of the whites.

The white community still had two very potent weapons at its disposal. The first was crude intimidation. The second lay in the arbitrary powers of county voter registrars to apply the registration requirements so that few, if any, blacks could get their names in the voting books. Let us first consider techniques of intimidation.

Intimidation

The white South has often used whatever force was necessary to keep blacks "in their place." One place in which blacks were to be kept was far from the ballot box. Stratagems to accomplish this end have frequently been of the crudest sort.

Traditionally the threat of physical harm has been the standby. In past decades blacks who demonstrated an interest in politics might be treated to a nocturnal visit by the Ku Klux Klan. With no attempt at subtlety, these vigilantes made clear that political activity would lead to beatings or worse. Although Federal laws prohibiting the intimidation of voters had been on the books since Reconstruction, they stood as lifeless as the statues of Confederate soldiers found in every Southern county seat.

In recent years fear of a visit by the Klan has not prevented some blacks from attempting to register. This heightened black political activity has resulted in the unleashing of repressive forces by the white community. Sometimes there has been harassment by local police: for example, civil rights activists have been subjected to what the Justice Department calls "baseless arrests." These misdemeanor arrests include disturbing the peace, minor traffic violations, trespass, obstructing the sidewalk, and using abusive language.[11]

For civil rights workers an arrest, even on the most trivial charge, could be a dangerous, costly experience. Conditions of incarceration might verge on the medieval. For example, in St. Augustine, Florida, civil rights demonstrators of both sexes were locked in an outdoor bullpen, exposed to the rain and humid, 90-degree heat.[12] In the privacy of the police station the defendant might be beaten by either the police or cellmates. While awaiting trial he might be unable to gain release because of excessive bail. Once brought to trial he would probably be convicted and given the maximum sentence or fine.[13]

Within the community, harassment might consist of shooting into, or firebombing buildings used by the Movement. Police, possibly nothing more than deputized Klansmen, might lurk outside of voter education project quarters and skulk along behind canvassers going door to door in search of prospective voters. Such police presence should not be construed as protective; rather, it has been intended to remind blacks of the displeasure with which "the man" has viewed such activities. Frightened blacks have been made aware that Big Brother is watching and may strike with a vengeance some moonless night.

At its most vicious, intimidation has taken the form of murder. Archetypical of this sort of violence has been the shot in the night to eliminate a Movement leader. The front porch assassination of Mississippi NAACP official Medgar Evers is a case in point. The most macabre example is of course the abduction, torture, and murder of three youths near Philadelphia, Mississippi, during Freedom Summer.

An example of physical intimidation, surprising even in the South for its openness, involved the registrar of Walthall County, Mississippi. A young civil rights worker accompanied two local residents who were seeking to register. The registrar drove them from his office, striking the leader on the head with a pistol butt. After stopping the bleeding, the assaulted youth reported the incident to the sheriff, who responded by arresting the victim for disturbing the peace.[14]

Little protection from either physical abuse or arrest has been afforded by early civil rights laws. One difficulty has been in proving the arrests to be baseless. If a person trying to register were to be arrested for a minor violation, it might be impossible for him to show that his arrest constituted a denial of equal protection. Without such a showing, there would be little likelihood that a higher court would free him. Moreover, even if the harassment were to be enjoined or the conviction overturned, those seeking to vote might remain un-registered.[15] Also, as punishment for bringing suit, the black plaintiff might be driven from the community.

A second aspect of intimidation has evolved from the economic dependence of most rural blacks on whites for jobs and loans. White store owners may refuse to sell to blacks, white bankers may turn down loan requests, and white landlords may evict offending tenants from their property. Even such a relatively well-off group as teachers are dependent for their livelihood on contracts let by white school boards.[16] To insure that whites are aware of the identity of the "uppity" blacks, the names of voting applicants have been printed in newspapers. If the threat of publicity did not dissuade blacks who were considering registration, whites in some towns have treated them like lepers, severing all commercial ties with them, even to the extent of refusing to gin their cotton. Unable to survive independently of the white community, blacks have frequently been forced to leave.[17]

Legal challenges to economic coercion have a mixed record of success. As with physical intimidation, court victories in this realm do not guarantee that the black man who was wronged will be registered. Nonetheless, there is some evidence that economic intimidation can be stemmed and registration achieved. Probably the clearest demonstration of a cause and effect relationship between successful Federal prosecution of white businessmen for economic coercion and increased black registration, occurred in two Tennessee counties. In 1960 Fayette and Haywood were the only predominately black counties in the state. No blacks were registered to vote in the latter and only 58 in the former. A registration drive added 325 blacks to the voting lists in Fayette County and 300 in Haywood. Local bankers and merchants refused loans or credit to the new registrants and landowners ordered tenants who had become voters to leave when the crops were in.[18] Department of Justice prosecution of local merchants and bankers ended these practices, thereby facilitating black registration. The fruit of the registration drive ripened in 1966 when seven blacks won local office in Fayette and two were elected in Haywood.[19]

Discrimination in Registration

The other major obstacle confronting potential black voters loomed before them as they completed the formal registration process. In the South registration of blacks has been carried out much like an initiation into a letterman's club, complete with hazing and a number of trivial tasks to be completed by the applicant. Completion of the requisite procedures, without assistance or advice from the registrar and in the face of open hostility on the part of the ruling whites, was often a formidable task.

There were four hurdles in registration which were manipulated so that virtually all whites cleared them, while most blacks were tripped up. The procedures—and these varied from state to state—found most useful by racist registrars were the requirements of literacy, ability to understand and interpret the Constitution, and good character. The processing of applicants was yet another point at which the blacks' quest for the ballot could be diverted.

From the multitude of available instances of discrimination, a few have been chosen as illustrative of the double standard used. Six blacks with doctorates were ruled illiterate in Alabama and five black teachers, three of whom has master's degrees, were judged too illiterate in a Mississippi city in which no whites ever failed the examination.[20] A white Mississippian was assigned the following section of the state constitution to interpret: "There shall be no imprisonment for debt." The following response was accepted as adequate, "I thank that a Neorger should have 2 years in collage befor voting because he don't under stand [sic]."[21] In Louisiana whites are often asked to interpret the following section of the state constitution: "No law shall be passed to curtail or restrain the liberty of speech or of the press." Among the white responses judged acceptable were, "I agree" and "Spoken in Right, Public."[22] Illiterate whites in some counties have been registered without even filling out the required application, while blacks have been rejected for the most trivial errors.[23] Elsewhere, uneducated whites have regularly been helped by registrars to complete the necessary forms; equally bewildered blacks have received no assistance. Registrars have also discriminated in the selection of constitutional passages which the aspiring voter must interpret. Mississippi whites have often been given the following sections to interpret:

> Section 8: All persons, resident in this state, citizens of the United States, are hereby declared citizens of the state of Mississippi.
> Section 240: All elections by the people shall be by ballot.[24]

Blacks have been confronted with sections such as the one below:

> Section 182: The power to tax corporations and their property shall never be surrendered or abridged by any contract or grant to which the state or any political subdivision thereof may be a party, except that the legislature may grant exemption from taxation in the encouragement of manufacturers and other new enterprises of public utility extending for a period of not exceeding five years, the time of such exemptions to commence from date of charter, if to a corporation; and if to an individual enterprise, then from the commencement of work; but when the legislature grants such exemptions for a period of five years or less, it shall be done by general laws, which shall distinctly enumerate the classes of manufactures and other new enterprises of public utility entitled to such exemptions, and shall prescribe the mode and manner in which the right to such exemptions shall be determined.[25]

The good character requirement was interpreted to require that a prospective voter present character vouchers signed by several registered voters. In a county in which no blacks were registered, it was often impossible to find whites who would vouch for a black. If there were some black voters, they were often limited in the number of prospective voters for whom they could vouch in one year.[26] Louisiana redefined its good character requirement to exclude anyone who participated in sit-ins or other civil rights demonstrations.[27]

In addition to the officially prescribed prerequisites to voting, there were other tactics available to registrars to impede black voting. The simplest of these was outright refusal to even permit blacks to register. Or, a registrar might—under Federal pressure—begin to register blacks but move at a snail's pace. An extreme example is a Mississippi registration office which has been able to handle 100 whites a day but found itself so overwhelmed by 700 blacks applying during a three-week period that the registration books were closed.[28]

Yet another pitfall in the application process has been the stringent review of the trivia involved in the process. For example, registrants were turned away in Louisiana for errors such as underlining instead of circling "Mr." on the registration card. Other blacks failed the test for not accurately computing their age to the exact year, month, and day.[29]

Even after letter-perfect completion of the forms, oaths, etc., requisite to registration, blacks encountered further unresponsiveness in the system. They might not be notified as to whether they had succeeded in running the gauntlet. If the registrar decided the applicant had failed, the latter was not permitted to see his application in order to learn the nature of his errors.

PROTECTING THE RIGHT TO VOTE

The first step toward limiting registrars' discretion is found in the Civil Rights Act of 1957. The Department of Justice was authorized to seek injunctive relief when blacks had been denied the vote for racial reasons. A prospective voter could turn to the Attorney General's office and seek a hearing in the Federal district court even if all of the state administrative remedies had not been pursued.[30] Violators of injunctions handed down under this act could be tried without juries at the option of the Federal judge.

While the terms of the 1957 act suggest much that could be done to facilitate black registration, results of the new law were disappointing. Between 1957 and 1960 only three cases were filed pursuant to its provisions, and they moved with glacial speed.[31] A partial explanation must be the minimal manpower commitments made for enforcement of the new law. Only one additional attorney was provided for by Title II of the act.

Nonetheless the terms of this law marked a new tack in civil rights protection and set a course to be followed in the future. Of its noteworthy elements, the first was the involvement of the Department of Justice as a protector of the blacks. Federal involvement could give courage to blacks, as well as pay for the expensive legal proceedings. A second feature was the provision of a remedy in the Federal court before the Gordian knot of state legal requirements was unraveled. This was the first of many Federal attempts to circumvent the dilatory tactics of Southern officials.

Another provision aimed at limiting local influence was the authorization of nonjury trials for people accused of practicing discrimination after being ordered to stop. This provision recognized that too many Southerners see nothing wrong in violating the law if doing so promotes segregation. In many counties it might have been impossible to find a dozen jurors who would convict officials of violating civil rights law. It was anticipated that Federal judges would be more willing to place law above personal preference.[32] Subsequent acts have been increasingly precise in specifying what constitutes discriminatory behavior. A second trend has been to provide alternative channels through which prospective voters could register. Keeping the patterns followed in Federal legislation in mind, we will now discuss the civil rights acts of the 1960s in some detail.

The first of these was the Civil Rights Act of 1960, designed to expedite voter registration. It provided that Federal judges or special referees could be authorized to register qualified blacks who had been turned down by local officials. Once a judge found a pattern or practice of discrimination, applicants were no longer at the mercy of racist registrars.

A second purpose of the Civil Rights Act of 1960 was to guarantee Federal prosecutors access to voting records. Examination of registration statistics provided essential data for the Department of Justice in prosecuting those accused of abridging voting rights. The 1960 law required preservation of voting statistics for 22 months after each election and made them available to the Attorney General.

As was noted about the 1957 act, the 1960 statute was slow in producing results. Between 1960 and 1962 the number of registered blacks in the South rose by only 17,000. (See Table 2-1.) In the first 16 months after enactment of the 1960 law the voter referee provision had yet to be used and there had been only one finding of a pattern or practice of discrimination.[33] Pursuant to the 1957 and 1960 statutes, by 1963 the Department of Justice had filed suits against 48 counties and the entire state of Mississippi.[34] Yet these efforts left untouched many Southern counties in which discrimination was equally pervasive. In 100 counties cited as denying the ballot to blacks in 1961, only 8.3 percent of the voting age blacks were registered two years later—and this in the wake of several registration drives and 36 suits filed by the Department of Justice.[35] In 1963 the Commission on Civil Rights observed:

An examination of the 100 counties where denials of voting rights were indicated in the *1961 Voting Report* compels the conclusion that racial discrimination persists and the policy of the Civil Rights Acts has been frustrated.[36]

While the general stagnation in black registration between 1960 and 1962 might have warranted an extension of the Commission's conclusion to much of the South, black registration grew rapidly during the next biennium. In 1964 there were some 683,000 more black

TABLE 2-1   *Voting age black southerners registered, 1940-1970*

Year	Number (in millions)	%	Average annual increase (%)
1970	.25	5	—
1947	.60	12	1.0
1956	1.24	25	1.4
1958	1.27	25	0.0
1960	1.46	29	2.0
1962	1.48	29	0.0
1964	2.16	43	7.0
1966	2.69	54	5.5
1968	3.11	62	4.0
1970	3.32	66	2.0

Sources: Donald R. Matthews and James W. Prothro, *Negroes and the New Southern Politics,* New York: Harcourt, Brace & World, 1966, p. 18; *V. E. P. News,* 4, January/February 1970, p. 3; "Voter Registration in Southern States," *Congressional Quarterly,* 28, December 11, 1970, p. 2952.
Note: For 1960, 1964, and 1966 figures in Matthews and Prothro are lower than those reported by the Voter Education Project, being 1.41 million in 1960, 1.91 million in 1964, and 2.31 million in 1966.

registrants than there had been in 1962. We cannot determine conclusively the cause for this 46 percent increase in black registrations but
there are several possible factors. It may be that new registrations
resulted from greater use of the provisions of the two civil rights acts.
This could have come about if activity by Department of Justice
attorneys convinced some registrars that the cost of noncompliance was
too high, thereby eroding their resistance. Or, the attention directed to
black registration by registration drives, Federal efforts, news coverage,
etc., may have prompted more blacks to attempt registration in areas
where discrimination was not practiced. Another possibility is that
registration increases reflect the heightened saliency of the 1964
presidential election, caused by the Republican nomination of a
candidate whose election was often perceived as detrimental to the civil
rights movement.[37]

Increased registration may also, in part, be attributable to the
passage of another civil rights law in 1964. Title I of this act specifically
forbade rejection of applicants for immaterial errors or omissions. It
provided that anyone with a sixth grade education was presumed
literate, thereby shifting the burden of proof to the state to prove
illiteracy rather than having the applicant prove his proficiency.
Literacy tests were to be conducted in writing and be available for
inspection by the examinee. Finally, a sweeping prohibition against the
application of different standards to blacks and whites sought to
eliminate discriminatory behavior in testing and processing black
applicants.

By 1964 it was apparent that many blacks, especially in Tennessee
and Florida, had succeeded in registering. As shown in Table 2-2, in
states on the periphery of the South, black registration was approaching
or exceeding 50 percent of those eligible.[38] These states, with smaller
proportions of blacks, were less susceptible to the phobias surrounding
black political emergence.

In the heartland of the South, the tier of states stretching from
Louisiana to South Carolina, plus Virginia, the civil rights laws had been
less effective. The paucity of success in enrolling black voters in these
states is demonstrated by the following statistics. Between 1958 and
1964 black registration in Alabama rose 5.2 percentage points to 19
percent, in Mississippi black registration increased 2 percentage points
to 6 percent during the decade ending in 1964.[39] The history of regis-

tration in Terrell County, Georgia, examplifies the quagmire through which prospective voters in the Black Belt had to slough. Registration practices in Terrell County were the first to be challenged under the Civil Rights Act of 1957. The district court held the act unconstitutional, but the decision was reversed by the United States Supreme Court.[40] Yet three years later and six years after passage of the 1957 act, black registration in the county had increased from 48 to 133. The latter figure constituted 3.4 percent of the eligible blacks; 95 percent of the whites registered.[41]

While black registration was often increasing, albeit very slowly, between 1956 and 1959 the number of registered blacks declined in 46 of Louisiana's 64 parishes. For example, in Red River the drop was

TABLE 2-2 Proportions of blacks and whites registered before and after the Voting Rights Act of 1965

	Registration before the act (% of voting age pop.)		Registration after the act (% of voting age pop.)	
	Black	White	Black	White
Alabama	19.3	69.2	51.6	89.6
Arkansas	40.4	65.5	62.8	72.4
Florida	51.2	74.8	63.6	81.4
Georgia	27.4	62.6	52.6	80.3
Louisiana	31.6	80.5	58.9	93.1
Mississippi	6.7	69.9	59.8	91.5
North Carolina	46.8	96.8	51.3	83.0
South Carolina	37.3	75.7	51.2	81.7
Tennessee	69.5	72.9	71.7	80.6
Texas	*	*	61.6	53.3
Virginia	38.3	61.1	55.6	63.4
TOTAL	35.5	73.4	57.2	76.5

Source: U.S. Commission on Civil Rights, *Political Participation,* Washington: GPO, 1968, pp. 12-13.
*Figures unavailable by race in *Political Participation:* 53.1% of total voting age population was registered. Voter Education Project estimates for 1964 are 57.7 and 53.3 for blacks and whites, respectively, *V.E.P. News,* 4, January/February, 1970, p. 3. V.E.P. estimates are often higher than are those in *Political Participation.*

from 1,360 to 16. Such dramatic disfranchising is made possible by a Louisiana law which permits the challenge and subsequent removal of improperly registered voters. In Washington Parish about 90 percent of the 1,500 registered black voters were purged often after White Citizens' Council members filed affidavits challenging registrants for "errors in spilling [sic]."[42] Once stricken from the lists, blacks might encounter difficulties in reregistering.

Instances such as these led the Commission on Civil Rights to the following evaluation of the first three statutes:

> The Civil Rights Acts of 1957, 1960, and 1964 . . .were unsuccessful attempts to compel state registration officials to apply their state voting standards fairly. Progress under these Acts was painfully slow, partly because of the intransigence of state and local officials and partly because of the delays inherent in the case-by-case litigation required under these statutes.[43]

The case-by-case route toward black participation was made even more tortuous by the refusal of some judges to apply standards established by the Supreme Court.[44] At times judges procrastinated for months before conducting hearings on matters pressed for by civil rights groups. During the hearings they sometimes badgered civil rights attorneys and their witnesses. Afterwards, more months would pass before a decision was rendered. Prior to passage of the Civil Rights Act of 1964, almost 18 months passed before the average voting rights case in Mississippi was decided; an appeal required another year.[45] During such protracted waits, discrimination continued unhindered. Some judges denied the existence of a pattern of discrimination in Black Belt counties where all the whites but none of the blacks were registered. Such evidence was dismissed as showing only that blacks were not interested in voting.[46]

To correct these and other deficiencies, the Voting Rights Act of 1965 was passed. The primary thrust of this new law was to facilitate black registration by supplanting the authority of local registrars. Rather than requiring blacks to assume the offensive in challenging discrimination, Congress decided that, prima facie, discrimination existed in states or counties in which less than 50 percent of the voting age public was registered or had voted in the 1964 presidential election. The act affected six states and some counties in North Carolina.[47] All tests and devices, e.g., literacy tests and good character requirements, as prerequisites to voting were prohibited in areas covered by the act. The new law insured that in counties where illiterate whites had long been permitted to register, the same standards would be applied to blacks now seeking to vote. The imposition of higher registration standards than had existed in the past was prohibited. In the absence of this stipulation, registrars who had permitted even the least-qualified whites to register could have enforced high standards in the future to preclude black registration. To prevent this, the only suffrage requirements tolerated were ones dealing with age, residence, and criminal record. In a subsequent court decision literacy tests in the seven states were judged inappropriate even when not used in a discriminatory fashion.[48] The Supreme Court concluded that literacy tests, regardless of how applied, were unfair since blacks were less well prepared to pass them due to disparities inherent in the South's dual school system. (See Chapter Four.)

To prevent hostile registration officers from continuing to turn away blacks regardless of Federal prohibitions, the Voting Rights Act authorized the appointment of Federal voting examiners in counties with a history of discrimination. Thus the extended, costly court litigation could be bypassed as the government turned from the prosecution of individual complaints to a search and destroy orientation. Obstinate local registration officials, aided and abetted by all manner of public and private people, had often proven more than a match for case by case prosecution.

A third provision of the Voting Rights Act was the blanket authorization for Federal poll watchers to be sent into counties where examiners had worked. The Federal presence on election day may help assuage fears of new voters; however, some civil rights workers have criticized the observers for being too passive and even at times hostile to blacks.[49]

In summary, the most salient features of the 1965 law were:

1. It authorized appointment of Federal officials to oversee registration and voting.
2. It swept aside the various tests and devices which could be administered discriminatorily to prevent black registration.
3. It obviated the need to transverse the legal maze in order to have one's rights established, by mathematically defining the existence of a presumption of discrimination.

The arrival of Federal examiners enabled qualified blacks to register without fear of being physically or verbally abused.[50] The registration of 300,000 new black voters during the first seven and one half months of application of the 1965 act gave the lie to the myth that blacks had little interest in politics.[51]

The rise in black registration following the Voting Rights Act boosted the size of the black electorate by 11 percent by 1966 and by another 8 percent two years later. The proportion of voting age blacks registered to vote increased from 43 to 62 percent in four years.[52]

While, as Table 2-2 shows, the proportion of blacks registered to vote increased in every state, it was greater in some states than others. As can be seen in Table 2-3, the mean increase in the six states in which Federal voting examiners have been active has been almost three times that in states not automatically covered by the examiner provision. The six examiner states were the ones with the least black registration in 1964. Increases are in large part the effect of blacks in these states catching up with their brothers in the other four. Before the act the range between Tennessee and Mississippi, the states in which black voting was most and least common, was 62.8 percentage points. In the post-act figures the range has shrunk to 20.5 percentage points—between Tennessee and South Carolina—and all of the states except Tennessee are within a range of 12.4 percentage points.

As a sidelight, white registration also increased substantially more in examiner than non-examiner states. To some extent the "catch up" hypothesis suggested to explain increases in black registration is appropriate here also. There is more to it, however. The three states in which white registration is highest (Alabama, Mississippi, and

TABLE 2-3   Increases in black and white registration after enactment of the Voting Rights Act of 1965

	Mean increase in voter registration (%)	
	Blacks	Whites
Six examiner states	28.2	15.1
Four Non-examiner states	10.4	1.9

Note: Texas is not included because of the absence of voting data by race before the act.

Louisiana) are the ones most closely associated with the "never" response to racial change. An ancillary hypothesis for increased white registration is that whites, fearful of black political power, registered to offset the influx of black voters in the more heavily black populated examiner states.

As demonstrated above, black registration has surged in states to which Federal voting examiners were sent. If attention is focused on the specific counties in which examiners worked, the impact of their presence becomes even clearer. As shown in Table 2-4 the rate of increase in black registration was more than twice as great in examiner as in non-examiner counties. The rise in examiner counties was 50 percent while in the other counties it averaged 22.3 percent. As the post-act figures show, Louisiana is the only state in which a smaller proportion of the eligible blacks registered to vote in examiner than in non-examiner counties. Federal examiners have been most active in Alabama, Mississippi, and Louisiana. More than 90 percent of the more than 150,000 blacks registered by Federal examiners were signed up in those three states. (See Table 2-5.)

In all, over 1 million additional black voters have been added to the rolls since 1964. This increase has been the product, no doubt, of a number of factors, only some of which involve the terms of the 1965 legislation and its antecedents.

Regardless of the terms of civil rights laws, their effect might have been muted in the absence of sufficient staff to enforce them. As the provisions of the laws have become more demanding, the number of Federal personnel involved in enforcement has grown. For example, in 1963 there were 20 attorneys in the Department of Justice's Civil Rights Division.[53] Fifty Department of Justice attorneys patrolled the South during the 1966 general elections.[54] In all, approximately 600 Federal officials were on hand for the 1966 elections, and a total of 1,500 were active in Southern elections in 1966 and 1967.[55]

The increase in Federal activity also becomes visible in the review of appropriations to the Department of Justice's Civil Rights Division contained in Table 2-6. This office, which has borne primary governmental responsibility for enforcing voting rights guarantees, spent its early years struggling along on skimpy funds. In fiscal 1966 it enjoyed a budgetary windfall, an unprecedented 95 percent increase. The expanded budget coincided with the Voting Rights Act.

The 1965 legislation differed from earlier laws by becoming operable immediately. Federal examiners signed up 27,463 new voters within three weeks of passage of the Voting Rights Act.[56] By 1967, 150, 345 new black voters had registered with Federal examiners.[57]

The rapidity and extent of Federal involvement following the 1965

TABLE 2-4   Proportions of blacks and whites registered before and after the Voting Rights Act of 1965 in examiner and non-examiner counties

	Registration before the act (% of voting age pop.)		Registration after the act (% of voting age pop.)	
	Black	White	Black	White
Alabama				
Examiner counties	14.8	57.3	59.3	87.2
Non-examiner counties	22.9	73.7	45.4	94.0
Georgia				
Examiner counties	10.3	85.1	62.8	100.0
Non-examiner counties	27.6	62.5	52.5	80.2
Louisiana				
Examiner counties	9.4	70.4	53.5	79.3
Non-examiner counties	37.1	82.0	60.2	95.4
Mississippi				
Examiner counties	8.1	83.7	70.9	90.8
Non-examiner counties	4.5	76.7	50.3	93.5
South Carolina				
Examiner counties	17.3	100.0	71.6	100.0
Non-examiner counties	38.1	75.4	50.5	81.2
TOTAL EXAMINER COUNTIES	11.9	67.2	61.9	83.4
TOTAL NON-EXAMINER COUNTIES	30.2	71.9	52.5	87.4

Source: U.S. Commission on Civil Rights, *Political Participation,* Washington: GPO, 1968, pp. 222-225.

act, in addition to expediting registration in the affected counties, had a broader influence. Registration also burgeoned in counties not visited by Federal examiners.[58] We can speculate that these increases resulted from the attempts of additional blacks to register as well as from more widespread willingness of registrars to comply with the law. Some

TABLE 2-5   *Number of blacks registered by Federal voting examiners between 1965 and 1967*

Alabama	60,316
Georgia	3,397
Louisiana	24,130
Mississippi	57,896
South Carolina	4,606
TOTAL	150,345

Source: U.S. Commission on Civil Rights, *Political Participation,* Washington: GPO, 1968, p. 223.

TABLE 2-6   *Appropriations for the Civil Rights Division, Department of Justice*

Fiscal year	Appropriations ($)	Increase ($)	Percentage increase
1959	490,000	—	—
1960	517,000	27,000	6
1961	650,000	133,000	26
1962	768,000	118,000	18
1963	811,000	43,000	6
1964	1,079,000	268,000	33
1965	1,255,000	176,000	16
1966	2,443,000	1,188,000	95
1967	2,459,000	16,000	1
1968	2,566,000	107,000	4
1969	2,770,000	204,000	8
1970	4,057,000	1,287,000	46

Source: Appropriations figures furnished by Senator Richard B. Russell (Democrat—Ga.).

blacks may have viewed the 1965 law as standing ready to protect their rights and for this reason have thought it worthwhile to attempt to register. Registrars may have preferred to enroll black applicants rather than persist in denials and risk being superseded by Federal examiners. Whatever the reason, within two months of the passage of the law 97,000 new blacks had registered in non-examiner counties in the five deep South states.[59]

Another significant contribution to rising black registration was the work of groups such as SNCC, CORE, NAACP, and the Voter Education Project (VEP). Their efforts sowed the crop of voters harvested in the sixties. VEP began registration efforts in 1962 and by 1968 had 175 programs in operation.[60] All told between 1966 and 1970, 510 voter registration programs were operating in the South.[61] By encouraging people and by giving civic training at freedom schools, thousands became politically motivated to attempt registration.

Data for three Southern states presented in Table 2-7 confirm that the combination of Federal and private efforts has been more successful in promoting registration than either has been operating alone. While the presence of either catalyst led to greater registration, counties with Federal examiners reported higher registration rates than did counties in which only the Voter Education Project had functioned. Except in South Carolina, registration rates were higher in counties in which both kinds of agent had been working than in counties visited by only one or the other.

The cumulative efforts of civil rights proselyting was augmented by several cultural factors. Even in areas not visited by civil rights workers,

TABLE 2-7   Percentage of blacks registered to vote in particular counties of the South

Voting rights agencies operating in the county	Registration (% of voting age blacks)		
	Alabama	Mississippi	South Carolina
Federal examiners and Voter Education Project	69.5	51.7	67.0
Federal examiners only	63.7	41.2	71.4
Voter Education Project only	57.6	34.9	51.6
Neither agency	45.4	24.2	48.8

Source: U.S. Commission on Civil Rights, Political Participation, Washington: GPO, 1968, p. 155.

blacks were informed of the Movement's progress by local preachers, word of mouth, and television. Blacks must have been alternately sickened by the beatings, snarling dogs, and mute rubble of destroyed homes and churches and cheered by scenes of the March on Washington[62] and the oratory of Martin Luther King. Thus the media may have helped knit together in spirit blacks on plantations and tenant farms, in the shotgun shacks along the unpaved roads in innumerable shantytowns, and in the tenements of urban ghettos. Many of these people could vicariously draw moral support and racial pride from the victories of the Movement in other parts of the nation. The media also helped spread the word that voter registration was the thing to do, that it was the way to demonstrate manhood, and that one could become a black rather than a "nigger." Thus was disseminated to black Americans a common goal and a common standard for self-evaluation.

Yet another cultural consideration has been the erosion of white opposition to black political participation. The younger generation of whites seems less bound to the precepts of white supremacy than were its elders.[63] Indeed, some sages have attributed change to the fact that a lot of funerals have laid to rest many of the most adamant opponents of civil rights. There have, of course, been some changes of attitude among Southerners. The passage of time has led to the mellowing of some beliefs. When limited desegregation did not result in the destruction of civilization, some people became less fearful. Others, while still opposing integration in principle, became reconciled to federally imposed changes. After unsuccessfully opposing each new Federal edict, some segregationists have probably been less vigorous in their resistance.

Not only are more people tolerant of change, but the costs which the unreconciled must pay to continue their discrimination have risen. Federal assumption of registration duties voided the powers of local registrars in some counties. The demonstration that the Federal government was prepared to effectively insure that blacks desiring to register could do so seemingly prompted compliance elsewhere so as to forestall Department of Justice intervention. Earlier when enforcement had been sparse and requirements lax, it was a simple matter to frustrate the purposes of laws. The costs—in terms of effort, and the probability of corrective action being instigated by Federal officials—rose appreciably after 1965.

The effect of the various forces in voter registration is that 66 percent of the eligible blacks were registered in 1970. This was 17 percent lower than figures for whites. Unless the Nixon administration becomes so enamored with the Southern strategy that it neglects civil rights entirely, the trend anticipated is a further diminution of racial differences in registration.

Poll Tax

Chronologically the last change in laws governing voting was the elimination of the poll tax. Its longevity may be attributable to the fact that it alone among the disfranchising tools was color-blind, taking the ballot from the poor of both races. A nominal sum of a dollar or two per year, the tax was nonetheless too much for sharecroppers and unskilled laborers, expecially when it was cumulative. That the vote was a privilege for which one should be willing to pay was not an idea original to the South.[64] Furthermore, the earmarking of proceeds of the tax for schools probably contributed to its long immunity from successful constitutional challenge.

By the 1960s all but four states[65] had eliminated the tax on their own volition, perhaps because other means existed to filter out virtually all blacks but no whites. The Twenty-fouth Amendment to the Constitution banished the tax from elections of Federal officials, and a Supreme Court decision[66] held that the poll tax infringed on rights guaranteed by the Fifteenth Amendment when applied to state elections.

The elimination of the poll tax after most other impediments to voting were already gone has permitted an attempt to measure its effect. In Harris County (Houston, Texas) the number of registered voters increased by almost 25 percent, i.e., by 96,405 people, with the demise of the tax.[67] In the subsequent general election more than 36,000 of these new registrants voted. However, contrary to expectations, blacks composed a *smaller* proportion of the electorate than when the tax was being levied. The proportion of the electorate that was white remained about the same while the proportion that was Mexican-American quadrupled (from 1.6 to 7.2 percent). Thus by the mid-sixties the poll tax was not a significant barrier to black participation—at least not in urban Houston.[68] While we cannot be sure of the applicability of these findings to areas where the population has only blacks and whites, there is one finding that is probably typical: a smaller proportion of those registering free voted than those who had paid the poll tax. It will take time for those previously disfranchised by the poll tax to acquire the voting habit.[69]

BLACK VOTING

The ability to register is, of course, not just an end in itself. Of more consequence is the right which registration entitles one to exercise. The limited available data suggest that the level of the office and the racial orientation of one or more of the candidates may be important in determining the extent to which blacks participate once they are registered.

A survey conducted in the early sixties found that among registered Southern voters, blacks were 58 to 78 percent as likely to vote as were whites. The likelihood that blacks would vote at the same rates as whites increased with the significance of the office. For President, 55 percent of the registered blacks and 78 percent of the registered whites voted. In school board elections, the figures were 28 and 48 percent respectively.[70] A study of turnout in Austin, Texas, for the decade ending in 1964 also found that white and black turnout figures varied with the significance of the office, with the proportion of registered blacks participating always less than that of whites.[71] Generally, the more extensive the constituency of the office, the greater the turnout was.[72] Thus 80 percent of whites and 62 percent of blacks registered voted in the presidential elections studied. Interestingly, while turnout for both races was low (42 percent and 32 percent of registered whites and blacks, respectively), the difference between the races was least in city council elections. Holloway and Olson relate this finding to Robert Lane's hypothesis that ethnics are particularly interested in local elections.[73] Scattered estimates of turnout rates made by the Southern Regional Council suggest that in 1966 between 30 and 74 percent of the registered blacks voted in various statewide races.[74]

Another determinant of black turnout is the breadth of choice available. When only segregationists are campaigning, blacks seem less inclined to vote. The entrance of predominantly black parties, such as the Mississippi Freedom Democratic Party and the National Democratic Party of Alabama (NDPA), into the political arena may fill the void left by the Tweedledum-Tweedledee alternatives offered by the national parties in some states. In 1970 the first three blacks elected to the South Carolina state legislature in modern times ran as members of the predominantly black United Citizens Party of South Carolina. Also in 1970 the NDPA claimed credit for 12 Alabama victories including a state legislator.[75] In the absence of a Republican challenge to George Wallace, the NDPA gubernatorial candidate amassed 16 percent of the vote.[76]

The presence of black candidates has a catalytic effect on black turnout. The candidacy of black Maynard Jackson in the 1968 Georgia senatorial primary caused black turnout to exceed white voting in urban Fulton County. Black registrants voted at the rate of 45.4 percent compared with 43.5 percent of the white registrants.[77] In Atlanta's mayoralty election in which Maynard Jackson was elected vice-mayor, 51 percent of the eligible blacks voted, as opposed to 43 percent of the whites. Low-income blacks participated more frequently than poor whites while upper-status samples of both races participated at comparable levels.[78]

Despite increases in black registration, general studies of voter turn-out suggest that blacks, being disproportionately poor and having fewer years of formal education, lower-status jobs, and less exposure to the mass media, would be less frequent voters than whites, even in the absence of intimidation and discrimination. After extensive study Matthews and Prothro conclude that individual attitudes, socio-economic characteristics, and the local environment are the most important predictors of black participation.[79] Briefly, the highlights of their research will be reported here.

The item most strongly associated with black voting is a series of psychological attributes. Of these the most important are party identifi-cation, strong political interest, knowledge about politics, and a sense of political efficacy.[80] For people who have been excluded from participation and cut off from political stimuli, it takes time before attitudes supportive of voting are acquired.[81]

Changes in socioeconomic status and the environment are helping to overcome the psychological factors associated with low participation rates. In their sample of Southerners of both races Matthews and Prothro found that young and well-paid blacks were as likely to be politically involved as were comparable whites. Racial disparities in participation decreased in the higher education and more prestigious occupational categories. On measures of political interest, blacks typically scored higher when amount of education was held constant. As more blacks achieve higher socioeconomic status, they can tap new information sources. With more information, interest in politics may increase.

Moreover, as the political system becomes more tolerant of blacks, their political participation may increasingly resemble that of whites. Matthews and Prothro report that in racially open Piedmont County, levels of apathy, political discussion, and voting are quite similar for both races. Black involvement will probably also be spurred when (as in Piedmont) there is an active black political club which gives endorsements and mobilizes voters. Indigenous activation and reinforcement is perhaps essential to overcome the socioeconomic and personal correlates of apathy discussed above. As barriers to participation collapse, interest can be translated into action. Success in the political arena should promote a sense of efficacy which in turn may stimulate greater interest.[82] Projecting, we may anticipate that as the black electorate becomes increasingly young, better educated, and more affluent, and moves into middle-class occupations, interest in politics will be translated into votes.

Diluting the Black Vote

With obstacles to black voting now being rooted out, registrars are often complying with the law, at least to the extent of permitting blacks to register. Some diehards, however, have developed techniques with which to dilute the force of black voting.[83] Several ploys have involved the drawing of constituency boundaries. In counties where blacks comprise a majority of some electoral districts but not a majority of the county, election procedures have been changed so that candidates run at large rather than from districts. Indications are that when it can be proved that these changes were adopted to thwart the election of blacks, they will be undone by the courts as infringements of Fifteenth Amendment rights.[84] A second effort, which has yet to be disallowed, is the subtle gerrymandering of districts so that blacks remain a minority.

Another set of subterfuges to prevent the election of black officials includes changes in the procedures by which aspirants initiate their candidacies. Lowndes County, Alabama, increased filing fees tenfold. In Mississippi an impediment was placed before the largely black Mississippi Freedom Democratic Party when the number of signatures required to place a name on the ballot was raised to ten times the previous figure.

To make it harder for blacks to elect one of their own in a multimember district, the "full slate" requirement has been adopted. Under this provision a ballot will not be tallied unless the voter has voted for as many candidates as there are posts to be filled. Thus if only one black is running in a district with four posts, blacks must contribute to the vote totals of three whites regardless of how distasteful they are. Since very few whites will vote for the black candidate, he is placed at a disadvantage.

The obstacles discussed so far may not prevent all blacks from achieving public office. Foolproof tactics have been to abolish the office, extend the terms of the white incumbents, and to change the mode of selection from election to appointment. Only the second of these has been struck down by the courts.

The full impact of black voting has been softened by the manner in which elections have been conducted. The effectiveness of black voting has been hampered in a number of ways, most of which if not constituting fraud, certainly verge on it. Blacks seeking to vote have been given misleading information; their ballots have been thrown out for minor errors; and black poll watchers have been banned from observing the count.

The last set of practices used to dull the cutting edge of black voting has involved the old standby, discrimination. White poll watchers have either refused assistance to illiterate blacks or have voted the ballots of illiterates for white candidates despite their pleas to be assisted by fellow blacks. Blacks have been excluded from precinct meetings and have had their names left off voting lists. White election officials have provided insufficient voting facilities in anticipation that many voters would be unable to wait or would tire before exercising the franchise. Another strategem has been to locate polling places in white business houses or in plantation company stores so that black voters must run a gauntlet of belligerent whites.[85]

Impact of Increased Black Voting

The increases in the number of blacks permitted to vote and the emergence of the competitive two-party system could result in black votes becoming essential for election victory. Just how meaningful has the influx of more than 2 million black voters since 1958 been in 1) electing members of their own race to public office, 2) providing the margin of victory for sympathetic whites, and 3) producing policy outputs desired by blacks? These are the questions which we will attempt to answer in this section.

Black votes will be most effective if mobilized en masse. In a society in which race is the overriding issue, bloc voting by one race may prompt coagulation of the other race around a single opposing candidate. Such racial polarity negates the influence of the black endorsement unless blacks constitute a majority or near majority of the electorate. Since the salience of race tends to vary directly with the size of the black component of the population, black electoral victories often necessitate a black majority.

Black political success occurred first in urban areas. Some Southern cities—notably Durham and Atlanta—with their less provincial populations have had a tradition of black participation for more than a generation. Recent Supreme Court decisions requiring electoral districts with equal numbers of people in conjunction with the concentration of urban blacks in ghettos has produced state legislative districts, city council wards, and school board districts in which whites are either absent altogether or are a minority. A growing number of Southern cities have witnessed the election of black public officials as black registration has risen. Some of the more notable successes have been the election of Maynard Jackson as vice-mayor of Atlanta (1969), the election of six members of the Nashville, Tennessee, City Council (1966), and the presence of 15 blacks in the Georgia General Assembly (1971), all from urban districts.

The greater success in electing blacks in urban than in rural areas is easily explainable. As mentioned earlier the proportion of the population which is black and the openness of the political system vary inversely. At least at this time many rural areas but only one major Southern city (Atlanta) have black majorities. Furthermore bigotry is associated with low income, low education, strong ties with tradition, and social backwardness and isolation. These characteristics are more prevalent in the country than the city. Rural whites have therefore more consistently resisted black voting than have their city kinsmen. Rural resistance has been augmented by greater power in the hands of rural whites. In the back-country South every black is directly or indirectly dependent upon whites for economic survival. In these areas most males exist as serflike tenants on white plantations. Their wives and daughters labor as domestics for white mistresses.[86] Even the few professionals are vulnerable, for if hard times befall the black community, the few black doctors, lawyers, insurance sellers, and other white-collar workers will soon thirst for the dried-up capital.

If in spite of all these obstructions an extensive registration effort enables blacks to mount a challenge to white domination, the latter's presence may manifest itself in yet another guise. Reference to the Lowndes County Freedom Organization (LCFO) in Lowndes County, Alabama, is enlightening on this point. The county was more than 80 percent black in 1960. In 1966 a registration drive led by charismatic firebrand Stokely Carmichael succeeded in enrolling more than 3,000 blacks on the voting lists, which constituted a majority of the county's electorate. In the face of this challenge white Democrats and Republicans united to defeat the LCFO slate for each of seven contested posts.[87]

Obviously some of the black voters in this election had spurned the candidate of their race. It is unlikely that the blacks who voted for whites were a detached group of concerned citizens who placed candidate qualification above race. Instead the victory of the whites was insured by frightened blacks who were brought by employers to the polls by the truckload. The whites saw to it that their tenants voted "correctly," giving them filled-out sample ballots which were voted for the blacks by white election officials.[88] Also contributing to the LCFO defeat was the difference in white and black turnout. A larger proportion of blacks than whites stayed away from the polls. It would be naive to deny that the absence of many blacks was fear-inspired.

Despite setbacks such as occurred in Lowndes County, black candidates have enjoyed some success in rural areas. By 1968 there were black public officials in some rural counties of every Southern state.[89] And in a few predominantly black counties, e.g., Macon and

Greene counties in Alabama, and Hancock County, Georgia, blacks control a variety of offices, from justice of the peace to county commissioner and sheriff. Another major gain was the election of civil rights leader Charles Evers as mayor of biracial Fayette, Mississippi, defeating the white incumbent of 18 years, "Turnip Greens" Allen.

If one's standard of success is percentage increase, then recent civil rights legislation has worked wonders in enabling blacks to win public office. In the fifties black officeholders in the South were rare indeed. Even after the first three civil rights acts they numbered fewer than 100. But by 1966 there were 159 and by the middle of 1969 there were 473 in the seven states affected by the Voting Rights Act alone.[90] However, in 1968 there were still many Black Belt counties without a single Negro officeholder—a witness to racial prejudice. Indeed, as recently as 1968, there were still five Deep South counties which had yet to register the first black. There were 65 other counties in which less than a third of the voting-age blacks had been registered.[91]

After the 1970 elections there were 665 black public officeholders in the South who had won public endorsement.[92] When Southern state legislatures convened in 1971, there were blacks sitting in each of them for the first time in generations. Where there have been black representatives for several years, there are indications that these men and women are increasingly becoming accepted by their peers and coincidentally are succeeding in their legislative endeavors. In systems where black members are less numerous and have less seniority, they may be less successful in achieving policy goals. However, the mere fact of their presence may be significant. They can serve both as watchdogs over white decision makers and as symbolic heroes for fellow blacks throughout the state.

In addition to electing hundreds of black public officials, the black vote has been decisive in a number of races pitting liberal and conservative white candidates. For example, black votes provided Lyndon Johnson with his margin of victory over Barry Goldwater in Alabama, Tennessee, Florida, and Virginia. Black votes have been responsible for the election of at least two Southern governors, several congressmen, and the mayor of Atlanta in recent years. Also in response to a growing black electorate, party organizations—even in George Wallace's Alabama—have accepted black members.[94]

A prime example of the role black votes may play in constituencies in which they are less than a majority is provided by elections in Durham, North Carolina.[95] As ethnic minorities have done in numerous American cities, blacks have bloc-voted for candidates endorsed by the Durham Committee of Negro Affairs (DCNA). The DCNA endorsement can mobilize at least 85 percent of the black voters behind the favored candidate. The bloc vote has provided the margin of victory in 57 percent of the contested mayoralty races and 61 percent of the contested city council races between 1946 and 1967. Because of the demonstrated ability of DCNA to play kingmaker, sound campaign strategy demands that as standard procedure white candidates solicit its endorsements by presenting their platforms before the organization's directors.

In an environment like Durham's, black voters become politically potent only when they can ally themselves with a segment of the white community. Consequently the black endorsement is valuable only when given to a moderate. Thus the candidacy of a radical closely attuned to the wishes of the black community may be sacrificed as the endorsement goes to a moderate likely to win. In the 1969 Atlanta mayoralty race such considerations caused a rift in the black community as the older, moderate black leaders endorsed white Sam Massell in preference to black Horace Tate in the primary.[96] The black vote was also split in the 1970 Georgia Democratic gubernatorial primary between black attorney C. B. King and white, moderate, former governor Carl Sanders.[97]

While the election of blacks or sympathetic whites to public office is an important gauge of black political participation, by itself it tells us little about the effect of increased participation. The presence of black men and women as elected officials unquestionably has symbolic value but is it the prelude to public policies more favorable to the black community? For instance, does increased black political participation lead to advances in desegregating various facilities? Or, on a more mundane level, are black votes converted into paved streets and improved garbage collection in black neighborhoods?

Unfortunately little research has been done on this question; therefore, we, like archaeologists, must content ourselves with drawing inferences from fragments. Nonetheless it seems safe to generalize that increased black participation has not expedited black acceptance into previously all-white institutions. School integration, access to public accommodations, open housing—none of these has proceeded as a result of heightened black voting. Rather these rights and their protection, at least in the South, have come from the Federal government—not from the courthouse, city hall, or state capitol. Southern cities and counties which permitted blacks access to the political arena have not expanded the scope of civil rights until prodded by Congress or the Federal courts.

While increased black political participation has not led to more integration, the rise in voting rates has not been devoid of significance. One change which seems to flow from Negro registration is that the more brutal racist tactics pass from the scene.[98] Acts such as burning churches, bombing homes, sniping, and beating those no longer docile have been far more prevalent in apartheid communities than in those where blacks have won the suffrage. Indeed it seems that white-instigated savagery in a community has increased as civil rights activities have moved toward a crescendo. Whites have been most aggresive when their one-race institutions have been hardest pressed by protestors. A few examples should be convincing. White housewives have taken to the streets to shriek obscenities only when a city's schools were first integrated. Once it became obvious that the Supreme Court edicts would be enforced, by Federal troops if necessary, passions soon cooled. Also, the dynamiting of black churches has generally occurred before the Movement has achieved its goals in the community, not after.[99]

Reduction of violence is, however, not the only benefit attributable to increased political participation. While black votes have not sundered barriers to physical integration, they have led to greater public spending for the ghetto. Black voting has often been followed by the paving of streets and regular collection of garbage in the ghetto. It has also opened the doors to various civil service jobs. As blacks came to constitute a significant part of the Atlanta electorate, they attained jobs with the city police force and with the county sheriff.[100] In Durham, North Carolina, in return for DCNA support, new fire stations and recreational facilities have been built in black neighborhoods.[101]

It is appropriate to ask why political participation has led to a more equitable distribution of public services but not to integration. A couple of factors are important. Significant is the fact that changes in the allocation of public benefits involve very few white people.

Employing black policemen and having them patrol the ghetto will go largely unnoticed. So also, improving ghetto facilities will not be met with the obstinacy which greets attempts to introduce blacks into previously all-white facilities. Some white supremacists have favored improving schools, hospitals, and other public facilities in black neighborhoods, hoping to thereby forestall demands for integration. In the face of imminent integration, whites are willing to honor the second half of the separate but equal doctrine.

A second explanation is closely associated with the first. Blacks have better access to decisions allocating public money than they do to decisions about integration. Local decisions on schools, public swimming pools, open housing, and public accommodations are typically made by an elected body. Except where blacks can elect a majority of the decision makers, it is unlikely that a city council or school board will decide to integrate facilities, unless so ordered by the Federal government. Moreover, decisions to raise and spend money for public improvements often require bond issues approved in referenda. When black votes hold the balance of power in a community, their political leaders can extract as the price of their endorsement promises that some of the goods to be bought by the bond money will be located in the ghetto. This strategy is unlikely to prompt racist opposition since it perpetuates segregation. Durham with its highly effective black political leadership illustrates the importance which black votes can have on bond referenda. In that city 60 percent of the referenda between 1945 and 1967 would have been defeated but for black support.[102] The black community thus has leverage which can be converted into new parks and playgrounds, and school improvements. In areas of the South in which blacks have been banned from political participation, the disparity between the level of public services provided to blacks and whites has often been greatest.

While support by the burgeoning black electorate is often a decisive element in elections, black votes do have some political costs. For every instance in which black votes have spelled the difference, one can perhaps cite a case in which a white backlash defeated a liberal candidate. Gains by blacks, political, social, and economic, have alienated many whites, 85 percent of whom, nationwide, feel that change is occurring too rapidly in civil rights.[103] Figures for the South would probably be even higher.

Black Leadership

An outgrowth of increased black political participation has been a change in the character of black political leadership. Even in the most repressive areas there were always one or more blacks who were assumed to speak for their community. As with most matters affecting blacks in the past, leaders existed because whites willed it. The whites wanted someone to whom they could communicate decisions relevant to the town's black population. In return for being the whites' delegate, the black man received a modicum of status among the whites, and with white status being the most important prestige ordering, he concomitantly received visibility and position in the black community.

Obviously the black leader was wholly dependent upon whites for his position. To retain it he had to tell whites what they wanted to hear while seeming to speak for his black brothers. While he might be able to win a few benefits for his community, he always had to seek these submissively. To *demand* some civil improvement probably would lead to replacement by a more circumspect successor.

With the acquisition of the suffrage and the changing tenor of the times, blacks have felt less need to beg and greater willingness to demand. The leaders of the past and their cautious words of expediency are rejected by young activists. Rather than approaching whites as supplicants, young blacks inspired by CORE and SNCC are seeking change through confrontation. Where the old leadership approached "Mr. Charlie" hat in hand, the new leaders organize marches, boycotts, and picketing and tell "Charlie-baby" how it's going to be.

Not only do the old and new differ in approach, but they have their eyes on different goals.[104] The traditional leaders sought to improve environmental conditions. They worked for better public services and higher pay, willing to play down demands for integration in return for improved segregated facilities. The Black Power generation, on the other hand, has been more concerned with demonstrating its manhood and exploding the myths of racial inferiority. Demanding immediate integration, some black leaders have found anything less than desegregation unacceptable. Their commitment to principle has been such that rather than enjoy segregated facilities, for example swimming pools, they have pressed for integration even if the result is that the services are denied to both races.

The background characteristics of the two sets of leaders also differ.

Leaders of the past tended to be older in years as well as in thoughts. They were generally of higher social and economic status than today's denim-clad demonstration leaders. Associated with the higher status of the conservative leaders was a greater economic reliance upon whites. The young leaders of today, like VISTA workers, have lived with the poor, sharing their humble fare. The going wage for SNCC workers has been $10.00 to $20.00 per week. These youths with minimal wants have been far less vulnerable to white economic threats.

The sudden change in personnel, goals, and tactics of the black leadership has confounded many whites. Since the new leaders have frequently come from outside the locale, whites have rationalized the changed goals and tactics as being purely the creation of outside agitators. Whites in the sleepy backwaters of the twentieth century fail to realize that the protestors would be shouting in the wind, had not the whole environment changed. It may be that in the past whites did know the thoughts and desires of "their colored people"—but no longer is this the case. Blacks have been caught up in a nationwide movement while some Southern whites' views are, at times, still limited to their county, or perhaps their own tradition-burdened state. Many poor blacks, having come to believe that they can win equal treatment with the support of the Federal government, chant "Black Power"—no longer paralyzed by fear of "the man."

SUMMARY

The thick underbrush of racism which had to be cleared before voting rights became a reality to Southern blacks has been described in this chapter. The first tentative paths have been gradually broadened until now most obstructions have been removed in most areas and two-thirds of all eligible blacks in the South are now registered. Of the many items which have been instrumental in fulfilling the terms of the Fifteenth Amendment, the penultimate was the enactment of a wide-ranging statute which effectively withdrew from local control much of the formal registration process. The Voting Rights Act with its meaningful enforcement provisions coincided with private registration efforts and attitudinal changes which facilitated massive black registration.

The growing black electorate has resulted in the election of sizable numbers of blacks and sympathetic whites to various offices. An accompaniment to the increased significance of the black vote has been some material benefits (paved streets, etc.); however, status gains have less frequently been an outgrowth of new black political potency.

The transformation of the political landscape of the South reveals the extent to which law—even when unpopular—can alter established behavior. Changes do not come readily but must be extracted through the application of pressure—sometimes great. Earlier Federal efforts failed because insufficient force was mustered to insure compliance. Many of these deficiencies were corrected in the Voting Rights Act of 1965.

NOTES

1. The difficulties encountered by a legislator in learning the wishes of his constituents are discussed in Warren E. Miller and Donald E. Stokes, "Constituency Influence in Congress," *American Political Science Review,* 57, March 1963, pp. 45-57; Lewis Anthony Dexter, *The Sociology and Politics of Congress,* Chicago: Rand McNally, 1969; Lewis Anthony Dexter, "The Representative and His District," in Robert L. Peabody and Nelson W. Polsby, eds., *New Perspectives on the House of Representatives,* 2d ed., Chicago: Rand McNally, 1969, pp. 3-29; John Wahlke et al., *The Legislative System,* New York: Wiley, 1962, pp. 267-286. The absence of voter knowledge and sophistication has been convincingly demonstrated in Angus Campbell et al., *The American Voter: An Abridgement,* New York: Wiley, 1964; Donald E. Stokes and Warren E. Miller, "Party Government and the Salience of Congress," *Public Opinion Quarterly,* 26, Winter 1962, pp. 531-546.
2. Quoted in William R. Keech, *The Impact of Negro Voting Rights,* Chicago: Rand McNally, 1968, p. 2.
3. "Blacks to Control Elections," *Atlanta Constitution,* January 29, 1970, reprinted in *V. E. P. News,* 4, January/February 1970, p. 4.
4. For only 13 percent of the whites did registration have this significance. Donald R. Matthews and James W. Prothro, *Negroes and the New Southern Politics,* New York: Harcourt, Brace & World, 1966, pp. 72-73.
5. Stokely Carmichael and Charles Hamilton, *Black Power,* New York: Vintage Books, 1967, pp. 104-105.
6. W. J. Cash, *The Mind of the South,* New York: Vintage Books, 1941.
7. Ten years earlier both of the Carolinas and Virginia each had a black congressman. Only a few years before the turn of the century there were more than 1,000 black officeholders in North Carolina. *Report of the United States Commission on Civil Rights, 1959,* Washington: GPO, 1959, p. 31.
8. Charles E. Silberman, *Crisis in Black and White,* New York: Vintage Books, 1964, p. 23.

9. The grandfather clause, a product of the Jim Crow era, excluded the descendents of voters prior to 1865 from having to pass a literacy test prior to registration. This was during a period when most Southerners of both races were illiterate. In Guinn v. U.S., 238 U.S. 347 (1915), this not too subtle technique for discrimination was judged unconstitutional.

10. Smith v. Allwright, 321 U.S. 649 (1944).

11. For a fuller discussion of this type of harassment see Donald S. Strong, *Negroes, Ballots, and Judges,* University: University of Alabama, 1968, pp. 13-20.

12. Leon Friedman, "The Federal Courts of the South: Judge Bryan Simpson and His Reluctant Brethren," in Leon Friedman, ed., *Southern Justice,* Cleveland: Meridian Books, 1967, pp. 187-213.

13. For examples see Elizabeth Sutherland, ed., *Letters From Mississippi,* New York: McGraw-Hill, 1965.

14. Anthony Lewis, *Portrait of a Decade,* New York: Random House, 1964, pp. 126-128.

15. Strong, op. cit., pp. 19-20.

16. Matthews and Prothro, op. cit., presents a poignant example of the bondage of fear which numbs the political sensitivities of teachers in repressive areas. See also U.S. Commission on Civil Rights, *Voting in Mississippi,* Washington: GPO, 1965, pp. 33-39; Gerald E. Stern, "Judge William Harold Cox and the Right to Vote in Clarke County, Mississippi," in Friedman, ed., *Southern Justice,* p. 170.

17. For additional instances in which economic intimidation has been used see U.S. Commission on Civil Rights, *Voting, 1961,* Washington: GPO, 1961, pp. 91-97.

18. Ibid., pp. 36-37.

19. U.S. Commission on Civil Rights, *Political Participation,* Washington: GPO, 1968, p. 220.

20. *Report of the U.S. Commission on Civil Rights, 1959,* p. 80; U.S. v. Lynd, 301 F.2d 818 (1962). In Terrell County, Georgia, where 95 percent of the eligible whites were registered, two blacks with masters and two with bachelors degrees were ruled illiterate by the local registrar. See *Voting, 1961,* p. 29.

21. Lewis, op. cit., p. 130.

22. *Voting, 1961,* pp. 64-65.

23. Ibid., provides numerous examples.

24. *Voting in Mississippi,* p. 14.

25. Ibid.

26. In Macon County, Alabama, voters could vouch for only two registrants per year. *Report of the U.S. Commission on Civil Rights, 1959,* p. 76.

27. *Voting, 1961,* p. 69.

28. See Strong op. cit., pp. 27-30, for this and other examples of dilatory practices.

29. Peter R. Teachout, "Louisiana Underlaw," in Friedman, ed., *Southern Justice,* p. 66.

30. Typically one must exhaust his administrative remedies, often a cumbersome process, before the courts will entertain his plea.

31. *Voting, 1961,* p. 136.

32. Kenneth Vines, "Southern State Supreme Courts and Race Relations," *Western Political Quarterly,* 18, March 1965, pp. 5-18. Vines reports that between 1954 and 1963 blacks won 29 percent of the racial cases before Southern state supreme courts but 51 percent of the cases in Southern Federal district courts. See also Michael Meltsner, "Southern Appellate Courts: A Dead End," in Friedman, ed., *Southern Justice,* pp. 136-154.

33. *Voting, 1961,* p. 136.

34. U.S. Commission on Civil Rights, *Civil Rights, 1963,* Washington: GPO, 1963, pp. 37-50.

35. Ibid., pp. 14-15

36. Ibid., p. 16.

37. In Austin, Texas, black turnout reached a ten year high in the Johnson-Goldwater contest. The level of black participation in this election has been interpreted as being caused by black antipathy for Goldwater. Harry Holloway and David M. Olson, "Electoral Participation by White and Negro in a Southern City," *Midwest Journal of Political Science,* 10, February 1966, pp. 115-116. In states in which registration was still possible, once it began to appear that Goldwater might capture the Republican nomination, some blacks may have seen this as sufficient cause to register.

38. The states are Florida, North Carolina, Tennessee, and Texas.

39. House of Representatives, Committee on the Judiciary, *Hearings, Voting Rights,* 89th Congress, 1st Session, 1965, p. 4.

40. U.S. v. Raines, 172 F. Supp. 552 (M. D. Ga. 1959), rev'd., 362 U.S. 17 (1960).

41. *Civil Rights, 1963,* p. 18.

42. *Report of the U.S. Commission on Civil Rights, 1959,* pp. 101-104. See also Robert F. Collins et al., "Clinton, Louisiana," in Friedman, ed., *Southern Justice,* p. 118; *Civil Rights, 1963,* p. 20.

43. U.S. Commission on Civil Rights, *The Voting Rights Act,* Washington: GPO, 1965, p. 8.

44. Evidence for this and succeeding points in this paragraph is found in several articles in Friedman, ed., *Southern Justice;* Meltsner, op. cit., pp. 136-140, 151-152; Stern, op. cit., pp. 168-172, 181-186; Friedman, *op. cit.,* pp. 188-192.

45. *Voting in Mississippi,* p. 53; Stern, *op. cit.,* p. 169.

46. For a more elaborate discussion of judicial behavior supportive of local racial practices see: Strong, op. cit.,; Friedman, ed., *Southern Justice,* passim. Refusal to find a pattern of practice of discrimination is significant because in the absence of such findings blacks could not be registered by

Federal judges and therefore, had to continue to seek registration through the county registrar.

47. Affected by the Voting Rights Act of 1965 are all of Alabama, Georgia, Louisiana, Mississippi, South Carolina, Virginia, and at least 26 North Carolina counties.

48. Gaston County v. U.S., 395 U.S. 285 (1969),

49. "LSCRRC Reports on Mississippi Elections," *V.E.P. News,* 2, January 1968, p. 3; "Rights Commission Reports Irregularities in Mississippi," *V.E.P. News,* 3, July 1969, p. 4.

50. See "Excerpts from Washington Speech by Vernon Jordon," *V.E.P. News,* 3, March 1969, pp. 4-5; Leon Lindsay, "Black Political Power at Stake," *Christian Science Monitor,* August 8 1969, reprinted in *V.E.P. News,* 3, August 1969, p. 4; Stern, op. cit., pp. 170, 181, 185.

51. Of these approximately one-third was registered by Federal examiners. See Matthews and Prothro, op. cit., p. 20.

52. *V.E.P. News,* 4, January/February 1970, p. 3.

53. *Civil Rights, 1963,* p. 25.

54. *Political Participation,* pp. 167-169.

55. Ibid., p. 157.

56. *Voting Rights Act,* p. 33.

57. *Political Participation,* p. 223.

58. By the end of 1969 Federal examiners had been sent to 64 of the 556 counties covered by the Voting Rights Act. "House Votes against Extending '65 Voting Act," *V.E.P. News,* 3, December 1969, p. 1.

59. *Voting Rights Act,* p. 30.

60. "175 Programs Funded by V.E.P. during 1968," *V.E.P. News,* 3, February 1969, p. 3.

61. "Voting Rights Act," *Atlanta Journal,* June 16, 1970, p. 18-A.

62. The March on Washington was a peaceful demonstration of 200,000 blacks and whites on August 28, 1963. Their goal was civil rights and equal job opportunities.

63. In his inaugural address Georgia's Governor Jimmy Carter said:

> Based on this knowledge of Georgians north and south, rural and urban, I say to you quite frankly that the time for racial discrimination is over. Our people have already made this major and difficult decision. . . . No poor, rural, weak, or black person should ever have to bear the additional burden of being deprived of the opportunity of an education, a job or simple justice.

Quoted in the *Atlanta Journal,* January 12, 1971, p. 5-A. Contrast this with statements in the 1959 inaugural address of Georgia's Governor Ernest Vandiver:

> I have been into almost every militia district of this state—I know the thinking of the people in the four corners of this state. . . We have only just begun to fight. The people of Georgia and their new governor say to the United States Supreme Court that we will fight it wherever it raises its ugly head, in these very streets, in every city, in every town, and in every hamlet. . . .

Quoted in *the Atlanta Journal,* January 13, 1959, p. 4. Vandiver, it is interesting to note, was more moderate on the race issue than was his major opponent in the Democratic primary.

64. At the time of the founding of the republic the suffrage was restricted to property owners and taxpayers. Indeed the requirement that one pay property taxes is still a prerequisite to voting in bond elections in some areas.

65. The four were Alabama, Mississippi, Texas, and Virginia.

66. Harper v. Board of Elections, 303 U.S. 663 (1966).

67. Dan Nimmo and Clifton McCleskey, "Impact of the Poll Tax on Voter Participation: The Houston Metropolitan Area in 1966," *Journal of Politics,* 31, August 1969, pp. 682-699. However in Austin, Texas, when assessment of the poll tax for Federal elections was voided only 862 whites and 61 blacks bothered to register. Holloway and Olson, op. cit., p. 106.

68. One can only speculate that in a poorer, racially oppressive, rural area, the poll tax may have been a greater handicap to blacks.

69. Nimmo and McCleskey, op. cit.

70. Matthews and Prothro, op. cit., p. 46.

71. Holloway and Olson, op. cit., pp. 110 ff.

72. Ibid. Exceptions are special senate elections and off-year gubernatorial elections.

73. Ibid., p. 112.

74. *Political Participation,* pp. 14-15.

75. "Nationwide Black Gains for Elected Office in 1970," *Congressional Quarterly,* 28, December 11, 1970, p. 2951.

76. *Congressional Quarterly,* 28, November 6, 1970, p. 2771.

77. Marvin Wall and Clarence Seebiger, "Post-Mortems of a Georgia Primary," *New South,* 24, Summer 1969, pp. 80-88.

78. Charles S. Rooks, *The Atlanta Elections of 1969,* Atlanta: Voter Education Project, 1970, pp. 27, 31.

79. Matthews and Prothro, op. cit., pp. 61-324.

80. These findings are in keeping with those of Campbell et al., op. cit.

81. Holloway and Olson, op. cit., p. 121.

82. Joe R. Feagin and Harlan Hahn, "The Second Reconstruction: Black Political Strength in the South" *Social Science Quarterly,* 51, June 1970, p. 56.

83. Much of the following material is taken from *Political Participation,* pp. 21-114. See also "LSCRRC Reports on Mississippi Elections," *V.E.P. News,* 2, January 1968, pp. 3-4; "Rights Commission Reports Irregularities in Mississippi," *V.E.P. News,* 3, July 1969, p. 4.

84. *Political Participation,* p. 24.

85. Carmichael and Hamilton op. cit., p. 16.

86. Paul Good, "Poverty in the Rural South," *New South,* 23, Winter 1968, pp. 51-62.

87. See Carmichael and Hamilton, op. cit., pp. 98-120, for this data and the material used in the following paragraph.

88. House of Representatives, Committee on the Judiciary, *Hearings, Voting Rights, Act Extension,* H.R. 4249 and H.R. 5538, 91st Congress, pp. 19-28.

89. *Political Participation,* pp. 212-221.

90. House Committee on the Judiciary Hearings, Voting Rights, p. 11; Feagin and Hahn, op. cit., p. 51.

91. *Political Participation,* pp. 225-256.

92. "Nationwide Black Gains for Elected Office in 1970," *Congressional Quarterly,* 28, December 11, 1970, p. 2951.

93. Much of the foregoing paragraph is based on Robert DeLeon, "Negro Elected Officials on Hot Seat," *Atlanta Journal Constitution,* November 30, 1969, pp. 1-C, 18-C.

94. In 1968, 93 blacks were delegates or alternates to the Democratic National Convention from Southern states. The number of blacks per delegation ranged from three to twelve. Five Southern states sent a total of 13 delegates and alternates to the Republican National Convention. Janet Wells, "Southern States Send 100 Negroes to Conventions," *V.E.P. News,* 2, July 1968, pp. 1, 3.

95. The following material is taken from Keech, op. cit., passim.

96. In the primary Tate polled 49 percent of the black vote while Massell received 44 percent of the vote. Rooks, op. cit., p. 6.

97. Some observers saw the gubernatorial contest as a power struggle between an established force in the black community, state Senator Leroy Johnson, and C. B. King. Steve Ball, Jr., "Johnson's Still the Champ After Black Leaders Spar," *Atlanta Journal-Constitution,* September 9, 1970, p. 6-A.

98. Suggested in Keech, op. cit., p. 98.

99. See, for example, the discussions of violence in Sutherland, op. cit., passim. Interestingly one of the most violent outbursts in opposition to school integration in years was the overturning of two buses carrying black children to a white school in Lamar, South Carolina, in March 1970. This insurgency occurred during a period in which the Nixon administration was seeking to decelerate the speed of integration. May it not have been that renitent whites perceived the Thurmond nurtured Nixon-Agnew Southern courtship as reopening the entire question of black-white equality for review?

100. *Report of the U.S. Commission on Civil Rights, 1959,* p. 547.

101. Keech, op. cit.

102. *Ibid.*

103. William Brink and Louis Harris, *Black and White,* New York: Simon & Schuster, 1966, p. 120.

104. See Everett Carll Ladd, Jr., *Negro Political Leadership in the South,* Ithaca, N. Y.: Cornell, 1966, pp. 145-232, for a fine description of leadership changes in two Southern cities. Some of Ladd's findings are utilized in this section.

CHAPTER THREE

Public Accommodations and Service:

The Appearance of Change

Frequently, the dominant group in a society—especially when it is distinguishable by race or ethnicity—will deny access to ostensibly public facilities to members of other castes, races, or ethnic groups. The Indian caste system and the treatment accorded colonials by their imperial overlords exemplify such behavior. The most pervasive contemporary system of segregation appears to be the apartheid policies of South Africa and Rhodesia. In the United States new immigrants were upon occasion barred from various public facilities. In the South blacks have traditionally either been denied the use of public facilities or else restricted to racially separate accommodations.

Since 1964 racial segregation in public accommodations has been declared unconstitutional. The civil rights act of that year was the culmination of numerous attempts to undermine the network of laws and customs which denied blacks equal access to public accommodations. In this chapter we shall trace the challenges to public accommodations discrimination both before and after 1964. We shall also suggest reasons for the amount of compliance with laws and court decisions affecting Southern practices in this sphere.

TYPES OF PUBLIC ACCOMMODATIONS AND DISCRIMINATION

While public accommodations discrimination was almost universal in the South until recently, there were variations in its practice. Discriminatory practices can be categorized both in terms of provision of services and on the basis of who the guilty party is.

With regard to provision of services, sometimes blacks and whites were restricted to using separate facilities, sometimes services were available to whites but not to blacks, and sometimes the same facilities were available to both races but on a segregated basis. Parks, pools, restaurants, and hotels exemplify facilities that blacks were banned from using simultaneously with whites, as was the case with schools. The separate but equal interpretation of the equal protection clause[1] prompted some Southern states and larger cities to maintain dual systems of public facilities. In some smaller towns, however, tax-supported facilities were provided only for whites. Thus many local governments in the South made no pretense of adhering to the separate but equal requirement in providing services other than education.

Another type of segregation has been more analogous to that found in employment—that is, blacks while eligible for employment in businesses throughout the South, were always limited to the lowest-status jobs. Similarly, blacks were permitted to attend public events and to ride on public conveyances but were confined to segregated seating areas. Southern ballparks had "nigger bleachers," and there were separate balconies in those theaters to which blacks were admitted.[2]

Discrimination in public accommodations was carried out by two agents—state and local government, and the business community. Schools, parks, and municipal stadia represent facilities owned by an arm of the state. In a second group are facilities which are privately owned and are open to the public, such as restaurants, motels, theaters, and commercial carriers.

Segregation in public accommodations rested upon both laws and folkways. Indeed it was a local segregation law which ushered in the first modern civil rights demonstration, the Montgomery bus boycott. This was triggered by the arrest of Rosa Parks who refused to vacate her seat in the white section of a city bus and stand in the packed aisle. Even in the absence of legally dictated segregation, the law was often an ally of businessmen who refused equal service to blacks. Those who challenged discrimination through sit-in techniques might be arrested for trespassing,[3] disturbing the peace,[4] and other misdemeanors. Once arrested, they languished in jail or posted bail, but in either case the subsequent litigation might last for years.[5]

If civil rights demonstrators were not arrested, they were often denied protection by the police. Some law enforcement officials often conveniently looked the other way while sit-in protestors were pummeled, cursed, and doused with ketchup, grease, and the like. In St. Augustine, Florida, deputized Klansmen were dispatched to break up protests challenging segregation practices of local motels, restaurants, and beaches.[6] This is reminiscent of tales of Southern law officers arriving at lynchings to direct traffic.

Public Sector

In the South virtually every service provided by the government was offered on a segregated basis. Separate hospitals and health centers looked after the health needs of blacks and whites. In public buildings, such as courthouses, whites and blacks drank from separate water fountains and urinated into segregated toilets. Justice was dispensed in courtrooms in which segregated seating was enforced and white and black witnesses took the oath using different Bibles. Those who were imprisoned were confined in racially homogeneous cells or were sent to work on the roads in uni-racial chain gangs. Some police departments had black officers, but these men were often forbidden to stop or arrest whites. In some cities they received no salary but were compensated with a portion of the fines levied on blacks whom they arrested. A standing joke in the South was that the only public facility not segregated was the highway system.

These and other similar instances of discrimination were tolerated so long as the equal protection clause was interpreted to permit separate but equal facilities for blacks and whites. The Supreme Court decision striking down the separate but equal doctrine (discussed in Chapter Four) opened the door for invalidation of state-required segregation in a variety of tax-supported facilities. Beginning with a 1955 decision on the constitutionality of a law requiring segregation at public beaches[7] and continuing through a 1968 case involving prison segregation,[8] Federal courts have expanded the range of state-owned desegregated facilities.[9]

In public accommodations, as has often happened elsewhere, some cities and towns have not discontinued discrimination until pressured to do so by either protestors or some arm of the government. However, once steps are taken to force compliance with the law, equal treatment has usually followed, particularly in the urban areas. Less frequently, equality has been attained through the closing of facilities so that they can be enjoyed by neither race.[10] At times individual whites avoid the effects of legal edicts by discontinuing use of facilities once black use reaches a certain level. The critical level varies seemingly depending upon the closeness of physical contact. For example, the presence of a handful of blacks can clear a municipal swimming pool of white bathers.[11] It requires many more blacks before whites give up the use of public beaches, parks, or tennis courts. Even the attendance of large numbers of blacks at sporting events does not result in a boycott by whites.

In the past many blacks were willing to settle for racially separate facilities as an improvement over no facilities at all for blacks. Increasingly, however, the sights of some young blacks have been set on status gains.[12] Thus there has been a growing willingness to confront the white power structure with an all-or-nothing proposition: Either open publicly owned facilities to everyone, or close them down!

Private Sector

The earliest successful cases challenging segregation practiced by private entrepreneurs involved commercial carriers. In 1946 the Supreme Court used the commerce clause of the Constitution to invalidate laws which required black interstate passengers to ride in separate train cars or at the rear of buses.[13] Such requirements were judged to be an unreasonable burden on the flow of interstate commerce. This interpretation, it should be noted, was quite narrow, being inapplicable to local carriers and to passengers who did not cross state lines in their travels. Also, no enterprise except commercial carriers was affected.

In other types of public accommodations few changes occurred before the sixties. True, in most states hotels and motels were under the common-law obligation to give board to any traveler requesting it, but this requirement went unenforced. Businessmen exercised the right to refuse service to whomsoever they chose, and in the South that often meant that all blacks were turned away, although some restaurants would sell food to blacks on a carry-out basis. The color line was so firm that the United States suffered loss of face before the whole world when Southern restauranteurs turned away visiting dignitaries from

Africa. Hotels and motels tolerated deviations from strict segregation only if the black guest was introduced as an Indian. Inns which offered lodging to the dogs of white travelers rejected black professionals, businessmen, and entertainers.

The legal position of white businessmen was that they could use their property as they saw fit so long as their activities were not illegal, immoral, or injurious to the general welfare. Extending the adage that a man's home is his castle, they contended that just as one could not be forced to let into his home someone whom he found unacceptable—regardless of the reason for this rejection—so also one could limit the clientele of his business. They further maintained that the owner's right to utilize his property as he sees fit is the most basic of freedoms. For, if the individual cannot control access to his property, they insisted, then there is no refuge where he can be safe from government interference.

Private businessmen also had the weight of legal precedent on their side. In 1883 the United States Supreme Court had ruled unconstitutional a section of the Civil Rights Law of 1875 which had extended the protection of Federal law to people denied service at businesses open to the public. The so-called Civil Rights Cases grew out of actions by black plaintiffs who had been turned away from hotels, theaters, and white railroad cars solely because of their race. The Court decided that the Fourteenth Amendment prohibited discrimination by the state but had no bearing on discrimination practiced by private individuals or corporations.[14] Consequently blacks who suffered the indignity of being denied service had no recourse. Privately owned businesses catering to the public were not even required to pay lip service to the separate but equal doctrine which set the pace in publicly operated institutions.

Denial of services was not only degrading but also inconvenient. One need only visualize a black family traveling on a rural stretch of interstate highway where motels and restaurants accepted only white customers, to comprehend the extent of the problem. To find lodging or a meal the weary family might have to drive miles out of the way. Even to press on to the next city having accommodations for blacks would not be a wholly adequate alternative. As the murder of Lemuel Penn[15] demonstrated, for blacks to be on a lonely Southern highway after dark might be sufficient provocation to be shot down.

The first protests by blacks were not, however, aimed at securing accommodations for the highway traveler. Indigenous blacks were not inconvenienced by the racial practices of motels in their own area. A denial of local service which was far more exasperating was the discriminatory practice at drug and dime store lunch counters. Southern entrepreneurs were eager for black dollars so long as they could be gathered without arousing local prejudices. Black customers were welcome in all other departments of these stores, being encouraged to buy everything except a meal. Thus black and white could sit side by side to try on shoes but not to eat.

Beginning in Greensboro, North Carolina, in February 1960 and spreading throughout the South, black college students and their white allies challenged these practices. Their protests took the form of sitting down at lunch counters and refusing to leave until served. Upon ignoring the owner's demands that they leave, the protestors might be arrested. By August of 1961 an estimated 70,000 people had participated in sit-in demonstrations; of these some 3,600 were arrested.[16] The sit-in tactic, since if the demonstrators were numerous enough they could halt the operation of the lunch counter, was more effective than marches or picketing. Where marches had at most caused whites only the temporary inconvenience of traffic congestion, sit-ins touched the business community in its most vulnerable spot, the pocket book.[17] The sit-in movement succeeded in opening hundreds of facilities to blacks.[18]

These privately arrived at agreements left facilities in Southern cities a confusing checkerboard of integration and segregation. Sometimes an owner would bow to black pressure and integrate his facilities, only to resegregate when picketed by whites or threatened with vigilante violence.[19] Blacks suffered the humiliation of entering an establishment which they thought was integrated only to find that they had been mistaken.

In addition, in trying to expand the range of services open to blacks, supporters of integration were involved in securing victories which in theory they had already won. Specifically, the requirement that interstate passengers not be forced to submit to local segregation practices had never been enforced in most of the South. Blacks still had to use separate waiting rooms and rest rooms, were turned away from terminal eating facilities, and often occupied segregated seating facilities while in transit. To challenge these clearly unconstitutional practices, young people rode buses through the South and refused to comply with local segregation laws. The historic Freedom Riders suffered verbal abuse, physical beatings, and even saw one of the buses on which they rode set afire.

As these challenges to discrimination were brought into the courts two constitutional points were raised. Situations involving interstate travel were decided under the commerce clause with its prohibition against activities impeding the free flow of commerce. The other tool available in protesting discriminatory treatment was the equal protection clause. This guarantee was, however, applicable only in instances in which it could be shown that the state or its agents had been parties to the discrimination.

Relying on the notion of state involvement, Federal courts struck down municipal ordinances requiring segregated facilities. Chief Justice Earl Warren, writing for the Court, argued that states had no power to require segregation.[20] He stopped short, however, of deciding that private persons could not continue to discriminate in their own business houses in the absence of laws to the contrary. The Court did, however, broadly define state action. In a case coming out of New Orleans where segregation was not required by local laws, a statement by the mayor that he would not tolerate restaurant integration was judged to constitute state action.[21] The rationale was that the mayor spoke as a public official and not as a private citizen. Unconstitutional state action was also found in the failure of a state to ban segregation when it could have done so. Thus a state was held to have a positive duty to require its lessee to conduct his business in a nondiscriminatory manner.[22]

In addition to voiding state and local laws requiring segregation in public places, the Supreme Court also swept aside laws used to harass sit-in demonstrators. Convictions of sit-in protestors were overturned in 61 of 81 cases reviewed by the Supreme Court.[23] The fact that whites reacted violently when peaceful blacks sought equal treatment was held to be an insufficient cause to interfere with the blacks' pursuit of their rights.[24] Arrests for trespass fell when it was shown that blacks were encouraged to spend money in all departments of a store except at the lunch counter. Having been encouraged to enter the store, they were not trespassing in seeking food services.[25]

The court decisions, however, did not cause the walls of segregation to come crashing down like those of biblical Jericho. While no figures are available, it is safe to say that prior to 1964 the number of Southern establishments willing to feed, lodge, or entertain both races were in the minority. To the extent that they existed, they were almost exclusively in urban areas. With the courts unable or unwilling to outlaw discriminatory practices unless state involvement, at least to the extent of tacit acceptance, could be demonstrated, free access to public accommodations seemed unlikely to come about in the absence of congressional action.

Soon after becoming President, Lyndon Johnson urged Congress to enact a public accommodations law as a lasting memorial to the slain John Kennedy. The President found an unwitting ally in Birmingham's "Bull" Conner who, by leading policemen wielding electric prods and high pressure fire hoses to disperse civil rights demonstrators, focused national attention on the continued existence of discrimination in the South. Title II of the Civil Rights Act of 1964, relying on the prohibition against interference with the flow of interstate commerce, forbade entrepreneurs to practice racial discrimination. Specifically, a businessman could not refuse service to blacks if 1) he served people traveling from state to state, or 2) a substantial portion of the products used in his business had moved in interstate commerce. By not defining what it meant by "a substantial portion" Congress left the decision up to the courts. Judging from cases involving the commerce clause, it appears that there is probably no business so small or regionalized that its activities do not have an effect on interstate commerce.[26]

Justifying the public accommodations section of the 1964 law by means of the commerce clause offered two advantages for enforcement. With virtually all businesses covered by the act, once a plaintiff demonstrated that discrimination existed—and few entrepreneurs who rejected black customers would deny it—the plaintiff had won. Under the equal protection clause, proof of state involvement in the discrimination would still be necessary for the plaintiff to win. A second advantage of using the commerce clause is that there is no court precedent holding an identical act unconstitutional. Recall from our earlier discussion of the 1883 Civil Rights Cases that a public accommodations act based on the enforcement clause of the Fourteenth Amendment was held unconstitutional when applied to the private sector. While the Supreme Court would probably have been willing to overrule its 80-year-old decision, the fact that it did not have to may have prompted compliance since it denied segregationists the criticism that the contemporary Court was striking at time-honored precedents. Moreover, using a congressional act rather than court action to state this policy goal may have given it a greater aura of legitimacy with some people. (We discuss this point at length in Chapter Eight.)

It appears that in much of the urban South blacks now have access to a wide range of services. Refusal to comply seems to be greatest in rural areas. Accumulation of precise data on the extent of compliance is made difficult, since exercise of rights to public accommodations had been on a freedom of choice basis. Thus until blacks seek service at a hotel, restaurant, etc., we do not know for sure whether discrimination is being practiced. We would expect, however, that with each passing year there is further testing of whether discrimination is practiced by a particular businessman. With such confrontations ultimately being decided in favor of the plaintiff, if it becomes necessary to pursue the matter in court, there is an ever-growing number of businesses open to blacks.

FACTORS ASSOCIATED WITH COMPLIANCE

Unlike other aspects of civil rights policy which we discuss in this book, the demise of the color bar in public accommodations was not greeted by near-universal resistance in the South. Some unreconstructed rebels, like Georgia's Lester Maddox who wielded an ax handle to drive black patrons from his restaurant, refused to comply. However many Southern businessmen acceded to the requirements of the public accommodations section of the 1964 law. In fact, rather than bemoaning the passing of a way of life, some businessmen sighed with relief as this vestige of a bygone era was laid to rest. Atlanta's Mayor Ivan Allen, Jr., spoke for many when he urged the Senate Commerce Committee to enact public accommodations legislation. As Allen noted, Congress' failure to act might be interpreted as tacit approval of racial discrimination and thereby undo the changes voluntarily made.[27]

Passage of public accommodations legislation facilitated compliance. Once all businessmen were required to open their doors to all customers they could desegregate, yet reply to white critics that they were doing so only because of Federal coercion. Thus they could integrate yet avoid being cast as traitors to their race. From an economic perspective, the absence of discrimination enabled Southern cities to compete more favorably for the lucrative convention trade.

Compliance was marred by some concerns, primarily restaurants and recreation operations, which resorted to the subterfuge of incorporating as private clubs in which membership was sold to any interested white for a nominal fee. This artifice has now been held to be unconstitutional.[28] Some lunch counters in drug and dime stores, particularly in rural areas, have reached a compromise with the demands of the law. They now serve blacks and whites but have removed the counter stools, tables, and booths. Biracial dining while standing up apparently poses less of a threat to some Southerners' values than does eating while sitting.

The apparent greater compliance with this statute than with many other civil rights laws requires an attempt at explanation. It would seem that the single most important factor was the attitude of many businessmen. These individuals undoubtedly frequently function as opinion leaders; therefore, their endorsement of the 1964 act endowed it with a degree of legitimacy in the eyes of many of their fellow citizens. With the business community in the main sanctioning compliance, since it was in its economic self-interest to do so, the potential mobs were lulled into acquiescence. Moreover the acceptance of desegregation by the business elite undoubtedly dissuaded many politicians from seeking to stir up opposition to the Federal law. If the people to whom one would turn for financial support in elections as well as general approval tolerated or encouraged the desegregation of public accommodations, the politician would be more likely to accept change than if he saw the situation as one in which racist appeals offered a political payoff.

A second factor is that the average white may feel less threatened by desegregation of public accommodations, than by integration elsewhere. Thus while 51 percent of a 1966 national sample did not want to live next door to a black family, only 16 percent found sitting next to blacks in restaurants or in buses objectionable.[29] Integrated schools and neighborhoods raise the specter of miscegenation to whites. There is less fear that matrimony will result from eating at the same restaurant.

Another consideration must be the type of people likely to seek service in privately owned public facilities. People seeking overnight lodging typically are of the middle class or richer. The same is true of those going outside of their neighborhood for a meal or for entertainment. Thus the customers who would be sharing public accommodations would often be social equals even if of different colors. The racist stereotype of a Negro is simply inappropriate when one thinks of blacks who are likely to dine at an Italian restaurant, or stay in a Holiday Inn. White fears and prejudices may be further allayed since blacks at integrated hotels, motels, and restaurants are relatively few in number—and tokenism has always been the guise in which integration has been most palatable to the majority race.

The class status of the white clientele likely to encounter blacks in public facilities is another consideration in understanding the degree of compliance. As is true of blacks, whites frequenting restaurants, hotels, and other establishments at which blacks are likely to be encountered tend to be of the middle or upper class. Being better educated, they probably are more tolerant; and being economically and socially secure, they may feel less threatened when in an environment in which blacks and whites are treated equally. Whereas other types of desegregation potentially affected the lower-class, redneck element of Southern white society, public accommodations integration is less likely to touch off the hair-trigger sensitivities of the white dirt farmers and mill workers.

Another factor ameliorating white fears is that many people, regardless of race, do not patronize daily or even weekly the types of business affected by the statute. Thus whereas integrated housing, schools, and employment mean daily interracial contact, the contact is neither as regular nor as frequent in public accommodations. In part, black presence in public accommodation facilities is less than in other spheres because fewer blacks can afford the services.

A last consideration in explaining the realization of public accommodations desegregation is the visibility of the discriminator's behavior. When a black seeks to utilize a public facility, he must be accepted or rejected; he cannot be told to fill out forms or to come back some other time. Attempts to register, gain employment, purchase a home, or integrate a school can be delayed through procedural subterfuges. Rejection of blacks in those areas can be more easily disguised as nonracial in nature. Integration, aside from public accommodations, is subject to tokenism, permitting defendants that are challenged to plead innocence of discrimination by arguing that there are a couple of black employees, a sprinkling of black students, or a handful of black voters. In public accommodations, demonstration of past token compliance does not ameliorate the guilt of the proprietor if he rejects a customer for racial reasons.

IMPLICATIONS

Compliance with Federal public accommodations decrees has become widespread in much of the South, particularly in urban areas. Court decisions of the late fifties and early sixties enlarged the range of publicly owned facilities to which blacks had access. After Congress moved to breach the obstacles to service for blacks in private concerns catering to the public, much of the business community acquiesced. Earlier arguments about the sanctity of property rights and the alleged un-American nature of the public accommodations act subsided soon after the Supreme Court upheld the statute in test cases.[30] Reasons for acceptance of the passing of segregation in public accommodations but not in other areas have already been suggested.

The long-run effect of the act is a major status gain for blacks. Henceforth they can patronize whatever facilities appeal to their tastes and are within the reach of their pocketbooks. In the immediate future the changes wrought by the disappearance of racial barriers may be of marginal consequence. Only the relatively thin strata of middle- and upper-income blacks can afford to patronize facilities (with the possible exception of hamburger joints and movie theaters) in which they are likely to encounter whites. Many poor blacks will continue to frequent primarily businesses which are located in all-black ghettos. Not until herculean economic advances are made which bring blacks beyond the immigrant stage can it be anticipated that they will fully enjoy the benefits of the 1964 act.

In the sphere of publicly owned services, the immediate potential has already been marked. Blacks began enjoying city parks and recreation centers, hospitals and clinics, libraries, etc., once their right to use these facilities was determined by the courts. Another court decision which has been implemented daily by thousands of blacks has been the right to take any vacant seat on a city bus. Government-owned facilities have attracted much greater black use because, unlike private businesses, their use does not have to be paid for.

NOTES

1. The separate but equal interpretation refers to Supreme Court decisions holding that so long as materially equal facilities were available to blacks and whites, it was permissable for Southern governmental units to enforce segregation. The rationale behind decisions of this type was that racial separation per se did not stamp either race as inferior. The myopic logic of the Court suggested that so long as facilities were equal, only the paranoid would find segregation distasteful. The landmark case of this type upheld a Louisiana law which required that blacks and whites occupy separate railway cars. Plessy v. Ferguson, 163 U.S. 537 (1896). Separate but equal was first judged unconstitutional when applied to educational institutions. Brown v. Board of Education, 347 U.S. 483 (1954). In the next few years similar decisions were handed down wiping away racial barriers in a number of other settings.
2. While blacks were limited to patronizing all-black theaters in the larger cities of the South, movie houses in some smaller towns and cities, particularly in Border states, admitted blacks but confined them to the balcony.
3. Peterson v. South Carolina, 373 U.S. 244 (1963).
4. Garner v. Louisiana, 368 U.S. 157 (1961); Bouie v. Columbia, 378 U.S. 347, 1964.
5. Hundreds of Freedom Riders convicted in Mississippi for breach of the peace waited more than three years as their cases were appealed. Anthony Lewis, *Portrait of a Decade,* New York: Random House, 1964, p. 92.
6. Leon Friedman, "The Federal Courts of the South: Judge Bryan Simpson and His Reluctant Brethren," in Leon Friedman, ed., *Southern Justice,* Cleveland: Meridian Books, 1967, pp. 194-199.
7. Mayor of Baltimore v. Dawson, 350 U.S. 377 (1955).
8. Washington v. Lee, 263 F. Supp. 327, Aff'd., 390 U.S. 333 (1968).
9. For a listing of the other cases and facilities which have been ordered to be provided free of segregation see William B. Lockhart, Yale Kamisar, and Jesse H. Choper, *Constitutional Rights and Liberties: Cases and Materials,* St. Paul, Minn.: West, 1970, p. 840.
10. Evans v. Newton, 382 U.S. 296 (1966).
11. The response of middle-class neighborhoods to blacks in the swimming pools has been to build pools to serve those living in the subdivision. The real losers have been lower-class whites too poor to swim anywhere but in public pools, which they avoid in the presence of blacks.
12. Everett Carll Ladd. Jr., *Negro Political Leadership in the South,* Ithaca, N.Y.: Cornell, 1966, pp. 145-232.
13. Morgan v. Virginia, 328 U.S. 375 (1946).
14. Civil Rights Cases, 109 U.S. 3 (1883).
15. Mr. Penn and Viola Liuzzo were victims of racially motivated shots fired into their cars at night from passing vehicles. Mr. Penn, a black officer in the Army Reserve, was slain a few miles outside of Athens, Georgia, as he drove

back to Washington from summer training at Fort Benning, Georgia. Mrs. Liuzzo, a white Detroit housewife was murdered as she drove a black youth back to Selma, Alabama, after the completion of a civil rights protest march on the state capitol.

16. Joel B. Grossman, "A Model for Judicial Policy Analysis: The Supreme Court and Sit-In Cases," in Joel B. Grossman and Joseph Tanenhaus, eds., *Frontiers of Judicial Research,* New York: Wiley, 1969, p. 427.

17. The sit-in as a challenge to segregated eating establishments was followed by kneel-ins at churches, wade-ins at beaches, and so forth. The technique has more recently been adopted by students in protests directed against college administrations and selective service boards.

18. Lewis, op. cit., p. 87.

19. For a graphic description see Leon Friedman, "The Federal Courts of the South: Judge Bryan Simpson and His Reluctant Brethren," in Friedman, ed., *Southern Justice,* p. 195.

20. Peterson v. South Carolina, 373 U.S. 244 (1963).

21. Lombard v. Louisiana, 373 U.S. 267 (1963).

22. Burton v. Wilmington Parking Authority, 365 U.S. 715 (1961).

23. Grossman, op. cit., pp. 439ff.

24. Garner v. Louisiana, 368 U.S. 157 (1961).

25. For a discussion see Loren Miller, *The Petitioners,* Cleveland: Meridian Books, 1967, pp. 392-409.

26. Wickard v. Filburn, 317 U.S. 111 (1942); Katzenbach v. McClung, 379 U.S. 294 (1964).

27. Testimony of Ivan Allen, Jr., Mayor of Atlanta, Hearings before the U.S. Senate, Committee on Commerce, "A Bill to Eliminate Discrimination in Public Accommodations Affecting Interstate Commerce," Senate 1732, 88th Congress, 1st Session, p. 866.

28. Daniel v. Paul, 395 U.S. 298 (1968).

29. William Brink and Louis Harris, *Black and White,* New York: Simon & Schuster, 1966, p. 136.

30. Heart of Atlanta Motel v. U.S., 379 U.S. 241 (1964); Katzenbach v. McClung, 379 U.S. 294 (1964).

CHAPTER FOUR

School Desegregation:
Nine Parts Deliberation and One Part Speed

In terms of the time, energy, and resources invested, progress in school desegregation has been the most elusive of all areas of civil rights. In fact it would not be too much to say that policy in this area has been a failure. After 15 years of litigation, demonstrations, and administrative actions approximately one of every six black students in the South attended a desegregated school.[1] A dramatic decision by the Supreme Court ordering an end to further delays in school desegregation,[2] implemented in some areas by massive busing, raised the number of black students attending predominantly white schools in the South to 39.1 percent in the fall of 1970.[3] Ironically, in the North only 27.5 percent of all black students were attending majority-white schools in the same period. There were still more students attending all-black schools in the South than in the North, but segregation seemed to be increasing in the North and decreasing in the South.

Success in this area, however, is even less than these modest figures indicate. In many of the schools that have been integrated in the South the most invidious kinds of racial discrimination persist.[4] In these schools the potential for alienation and confrontation seems to be rising.

It will be the purpose of this chapter to analyze events surrounding the struggle over school desegregation in the hope of casting some light on the factors that have impeded progress and to reflect on the implications of nondiscriminatory school systems.

THE BROWN DECISION

Until 1954, 17 states and the District of Columbia required racial segregation in public schools.[5] Four other states permitted school districts to opt for segregation without requiring it statewide.[6] Desegregation efforts began in 1954 when the Supreme Court, in the now famous *Brown* v. *Board of Education of Topeka,*[7] ruled that racial segregation in public schools is unconstitutional because separate facilities are inherently unequal. The Court did not stipulate how the states were to correct inequities or what deadline would be imposed. Instead the Court invited interested parties to prepare briefs directed at means for implementing the Court's orders. Representatives of ten Southern and Border states advised the Court on how the object of the *Brown* decision might be realized. The state officials cautioned against the issuance of specific instructions or set guidelines by the Court, recommending that the determination of whether school districts were in compliance with *Brown* be left to Federal district courts. Thurgood Marshall and his staff of NAACP lawyers implored the Court to set September of 1955 or 1956 as the deadline for ending segregation, and to issue explicit instructions to the district judges.[8] Marshall argued that black children ought to be able to enjoy constitutionally guaranteed rights immediately, not at some distant time in the future.

The Court rejected Marshall's advice. In its implementation decision (sometimes known as *Brown II*) handed down in 1955, the Court explained that the diversity of local conditions dicated a policy that would make room for exceptional situations. Federal district judges were ordered to supervise desegregation within these boundaries:

1. Remember that school authorities, not the courts, have the primary duty for determining how and when schools should be integrated.
2. Require the school board, however, to make a prompt and reasonable start toward full compliance with the May 17, 1954 ruling.
3. Once such a start has been made, the board may be given additional time to complete integration.
4. The burden rests on the school board to establish the need for additional time. Do not grant a postponement unless you are convinced the board is acting in good faith to bring about

integration at the earliest practicable date. Among the factors which may be considered in deciding whether a school district may delay integration are necessary administrative rearrangements, adjustments of the transportation system, revision of school district lines to accommodate the altered situation, revision of local laws and regulations.

5. Do not allow school boards to postpone integration merely because the board members or their community favor segregation.
6. Plans calling for desegregation by steps are permissible, provided authorities, acting in good faith, are proceeding with all deliberate speed.
7. Retain jurisdiction during the period of transition.[9]

THE FIRST TEN YEARS: THE JUDICIAL ERA

Save for an occasional Texas or Arkansas district with few black pupils, the South made no voluntary move to comply with *Brown.* In the Border states of Delaware, Maryland, West Virginia, Kentucky, Missouri, and Oklahoma, however, immediate progress was made. Although some difficult problems had to be overcome, school districts in these states moved steadily toward desegregation. Cities such as St. Louis, Baltimore, Washington, Kansas City, and Louisville demonstrated that large cities with substantial numbers of black citizens could desegregate without violence or disruption.[10]

In the Southern states, however, there was no progress, and hostility to desegregation was growing as every effort was made to fight the Supreme Court's decision. Aspiring politicians vied with one another in promising the extremes to which they would go to prevent integration. In Georgia "Marvin Griffin was nominated for Governor . . . on the pledge: Come Hell or high water races will not be mixed in Georgia schools."[11] In Virginia the Governor announced: "I shall use every legal means at my command to continue segregated schools."[12] George Wallace told the people of Alabama: "I draw the line in the dust and toss the gauntlet before the feet of tyranny and I say segregation now, segregation tomorrow, segregation forever."[13]

In the Deep South the chosen path of massive resistance called for law after law designed to "legalize" circumvention of *Brown.* This "litigate and legislate" strategy called for the extended litigation of each of the questionable integration-thwarting statutes. When one law was overruled by the courts, by a long and costly process, the legislature or local school board merely passed another law or regulation designed to preserve the status quo (hence the popular saying, "As long as we can legislate we can segregate.").

In resisting *Brown* Southern solons displayed far more ingenuity, energy, and boldness than they ever expended in resolving the problems of poverty, illiteracy, malnutrition, and illness which have plagued the region. A multitude of laws encompassing everything from Calhoun's moth-eaten nullification doctrine to the self-destructive proposal that the public schools be closed were hastily enacted. In Texas the progress that had been made immediately after *Brown* was reversed by a state law that withheld state funds from school districts that integrated without prior approval having been registered by the district's citizens in a referendum.[14] The Georgia, Alabama, and Virginia legislatures forbade desegregation even when ordered by Federal courts.[15] Several states offered tuition grants to parents of white children wishing to send their children to private schools to avoid desegregation.[16] In Arkansas and Virginia where integration had been ordered by the courts, public schools were closed, denying an education to both blacks and whites. These and other laws were passed with full knowledge that they contravened Federal law and were therefore unconstitutional. That these statutes were obviously illegal brought no shame to the policy makers who violated the meaning if not the letter of Federal law. Instead, obstructionist state legislators were honored as folk heroes in the best Johnny Reb tradition.

Defiance achieved new respectability when in 1956, 96 members of the United States Congress signed the Southern Manifesto. The Manifesto condemned the *Brown* decision, commended those Southern states that had announced a policy of resistance to desegregation, and declared an intention to use "all lawful means" to bring about a reversal of the decision.

Official acts such as these gave the trappings of legitimacy to the resistance movement, and by placing ends above means encouraged the worse elements in Southern society to take any steps perceived necessary (including violence) to stop desegregation. Local recalcitrance became something of an art. Jack Peltason describes the segregationists at work:

Their strategy is relatively simple. Mobilize political power to discourage any school board or any judge from moving against segregation. Create obstacles to make it difficult or dangerous for any Negro to carry the issue before a judge. If these moves fail, persuade the judge not to issue an injunction, and if he does issue one, persuade him that it need not call for any actual desegregation. If all this fails, then find ways to circumvent the injunction.[17]

Using such tactics, segregationists brought what little voluntary integration there had been to a halt by 1957. The tone for future events had been set by the most rabid racists in the South.

Large-scale violence was less frequent in the South after *Brown* than many southerners (sometimes gleefully) had predicted, but it was present, sometimes in very dramatic form. In 1957 mobs turned black children away from Central High School in Little Rock, Arkansas. President Eisenhower, after publicly vacillating about what stance the Federal government should take, finally ordered Federal troops to the school to insure peaceful integration. A similar crisis developed in New Orleans in 1960, where mobs ran through the streets assaulting innocent people, and a band of screaming women (known as the "cheerleaders") demonstrated outside an integrated school before national television. In Birmingham, Alabama, in 1963 an orgy of mob violence resulted from a court order desegregating a number of previously all-white schools. White students boycotted the schools, and rioting whites killed at least three blacks. During this same troubled period, a black church was bombed—killing four little girls at Sunday School and injuring 23 others.

The absence of violence in other parts of the South usually denoted the lack of even token desegregation. The paucity of progress was beginning to tax the Supreme Court's patience. In a 1963 case the Court cautioned that it was "never contemplated that the concept of 'deliberate speed' would countenance indefinite delay in elimination of racial barriers in the South."[18] Even more significantly, the Court added: "the basic guarantees of our Constitution are warrants for the here and now and unless there is an overwhelmingly compelling reason, they are to be promptly fulfilled."[19] In 1964 the Court warned that integration had proceeded with "entirely too much deliberation and not enough speed."[20] In this case the Court held that the closing of public schools in Prince Edward County, Virginia, while other public schools remained open in the state, denied black students equal protection of the laws as guaranteed by the Fourteenth Amendment. The Court also ruled that states could not give tuition grants or tax breaks to parents who sent their children to private, segregated schools to avoid attending integrated schools. In another 1964 case the Court upheld a district court decision ordering Duval County (Florida) school officials to stop assigning teachers in its school system on a racial basis.[21]

Congress finally became meaningfully involved in the school desegregation struggle with the passage of the Civil Rights Act of 1964. For the first ten years after *Brown,* the judiciary had assumed almost total responsibility for effectuating school desegregation. As Table 4-1 shows, the judiciary's success was extremely limited. Texas, with 5.5 percent of its black students attending schools with whites, led the South. Seven of the eleven Southern states had not achieved even 1 percent racial integration. In contrast the six Border states made more progress in the first two years following *Brown* than the South did in ten years. By the 1963-64 school year, three of the Border states had achieved over 50 percent racial mixing, and two others over 40 percent. Before proceeding to an analysis of the impact of the 1964 act, we will analyze why judicial efforts to achieve school desegregation were so unsuccessful in the first decade after *Brown.*

FACTORS IMPEDING INTEGRATION
DURING THE FIRST DECADE

The Wrong Branch of Government

It was unfortunate that the first branch of government to recognize the right of black Americans to an equal education had to be the Supreme Court. For a number of reasons the Supreme Court was a less desirable vehicle for this new policy than either of the other branches of government. The *Brown* decision represented policy in the purest sense. Policy making is a function of courts,[22] but the public generally sees their function as one of simply interpreting law. In interpreting the law, however, courts frequently have considerable latitude in making decisions. Few laws are so specific that a judge has no discretion in deciding new problems subsumed under the law. Such decisions constitute policy. The public becomes aware of the Court's policy-making role

TABLE 4-1 Progress in school desegregation by percentages of black pupils in public schools with whites (1954-1970)

	54-55	55-56	56-57	57-58	58-59	59-60	60-61	61-62	62-63	63-64	64-65	65-66	66-67
South													
Alabama	00.0	00.0	00.0	00.0	00.0	00.0	00.0	00.0	00.0	00.0	00.0	00.4	04.4
Arkansas	00.0	00.0	00.0	00.1	00.1	00.1	00.1	00.1	00.2	00.3	00.8	06.0	15.1
Florida	00.0	00.0	00.0	00.0	00.0	00.3	00.0	00.3	00.7	01.5	02.7	09.8	22.3
Georgia	00.0	00.0	00.0	00.0	00.0	00.0	00.0	00.0	00.0	00.1	00.4	02.8	08.8
Louisiana	00.0	00.0	00.0	00.0	00.0	00.0	00.0	00.0	00.0	00.1	01.1	00.9	03.4
Mississippi	00.0	00.0	00.0	00.0	00.0	00.0	00.0	00.0	00.0	00.0	00.0	00.6	02.5
North Carolina	00.0	00.0	00.0	00.0	00.0	00.0	00.0	00.1	00.3	00.5	01.4	05.2	15.4
South Carolina	00.0	00.0	00.0	00.0	00.0	00.0	00.0	00.0	00.0	00.0	00.1	01.7	05.6
Tennessee	00.0	00.1	00.1	00.1	00.1	00.1	00.2	00.8	01.1	02.7	05.4	16.3	28.6
Texas	00.0	01.4	01.4	01.4	01.2	01.2	01.2	01.3	02.3	05.5	07.8	17.4	44.9
Virginia	00.0	00.0	00.0	00.0	00.0	00.1	00.1	00.2	00.5	01.6	05.2	11.0	25.3
Border													
Delaware	01.9	11.0	28.5	36.2	43.7	44.1	45.0	53.7	55.9	56.5	62.2	83.3	100.0
Kentucky	00.0	00.8	20.9	28.4	27.5	38.9	47.2	51.2	54.1	54.4	68.1	78.1	90.1
Maryland	05.1	13.9	19.1	22.1	32.4	29.3	33.6	41.5	45.1	41.8	50.9	55.6	65.3
Missouri	*	*	*	*	*	42.7	41.7	41.4	38.9	42.1	42.3	75.1	77.7
Oklahoma	00.0	*	08.7	18.2	21.2	26.0	24.0	25.6	23.6	28.0	31.7	38.3	50.8
West Virginia	04.3	*	*	38.7	39.8	50.0	66.6	62.0	61.4	58.2	63.4	79.9	93.4

Source: Figures for years 1954-1967 compiled from various editions of Southern Education Reporting Service, *Southern School News* by Thomas R. Dye, ed., *American Public Policy: Documents and Essays* Columbus, Ohio: Merrill, 1969, pp. 18-19.
Note: These figures exaggerate progress achieved because only a few blacks attending a majority white school (or vice versa) hikes the figures significantly although many minority schools persist. HEW's figures are more revealing since they indicate the percentage of black students attending 49.9% minority schools. No state figures are available after the 1966-1967 school year.

*No data is available.

only in dramatic situations, e.g., *Brown.* In landmark cases many citizens question the Court's authority to make such a decision, perhaps because of the natural belief of Americans that important policy should be made by more representative branches of the government. When there is doubt about the Court's right to make a decision, qualms about legitimacy arise which ultimately diminish compliance. This happened in the wake of *Brown,* as a sizable minority of the public, a majority in the South, thought the Court had overstepped its authority, and therefore refused to obey the decision.

Congress would have been a much better agent of the policy unveiled in *Brown* because there would have been less doubt about the legitimacy of the decision. Even after the Supreme Court handed down *Brown,* if Congress had voiced its approval of the decision, the Court's path would have been easier. However, Congress never sanctioned the Court in a unified and meaningful way until the Civil Rights Act of 1964 and much had transpired in the interim.

Congressional action would have had a number of other advantages over a court decision. Congress is much better prepared to formulate a uniform standard for all school districts, and Congress has the financial resources necessary to supervise and regulate individual school boards and other local officials. The court's ability to enforce its decisions, on the other hand, is extremely limited since its power and prestige rest primarily on respect for the law.[23] When respect breaks down, the court must largely depend on the other branches of government to enforce its decisions. Additionally, courts are not designed to work quickly or cheaply. The advisory process is slow and deliberative by nature. Courts do not give advisory opinions, so each new situation must receive a full hearing. The courts then are not readily suited for initiating and enforcing new, controversial policy. They are best suited to serve as an ally or watchdog for and over other policy-making agencies and for legitimizing acts of the executive and legislature. But in 1954, in the face of congressional and executive inaction, the Supreme Court forged a new policy, and the struggle was on.

An Ambiguous Start

Even as the Supreme Court decided to lead the way, it made several tactical errors.[24] The Supreme Court's failure to formulate specific standards to guide enforcement of its decisions turned out to be a serious mistake. Terminology such as "all deliberate speed," "good faith," and "at the earliest possible date" was much too ambiguous. Such terms could be litigated, legislated, stretched, and distorted in a million ways. The South was quick to realize that it had won a victory when the Court failed to establish any specific standards for desegregation. Georgia's Governor Ernest Vandiver reacted to *Brown II* by saying: "I think the Supreme Court in some small measure attempted to correct an obnoxious decision."[25] In Florida *Brown II* was read over the public address system to the assembled members of the state legislature and was greeted with cheers.[26]

The Reluctant Bride: United States District Courts

The Supreme Court compounded its problems by charging the United States District Courts with applying and enforcing its decision. The district courts are particularly ill-suited to play the role of middleman in a cultural war. They are creatures of the environment over which they exercise jurisdiction. Their immersion in local culture and traditions makes them extremely vulnerable to parochial pressures from which the Supreme Court is largely isolated. The district courts can easily enforce and interpret standards set down by the Supreme Court, as long as those standards are specific and embodied in direct and unambiguous commands, but they are poorly suited for making and enforcing unpopular policy decisions. Additionally, Southern district judges have usually grown up with, and have been socialized to accept, the mores and culture they are expected to regulate. It is not surprising that in some instances district judges share the biases of the regions they serve, and that these biases are sometimes reflected in their decisions. When *Brown II* was being heard before the Supreme Court, S.E. Rogers representing South Carolina asked the Supreme Court to let the South take its segregation problems to the district courts, admitting that if it could "there would be no integration perhaps not until 2015 or 2045."[27]

The Supreme Court passed the pressure, then, to the agents least able or willing to handle it. State officials and private citizens alike put pressure on their district judges to ignore *Brown*. As Peltason says: "Segregationists lost their case at the Supreme Court, but they demanded that the district judge save their cause."[28] Many district judges were more than willing to do so. As late as 1963, Judge E. Gordon West of the Eastern District of Louisiana wrote in a school desegregation case:

> I could not, in good conscience, pass upon this matter today without first making it clear, for the record, that I personally regard the 1954 holding of the United States Supreme Court in the now famous Brown case as one of the truly regrettable decisions of all times. Its substitution of so-called "sociological principles" for sound legal reasoning was almost unbelievable. As far as I can determine, its only real accomplishment to date has been to bring discontent and chaos to many previously peaceful communities, without bringing any real attendant benefits to anyone.[29]

Judge West's opinions were shared by many district judges and were reflected in varying degrees of subtlety in their decisions. The Fifth Circuit Court of Appeals had to reverse dozens of cases in which district judges ruled against black plaintiffs when their right to judicial relief was unambiguous.[30] In some instances, district judges had to be reversed more than one time on the same case. In 1967 the Fifth Circuit in reviewing a district court case observed:

> This is the fourth or fifth appearance of this case in this court, considering both temporary measures and appeals on the merits. We simply do not consider it worthwhile to take the time to canvass the exact number of times in which we have been called upon to correct the actions of the District Court for the Southern District of Georgia which have been brought to us for review.[31]

The Lack of Executive Backing and Leadership

Not all Southern district judges are segregationists, and some of them tried manfully to apply the new decision as conscientiously as possible. Most district judges who did try to enforce *Brown* in the years immediately after the 1955 decision did not find it a very rewarding experience. The extreme vulnerability and isolation of district judges were soon made clear. To be effective the district courts need the power and prestige of the Federal government behind them. For the most part, that support never came during the Eisenhower years. Eisenhower's approach to all governmental activity was laissez faire, especially in his earliest years in office. He always believed that the Presidency should be above the day-to-day struggles of politics, and his attitude toward racial equality was no different. Eisenhower gave segregationists hope by refusing to endorse *Brown* and by constantly cautioning that progress in civil rights could only be gained over a long period. As Peltason points out:

> Segregationists did not expect the President or the Department of Justice to espouse segregation. But it suits their purpose almost as well if these officials stay out of the fight.[32]

Eisenhower's aloofness extended even to refusing on some cases to back up Federal district judges when their decisions were defied. "Eisenhower insisted that the refusal to obey the federal courts could not be dealt with by law enforcement but only by moral conversion."[33] Eisenhower had no intention of guiding the transformation, however, and the result was that district judges soon learned that if they enforced the law in good faith and found themselves facing a hostile mob, a recalcitrant governor, a determined legislature, or an immovable school board, they could not be sure of being backed up. Ominous examples began to crop up. In Texas in 1956 a district judge ordered a local school district to desegregate. The school board followed the court's decision, but Governor Shivers ordered the Texas Rangers to turn black children away from the schools. Eisenhower not only did not send Federal troops to back up the judge; he told a news conference that he had not been paying attention to the situation.[34] The result was that the district judge's order was ignored, and other judges were given an example of what could happen if they enforced the law. Peltason calculates that "between 1954 and 1960 there were at least twelve incidents in which rioters, sometimes with the tacit encouragement of state and local officials, tried to thwart the execution of a federal court order."[35] In only five of these cases did Federal executive authorities intervene, and "they did so in these instances only after local officials begged for help."[36] The lesson for the district judge was obvious: "desegregate and you get trouble; refuse to do so and you are a hero."[37]

Eisenhower's detachment also had repercussions for moderate office-holders in the Southern and Border states.[38] The same pressure put on district judges by rabid segregationists was also applied to public officials who dared to espouse moderation. Arguments that the law would have to be obeyed were undermined by Eisenhower's willingness to let defiance go unchallenged. The state legislatures seized the opportunity by passing laws designed to keep moderates from obeying the law. The accumulation of pressures made it perilous for local officials to make any effort to obey the law except in the face of extreme Federal coercion. Local officials soon realized that the Federal government was taking no steps to punish the disobedient, so the easiest and safest route was to do nothing.

The Lack of Activity by Black Citizens

The failure of Congress, the President, and local officials to take any positive measures to aid the school desegregation effort was matched, in large part, by a lack of activity on the part of black Americans. Although black citizens placed sustained pressure on officials in a few cities during the first ten years after *Brown,* efforts were sporadic and extremely limited where racial equality was most lacking. Undoubtedly many black Americans overestimated the forces at work on their behalf. Additionally, most rural blacks of the Southern and Border states could bring pressure to bear on local officials only at considerable risk. Segregationists made every effort to bring reprisal against blacks who responded to the Supreme Court's beckoning. Economic coercion in the form of lost jobs, credit termination, loan recalls, and revocation of leases was applied to many black citizens who sent their children to previously all-white schools or served as a plaintiff in a civil rights suit.[39] Other blacks had shots fired into their homes, were beaten, and were intimidated in a variety of ways; several civil rights workers were killed.[40]

Also, until 1964 there was no easy way for a black citizen to secure his rights. If he was willing to brave the segregationists in his community, he had to hire an attorney and bring a suit before the district court at considerable personal expense. The same forces that kept black citizens from speaking up also kept many lawyers of both races from taking civil rights suits. Thus, even if a black citizen had the courage and the money to bring a suit, he might not be able to find an attorney to represent him. Most of the more important civil rights suits were therefore brought before the courts by civil rights organizations, such as the NAACP. In many instances even civil rights organizations could not bring a suit, because no black citizen was willing to serve as plaintiff.

Civil rights organizations have also had a multitude of problems in the South, and have not been as strong or well organized as many people have believed. In several Southern states the NAACP had to fight off determined efforts by state officials to expel them from the state on trumped-up charges. In Alabama the effort was successful for a number of years because a bigoted judge joined forces with state officials.[41] Most civil rights groups have also had to labor under the burden of limited resources and personnel, forcing them to work in concentrated areas. There are 4,466 school districts in the Southern and Border states, and most of them have never seen a well-organized or determined civil rights demonstration.

School boards, then, have been under much less pressure from integrationists than one might expect. In a study of school desegregation in 15 major cities across the nation, Robert Crain et al. centered attention on the pressures placed on school boards by various groups.[42] They found that civil rights groups were not very active or effective in influencing board members. Even when civil rights organizations did put pressure on school boards, little progress resulted because the board members were most likely to follow their own biases.[43] Another limiting factor was that the civil rights organizations were frequently "symbol oriented,"[44] i.e., they were more interested in getting school boards to accept the principle of racial equality than in forcing full compliance with the law. Frequently boards could mouth the words of desegregation without doing much integrating. Boards which desegregated but never publicly made a commitment to racial equality were often subjected to more criticism than those boards that made the commitment but failed to integrate. The symbol of progress took the place of tangible deeds.

THE ADMINISTRATIVE-JUDICIAL ERA: 1964-1970

With the passage of the Civil Rights Act of 1964, leadership in school desegregation passed to the Department of Health, Education, and Welfare. HEW was charged with enforcing Title VI, which provided that any beneficiaries of Federal financial assistance who practice racial discrimination could have their funds terminated. Since all public schools depend on substantial Federal subsidies, the government had a new and potent weapon to use against discrimination. The 1964 act also authorized the Attorney General to bring desegregation suits where there was a private complaint.

Even with these new arrows in the administration's quiver, integration in the South came painfully slowly. Enforcement of Title VI did not meaningfully get under way until the 1965-1966 school year. HEW formulated a set of guidelines to be followed in enforcing Title VI. Basically the guidelines accepted gradualism and set 1967 as the target date for complete desegregation of all public schools. School districts were required to make a substantial good faith start toward integration by the fall of 1965. "Good faith start" was defined to "include the first and any other lower grade, the first and last high school grades, and the lowest of junior high where schools are so organized."[45] HEW allowed a school district to use any of three methods to show compliance: 1) execution of an Assurance of Compliance, stipulating that race, color, or national origin was not a factor in student assignment, reassignment, or transfer; that faculty and staff were not segregated; that the facilities, activities, and services of the school system were not segregated; and that no other vestige of segregation remained; 2) submission of a final order by a U.S. court requiring desegregation, plus a report indicating the willingness of the school system to comply, and the progress made to date; or 3) submission of a desegregation plan approved by the United States Commissioner of Education. This plan would have to show that the school system had adopted a workable desegregation plan. Freedom of choice was acceptable, but the burden of proof was on the school system to show that the plan would effectuate meaningful desegregation.

Using guidelines in place of slow case-by-case litigation, the first integration was achieved in many Southern districts. By September 18, 1965, 98 percent of the school districts in the Southern and Border states claimed to have met the minimal requirement of integrating at least four grades. This figure is deceptive, for while the percentage of school districts in compliance may have been high, the number of black children attending mixed schools was very small, as a glance at Table 4-1 will reveal.

In the 1966-1967 school year HEW made a few changes in its guidelines and continued enforcement efforts. Progress was slow, but better than in previous years. "In the 11 Southern states, 12.5 percent of Negro students attended schools with white students in the fall of 1966, compared with 6 percent in 1965."[46] By the end of 1966 the Department of Justice "had filed or joined its 93rd desegregation suit under the 1964 Act."[47] By February 7, 1967, HEW had cut off Federal funds to 34 school districts and had initiated final termination proceedings against 157 more.[48] During the next 11 months funds to 122 school districts were terminated.[49] Administration efforts received a further boost when a district court ordered desegregation to begin in all Alabama schools by fall, 1967, marking the first time a whole state had been ordered to desegregate. The court based its statewide injunction on the conclusion that state officials had "through their control and influence over local school boards flaunted every effort to make the Fourteenth Amendment a meaningful reality to Negro school children in Alabama."[50] The state was also ordered to develop remedial programs for black students, to overcome the effects of past discrimination.

In a similar action the Fifth Circuit Court of Appeals affirmed a district court decision upholding HEW guidelines and ordering desegregation of all grades by the fall of 1967 in six Southern states—Alabama, Georgia, Florida, Louisiana, Mississippi, and Texas.[51] The court said the school boards "have the affirmative duty under the Fourteenth Amendment of the United States Constitution to bring about an integrated, unitary school system in which there are no Negro schools and no white schools—just schools."[52] The court also stated that school officials had a positive obligation to overcome the effects of dual school systems by integrating facilities, faculties, and activities. The Supreme Court refused to hear the case on appeal, thereby upholding the Appellate Court opinion. In the same year the Supreme Court held that "free choice" and "free transfer" plans would be acceptable only if desegregation resulted. Where other methods would work faster, the Court ruled, they must be used [53]

HEW's attention up to this time had been confined almost exclusively to discriminatory practices of Southern schools. Attention was expanded to the magnitude of segregation nationwide by a 1967 report of the U.S. Commission on Civil Rights. The findings were not encouraging: "Racial isolation in the schools . . . is intense whether the cities are large or small, whether the proportion of Negro enrollment is

TABLE 4-2   Extent of elementary school segregation in 75 school systems

City	Percentage of blacks in 90-100% black schools	Percentage of blacks in majority-black schools	Percentage of whites in 90-100% white schools
Mobile, Ala.	99.9	99.9	100.0
Tuscaloosa, Ala.	99.6	99.6	100.0
Little Rock, Ark.	95.6	95.6	97.1
Pine Bluff, Ark.	98.2	98.2	100.0
Los Angeles, Calif.	39.5	87.5	94.7
Oakland, Calif.	48.7	83.2	50.2
Pasadena, Calif.	None	71.4	82.1
Richmond, Calif.	39.2	82.9	90.2
San Diego, Calif.	13.9	73.3	88.7
San Francisco, Calif.	21.1	72.3	65.1
Denver, Colo.	29.4	75.2	95.5
Hartford, Conn.	9.4	73.8	66.2
New Haven, Conn.	36.8	73.4	47.1
Wilmington, Del.	49.7	92.5	27.3
Miami, Fla.	91.4	94.4	95.3
Tallahassee, Fla.	99.7	99.7	100.0
Americus, Ga.	99.3	99.3	100.0
Atlanta, Ga.	97.4	98.8	95.4
Augusta, Ga.	99.2	99.2	100.0
Marietta, Ga.	94.2	94.2	100.0
Chicago, Ill.	89.2	96.9	88.8
East St. Louis, Ill.	80.4	92.4	68.6
Peoria, Ill.	21.0	86.9	89.6
Fort Wayne, Ind.	60.8	82.9	87.7
Gary, Ind.	89.9	94.8	75.9
Indianapolis, Ind.	70.5	84.2	80.7
Wichita, Kans.	63.5	89.1	94.8
Louisville, Ky.	69.5	84.5	61.3
New Orleans, La.	95.9	96.7	83.8
Baltimore, Md.	84.2	92.3	67.0
Boston, Mass.	35.4	79.5	76.5
Springfield, Mass.	15.4	71.9	82.8
Detroit, Mich.	72.3	91.5	65.0
Flint, Mich.	67.9	85.9	80.0
Minneapolis, Minn.	None	39.2	84.9
Hattiesburg, Miss.	98.7	98.7	100.0
Vicksburg, Miss.	97.1	97.1	100.0
Kansas City, Mo.	69.1	85.5	65.2
St. Joseph, Mo.	39.3	39.3	91.3
St. Louis, Mo.	90.9	93.7	66.0

TABLE 4-2 *(Continued)*

City	Percentage of blacks in 90-100% black schools	Percentage of blacks in majority- black schools	Percentage of whites in 90-100% black schools
Omaha, Nebr.	47.7	81.1	89.0
Newark, N. J.	51.3	90.3	37.1
Camden, N. J.	37.0	90.4	62.4
Albany, N. Y.	None	74.0	66.5
Buffalo, N. Y.	77.0	88.7	81.1
New York City, N. Y.	20.7	55.5	56.8
Charlotte, N. C.	95.7	95.7	94.7
Raleigh, N. C.	98.5	98.5	100.0
Winston-Salem, N. C.	88.7	95.1	95.6
Cincinnati, Ohio	49.4	88.0	63.3
Cleveland, Ohio	82.3	94.6	80.2
Columbus, Ohio	34.3	80.8	77.0
Oklahoma City, Okla.	90.5	96.8	96.1
Tulsa, Okla.	90.7	98.7	98.8
Portland, Oreg.	46.5	59.2	92.0
Chester, Pa.	77.9	89.1	37.9
Harrisburg, Pa.	54.0	81.3	56.2
Philadelphia, Pa.	72.0	90.2	57.7
Pittsburgh, Pa.	49.5	82.8	62.3
Providence, R. I.	14.6	55.5	63.3
Columbia, S. C.	99.1	99.1	100.0
Florence, S. C.	99.1	99.1	100.0
Sumter, S. C.	99.0	99.0	100.0
Knoxville, Tenn.	79.3	79.3	94.9
Memphis, Tenn.	95.1	98.8	93.6
Nashville, Tenn.	82.2	86.4	90.7
Amarillo, Tex.	89.6	89.6	98.3
Austin, Tex.	86.1	86.1	93.1
Dallas, Tex.	82.6	90.3	90.1
Houston, Tex.	93.0	97.6	97.3
San Antonio, Tex.	65.9	77.2	89.4
Richmond, Va.	98.5	98.5	95.3
Seattle, Wash.	9.9	60.4	89.8
Milwaukee, Wis.	72.4	86.8	86.3
Washington, D. C.	90.4	99.3	34.3

Source: U.S. Commission on Civil Rights, *Racial Isolation in the Public Schools,* Washington: GPO, 1967, pp. 4, 5.

Note: Percentages shown in this table are for the 1965-1966 school year, except for Seattle, Wash. (1964-1965), Los Angeles, Calif. (1963-1964), and Cleveland, Ohio (1962-1963).

large or small, whether they are located north or south."[54] Table 4-2
shows the extent of elementary school segregation found in 75
American cities.

> In these cities 75 percent of the Negro students are in elementary
> schools with enrollments that are nearly all-Negro (90 percent or
> more Negro), while 83 percent of the white students are in nearly
> all-white schools. Nearly 9 of every 10 Negro elementary school
> students attend majority-Negro schools.[55]

Even worse were indications that black students were becoming more,
instead of less, segregated in many parts of the United States. For
example, Table 4-3 shows the increasing segregation of black elementary school children in 15 Northern cities. Racial isolation was increasing because blacks were migrating to the cities and whites were moving
to suburbia. A good example is provided by Cincinnati, Ohio, where
black enrollment doubled in the last 15 years, but the number of black
children attending majority-black schools almost tripled.[56]

In the South the proportion of blacks in totally black schools has
decreased but the actual number of black students studying in racially
isolated schools has increased. This has been caused by slight desegregation combined with a much higher ratio of black students in the public
schools.[57]

New guidelines issued by the Johnson administration in 1968
brought Northern school systems into the controversy. De facto
segregation (segregation caused by housing patterns) was not outlawed,
but disparities in the caliber of education found in black and white
schools were condemned.[58] This meant that school facilities, curriculum, faculty, services, and per-pupil expenditures would have to be
equalized within a school system. The guidelines also required the
eventual elimination of segregation by planning new schools, renovating
old ones, and setting up appropriate school zones, feeder patterns, and
school transportation patterns.[59] The guidelines for the South
remained the same except that the percentage guides for free choice
plans were dropped, since the Supreme Court had elaborated the
standards that would make such plans acceptable.

Despite a flurry of Federal activity in 1968, progress in school
desegregation was minimal. A national survey by HEW found

> [a] shockingly low desegregation ratio on a national basis, with only
> 23.4 percent of the Negro students in the nation's public elementary

TABLE 4-3　Changes in numbers and proportion of black elementary enrollment in 90-100 percent black and majority-black schools in the North

City	Year	Number in 90-100% black schools	Percentage of total black enrollment	Number in majority black schools	Percentage of total black enrollment	Year	Number in 90-100% black schools	Percentage of total black enrollment	Number in majority black schools	Percentage of total black enrollment
Cincinnati	1950	3,981	43.7	6,442	70.7	1965	11,155	49.4	19,868	88.0
Milwaukee	1950*	1,316	51.2	1,716	66.8	1965	14,344	72.4	17,204	86.8
Pasadena	1950	0	0.0	196	26.2	1965	0	0.0	3,240	71.4
Philadelphia	1950	29,555	63.2	39,633	84.8	1965	66,052	72.0	82,704	90.2
Pittsburgh	1950	3,226	30.4	5,408	51.0	1965	9,226	49.5	15,428	82.8
Indianapolis	1951	7,637	83.2	8,101	88.2	1965	15,426	70.5	18,423	84.2
Cleveland	1952	12,369	57.4	18,174	84.4	1962	41,034	82.3	47,160	94.6
Oakland	1959*	1,110	7.7	10,274	71.1	1965	9,043	48.7	15,455	83.2
Detroit	1960	62,391	66.9	84,939	91.1	1965	77,654	72.3	98,274	91.5
Buffalo	1961	9,199	80.5	10,212	89.4	1965	13,106	77.0	15,097	88.7
San Francisco	1962	1,579	11.6	10,334	75.8	1965	3,031	21.1	10,369	72.3
Chester, Pa.	1963	2,961	71.1	3,573	85.8	1965	3,499	77.9	4,001	89.1
Harrisburg, Pa.	1963	2,103	58.1	2,994	82.7	1965	2,025	54.0	3,048	81.3
Springfield, Mass.	1963	0	0.0	1,989	58.8	1965	567	15.4	2,651	71.9
New Haven	1963	1,196	22.5	3,769	71.0	1965	2,171	36.8	4,329	73.4

Source:　U.S. Commission on Civil Rights, *Racial Isolation in the Public Schools*, Washington: GPO, 1967 p. 9.
*Estimated figures based on census and school enrollment data.

and secondary schools attending schools of predominately white (non-minority) enrollment, and with 61 percent of the Negro students isolated in 95 to 100 percent minority schools.[60]

In the South the situation was worse: only 18.4 percent of the black students in the 11 Southern states and only 10.5 percent in the five states of Alabama, Georgia, Louisiana, Mississippi and South Carolina attended majority-white schools in the spring of 1969.[61]

Years of bitter struggle had produced very little change. HEW concluded that a major reason was the existence of a large number of all-black schools—in both the North and South—created by segregated living patterns. HEW interpreted the 1967 decision obligating school systems to establish "an integrated, unitary school system in which there are no Negro schools and no white schools—just schools," as authority for ordering busing to overcome segregated living patterns. This decision was destined to be the center of considerable controversy.

The New Administration: Nixon's Slowdown

The lack of substantial progress in school desegregation was further impeded by a change in administrations in 1969. In his 1968 campaign, Nixon made it clear that he opposed busing and favored preservation of the neighborhood school. His general support for school desegregation was vague, but it appeared to be weak. He endorsed the *Brown* decision, but as one newspaper said "he opposed virtually every effort short of divine revelation for stepping up the segregation process." [62] Senator Strom Thurmond of South Carolina and other influential Southern Republican politicians stumped the South spreading the word that Nixon would soften HEW guidelines if elected President. With the help of the Southern states, Nixon won the election in a squeaker.[63]

In the first few months of his administration, Nixon took no clear stand on HEW guidelines. His Secretary of Health, Education, and Welfare, Robert Finch, and Director of HEW's Office of Civil Rights, Leon Panetta, were both liberals committed to enforcing the guidelines established during the Johnson administration. The result for the first few months was business as usual. Although outraged Southerners who had been promised relief by Thurmond applied considerable pressure on Nixon, enforcement continued unabated. Finch and Panetta persevered despite persistent rumors that the guidelines would be softened and efforts to achieve desegregation in the South would be deemphasized.

Nixon finally put his particular stamp on the desegregation movement in July, 1969, when Attorney General John Mitchell and Secretary of Health, Education, and Welfare Robert Finch jointly announced "new coordinated procedures" for the Federal effort to desegregate public schools. The thrust of the statement suggested that Nixon intended to pursue school desegregation by offering a plan that would hopefully please everyone. In effect the present deadlines were to be "both relaxed and, maybe, hopefully enforced."[64] Equivocation constituted the core of the new approach. The new procedures were:

1. The major focus of Federal efforts to desegregate elementary and secondary schools will be through litigation brought by the Department of Justice. The use of HEW's administrative proceedings backed by the threat of a termination of Federal funds, will be de-emphasized.
2. The two Departments will begin a substantial program of desegregation in areas of the North, the Midwest, and the West, where *de facto* racial segregation in schools results from discriminatory housing patterns.
3. The Department will refuse to require the completion of desegregation in all districts by "a single arbitrary date" or by means of "a single, arbitrary system."
4. The Department will continue to accept freedom-of-choice plans where such a plan "genuinely promises" to achieve desegregation at an early date.
5. HEW will provide more advice and assistance to school districts undergoing desegregation.
6. The Departments intend to recommend legislation to provide a selective infusion of federal funds for such needs as school construction, teacher subsidies and remedial education to aid desegregation.[65]

The statement contained strong language to the effect that the new procedures would be enforced vigorously and that every effort would be made to achieve full compliance by autumn 1969, but it also contained a loophole. It stated that some school districts might require a "limited delay" in achieving full desegregation, and that bona fide excuses would be acceptable. This phrase reflected a hesitancy that Nixon had expressed about the formulation of uniform standards and deadlines. Nixon felt that more consideration should be given to the "special problems and considerations" of particular school districts, and that a more flexible policy was desirable. The decision to deemphasize fund cutoffs also reflected Nixon's reservations about this technique as a means of gaining compliance.

Most civil rights organizations and a large part of the news media saw the statement as an attempt by Nixon to back off on school desegregation. The activities of the administration in the next few months supported these predictions. In the summer of 1969, HEW and the Department of Justice asked the district courts to allow 30 recalcitrant Mississippi school districts under orders to desegregate that fall another year of preparation. Also, in Alabama and South Carolina, school districts were given another year's delay. It was obvious that the administration had decided to adopt a rather generous definition of bona fide delays. The administration's actions were strongly criticized by many persons concerned with civil rights. A revolt even developed among attorneys in the Civil Rights Division of the Department of Justice: 65 of the 100 attorneys in the division signed a petition labeling the administration's policy on civil rights as "inconsistent with clearly defined legal mandates."[66] They also expressed grave concern about "events of recent months which indicate to us a disposition on the part of responsible officials of the Federal government to subordinate clearly defined legal requirements to non-legal considerations."[67]

Public revolts among the troops are rare in Washington and undoubtedly caused the administration some embarrassment. The smoke had hardly cleared before the Supreme Court added to the administration's problems. Black plaintiffs in the Mississippi school districts scheduled for another year's delay appealed to the Supreme Court for relief, charging that the delays were not justified. After a full review, the Supreme Court unanimously overruled the delays and ordered immediate desegregation. In *Alexander v. Holmes* the Court used its most unequivocal language to date:

> Continued operation of racially segregated schools under the standard of all deliberate speed is no longer constitutionally permissible. School districts must immediately terminate dual school systems based on race and operate only unitary school systems . . . [defined

as one]: "Within which no person is to be effectively excluded from any school because of race or color."[68]

The administration set about implementing the Court's order. The President told a national television audience that he did not agree with the Court's decision but that he was obligated to obey. The pace of government efforts quickened after *Alexander* and many Southern schools were forced to integrate. In a number of district court cases, school districts were told to desegregate both students and faculty in the middle of the school year. Busing of both white and black students began on a large scale amidst an almost deafening hue and cry.

By January 1970, busing of schoolchildren to achieve racial balance had become the biggest controversy in the racial struggle. Parents and politicians, both North and South, were pressuring Congress for relief. In February Nixon once again expressed his opposition to busing, but the district courts continued to order desegregation at a rate that could be achieved only by busing. The South searched frantically for a means of deflecting the heat. In February Congress passed a bill requiring the pursuit of desegregation in the North as vigorously as in the South. The provision had been introduced as an amendment by Senator John Stennis of Mississippi. The Senator admitted that he had no interest in seeing more school desegregation in the North; he simply hoped to dilute the resources of HEW and the Department of Justice so as to reduce pressure on the South. Additional bills were introduced by Southern congressmen which would have prohibited busing of students to achieve racial balance, but they were not passed by Congress.

Signs of extreme pressure being placed on the White House became evident again in February with the resignation of Leon Panetta, Director of the Department of Health, Education, and Welfare's Office of Civil Rights. Panetta charged that White House aides undermined tough enforcement of antidiscrimination laws, and said his resignation was forced by protests from racist members of Congress that were heeded at the White House. Panetta expressed dismay "at the tendency of this administration to buy and sell everything, including its stand on civil rights, for political profit."[69] The resignation highlighted the absence of sustained Presidential leadership of the civil rights movement. Rumors were current that President Nixon had formulated a "Southern strategy" designed to attract large numbers of Southerners to the Republican party to strengthen his reelection bid in 1972. Nixon denied that there was such a thing, but few observers doubted that Nixon was trying hard to bring the South into the Republican camp. As Democratic Senator Ernest Hollings saw it: "The goal of the Nixon administration seems to be to convince the South that there is a Southern Strategy while convincing everyone else that there is not."[70]

The progress brought about by *Alexander* v. *Holmes* continued; school districts in cities as large as Atlanta made extensive desegregation efforts. Still the controversy over busing was far from settled. In early March one of the most blatant instances of racial violence in the past two decades occurred in Lamar, South Carolina. Buses filled with black children being transferred to previously all-white schools were met by a mob of white adults armed with ax handles, chunks of cement, and chains. The mob clashed with state troopers, and managed to turn two of the buses over, injuring several children and troopers. Many persons placed the blame for this incident on Nixon's faltering civil rights stance. They argued that his backdown on enforcement had encouraged recalcitrant Southerners to believe that they would not have to desegregate. Nixon, feeling that the administration's position needed clarification, sent his Vice President, Spiro T. Agnew, before a national television audience to proclaim the outrage of the administration over the incident. Agnew stated that every effort would be made to fully prosecute those involved in the incident, and that desegregation policies would be pursued vigorously nationwide.

On March 24, 1970, President Nixon went before a national television audience to explain his position on school desegregation. Basically, Nixon sought to convince critics that he supported school desegregation and to stem fears that his administration was backing off on enforcement. Nixon affirmed that where the Supreme Court has ruled, its word is law. He believed, however, that the Court had left a number of questions unanswered, and in those areas he felt free to set policy. Nixon interpreted the Court to say that segregation imposed by law or official action (de jure segregation) was illegal and must be eradicated, but de facto segregation resulting from living patterns is natural and not illegal. Obviously Nixon viewed the distinction between de jure and de facto segregation as a means by which he could prosecute official segregation while preserving neighborhood schools and avoiding busing. The distinction made for integrating schoolchildren did not apply, Nixon said. to teachers, facilities, and services which would have to be fully integrated and equalized. Nixon further proposed to spend $500 million in 1970 and $1 billion in 1971 to improve the quality of racially impacted schools.

There was disappointment among both Southerners and civil rights leaders. Many Southerners were disappointed that Nixon did not support freedom-of-choice school plans, except where they achieved meaningful desegregation. Senator James Eastland of Mississippi summed up considerable Southern sentiment: "It appears the President has declared a policy of separate but equal schools in the North. But, at the same time, he has reaffirmed the Federal government's policy of pursuing planned integration in the South."[71] Civil rights leaders felt that Nixon's policy would simply maintain the status quo in much of the country.

It is hard to avoid the conclusion that Nixon embraced the distinction between de facto and de jure segregation in a belated attempt to justify his reservations about busing. Nixon had never officially made such a distinction before, and it conflicted with the guidelines set down in the joint statement issued by Attorney General Mitchell and HEW Secretary Finch. There is also some doubt that Nixon interpreted the Supreme Court's decisions correctly. When the Court says that there can be no black or white schools, "just schools," it may mean that all-black or all-white schools are illegal.

In keeping with his interpretation of *Alexander,* Nixon ordered a toughening of policy against de jure segregation for the 1970-1971 school year. During the summer of 1970 top officials from the Justice and HEW departments met with school officials from recalcitrant districts and delivered the message that all districts would desegregate or be taken to court. By the end of August suits had been filed against 412 districts and statewide suits were brought against Texas and Mississippi By the fall of 1970 the administration was claiming almost total success in school desegregation with 97 percent of all Southern school *districts* operating under a voluntary or court-ordered desegregation plan. In the past, success had been measured by the number of students attending integrated schools. The new standard greatly exaggerated the amount of progress actually achieved and gave the dangerous impression that the goal of fully integrated schools was virtually achieved. A survey completed in June of 1971 revealed that in fact 60.9 percent of the black students in the South and 72.5 percent in the North were still in segregated schools (See Table 4-4).[72]

Another survey found that the 97 percent figure had been achieved only by acceptance of hundreds of basically inadequate desegregation plans.[73] Obviously the administration was more interested in the appearance of change than the real thing. Many of the plans left blacks segregated or disproportionately placed the burden for integration on them. In many instances physically sound black schools were closed and black students were bused to old and overcrowded white schools. These arrangements were made to alleviate fears of white parents about their children attending previously black schools. The feelings of blacks were not given the same consideration.

There was also evidence of racist policies in many newly integrated schools which daily reminded blacks that their basic equality was being denied. For example, in 123 newly integrated districts, segregated classrooms were found.[74] In 40 districts students were segregated in the classroom. In some instances dividers had been placed down the middle of the room with whites on one side and blacks on the other. Twenty-one districts had segregated facilities such as lunchrooms, dressing rooms, showers, and recreational areas.[75] Segregated buses were found in 89 districts.[76] In some districts where blacks and whites were allowed to ride the same buses, blacks were required to sit in the back of the bus.

Discrimination in extracurricular activities was found in 126 districts.[77] Discrimination was found in social activities (in one case the senior prom was ruled to be by invitation only—no blacks were invited),[78] athletics, cheerleader selection, band membership, and student government. In one instance "when a black student was elected eleventh grade class president in Waskom, Texas, the school board met and decided that last year's officers would serve again."[79]

Integration of black schools also frequently led to the loss of all black identity.[80] Of 321 black schools integrated under the new integration plans, 188 had their names changed. School trophies, colors, mascots, and symbols frequently disappeared. In some areas black schools were integrated only after insulting efforts to "deniggerize" the school were carried out (replacement of all toilet seats, fumigation of the school, etc.).

Integration also contained a high cost for many black administrators

TABLE 4-4   Number and percentage of blacks by geographic area attending school at increasing levels of isolation, fall 1968 and fall 1970 elementary and secondary school survey

	Total pupils	Black pupils	% black	Percentage of blacks attending						
				0-49.9% minority schools	50-100% minority schools	80-100% minority schools	90-100% minority schools	95-100% minority schools	99-100% minority schools	100% minority schools
Continental U.S.										
1968	43,353,568	6,282,173	14.5	23.4	76.6	68.0	64.3	61.0	53.0	39.7
1970	44,877,547	6,707,411	14.9	33.1	66.9	49.4	43.3	38.2	28.0	14.0
North and West (32 states)*										
1968	28,579,766	2,703,056	9.5	27.6	72.4	57.4	50.7	44.3	30.9	12.3
1970	29,451,976	2,889,858	9.8	27.5	72.5	57.6	51.1	44.6	30.4	11.9
Border (6 states)† and D. C.										
1968	3,730,317	636,157	17.1	28.4	71.6	63.8	60.2	57.9	46.3	25.2
1970	3,855,221	667,362	17.3	29.8	70.2	60.6	57.0	53.3	44.1	23.1
South (11 states)**										
1968	11,043,485	2,942,960	26.6	18.4	81.6	78.8	77.8	77.0	74.8	68.0
1970	11,570,351	3,150,192	27.2	39.1	60.9	39.4	33.4	29.2	22.4	14.1

Source: Adapted from *HEW News*, U.S. Department of Health, Education, and Welfare, June 18, 1971.

Note: Minute differences between sums of numbers and totals are due to computer rounding. Districts with fewer than 300 pupils are not included in the survey.

*Alaska, Ariz., Calif., Colo., Conn., Idaho, Ill., Ind., Iowa, Kans., Maine, Mass., Mich., Minn., Mont., Nebr., Nev., N. H., N. J., N. Mex., N. Y., N. Dak., Ohio, Oreg., Pa., R. I., S. Dak., Utah, Vt., Wash., Wis., Wy.

†Del., Ky., Md., Mo., Okla., W. Va.

**Ala., Ark., Fla., Ga., La., Miss., N. C., S. C., Tenn., Tex., Va.

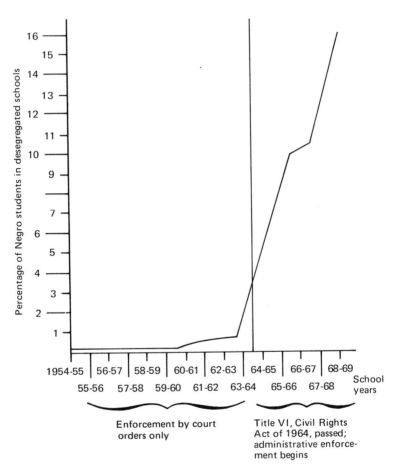

FIGURE 4-1 Percentage of Negro students attending desegregated schools in seven Southern states. The states involved are Alabama, Georgia, Louisiana, Mississippi, North Carolina, and Virginia. Save for North Carolina and for Virginia, in none of these states did the percentage of Negro students attending desegregated schools, whether under court orders or administrative enforcement, ever exceed 16%. Source: U.S. Commission on Civil Rights, *Federal Enforcement of School Desegregation,* Washington: GPO, 1969, p. 36.

and teachers. In fact, 34 districts dismissed black principals, 194 demoted black principals, 127 dismissed black teachers, and 103 demoted black teachers.[81] In many instances the dismissed black personnel were replaced with newly hired white personnel.

Obviously, all these policies place a heavy burden on black patience and faith in the political system. In many instances blacks have been placed in a more abrasive environment than before and the potential for confrontation is obvious.

FACTORS IMPEDING PROGRESS DURING THE ADMINISTRATIVE–JUDICIAL ERA

When Congress finally became significantly involved in the civil rights movement following passage of the Civil Rights Act of 1964, progress in school desegregation improved considerably as Figure 4-1 shows. The overall rate of progress was still, however, disappointingly slow. Change undoubtedly would have been greater except that, even after the 1964 act, Federal commitment to achieving racial desegregation remained limited. The absence of a strong commitment to ending segregation was reflected in both the enforcement and content of the guidelines. We have examined some of the problems with Federal guidelines and enforcement efforts but the topic deserves more attention.

Enforcement of the Gudelines

For years HEW guidelines were not enforced with anything approaching rigor. Each administration enforced the guidelines with exaggerated timidity because it was unwilling to risk alienating the South sufficiently to drive it away from a particular party. Each administration's approach to school desegregation combined a delicate mixture of force, encouragement and leniency. In the final analysis, each administration has come closer to filling the role of conciliator than to that of enforcer of the law. Obdurate local officials were soon aware that the government's commitment was weak and that administration positions could be either avoided, diluted, or dissipated by opposition. Frequently opposition took the form of a flat refusal to obey the law, and sometimes it was cloaked in sophisticated arguments designed to make federal officials believe that the district could not obey the law.

Misleading Federal officials became something of an art, and the Nixon administration was particularly vulnerable.[82]   Federal bureaucrats played into the hands of lagging officials by assuming that the latter could be expected to act in good faith. After a decade of dishonesty, the assumption of good faith was worse than naive.

In part, however, Federal officials had to act on a presumption of good faith since Congress never provided HEW with sufficient personnel to properly oversee all the recalcitrant school districts. By 1970 HEW had only 35 professional (nonclerical) employees working in the South and 40 in the North. The largest number HEW ever had in the South was 48 in 1968. Since this miniscule force could not effectively oversee 4,466 school districts, many schools continued to receive funds while making no progress. On several occasions Congress turned down or cut budget requests to hire additional employees.

Another factor which forced presumptions of good faith was that HEW has always been slow to obtain and tabulate statistics on integration progress. The absence of data frequently thwarted HEW's attempts to locate and apply pressure to dilatory districts. School districts lost Federal funds or had cases brought against them, only when progress was minimal in all areas. Schools that made modest efforts to integrate students, but failed to desegregate facilities, staff, and services as the guidelines required, were generally left alone.

Enforcement was also hampered by a tendency to vacillate on

TABLE 4-5   *Comparison of enforcement by private litigation with Federal enforcement in seven Southern states**

State	Percentage of all black pupils attending integrated schools	
	1963-64 school year	1968-69 school year
Alabama	.007	7.4
Georgia	.052	14.2
Louisiana	.602	8.8
Mississippi	.000	7.1
North Carolina	.537	27.8
South Carolina	.003	14.9
Virginia	1.63	25.7

Source: *U.S. Federal Enforcement of School Desegregation,* Commission on Civil Rights, Washington: GPO, 1969, p. 31.

standards and deadlines. Standards were frequently established but not enforced. This policy encouraged foot-dragging, and caused moderates to fear doing too much because it was not clear that other districts would be forced to keep the pace. If one community's officials ended up doing more than others, it would place them in a bad light with their constituents.

The Nixon administration has been the most guilty of vacillation, inconsistency and weakness. In fact, the desegregation procedures jointly announced by Nixon's Secretary of Health, Education, and Welfare and Attorney General amounted to a blueprint for failure. The statement deemphasized the technique that had proven best at achieving school desegregation in recalcitrant school districts (HEW fund cutoffs), and adopted a technique that had proven bankrupt before (individual negotiations with school boards backed by litigation brought by the Department of Justice).[83] Individual negotiations were first tried in 1965 by HEW but were abandoned because of the enormity of the job. Also, in a 1969 report, the U.S. Commission on Civil Rights demonstrated that more progress was made at HEW's behest than by judicial proceedings.[84] Table 4-5, showing the progress made in districts operating under HEW guidelines compared to that of districts operating under court order, provides faint hope that meaningful progress would have been achieved under the new procedure. The Commission pointed out that in adding Title VI to the Civil Rights Act of 1964, Congress sought to relieve the courts of the major burden for achieving compliance.[85] Judges had expressed considerable relief when Title VI was passed and had every reason to be disappointed with Nixon's new strategy. For example, Judge Brown of the Fifth Circuit explained:

These executive standards, perhaps long overdue, are welcome. To many, both on and off the bench, there was great anxiety in two major respects with the *Brown* approach. The first was that probably for the one and only time in American constitutional history, a citizen—indeed a large group of citizens—was compelled to postpone the day of effective enjoyment of a constitutional right. . . . Second, this inescapably put the Federal Judge in the middle of school administration problems for which he was not equipped. . . . By the 1964 Act and the action of HEW, administration is largely where it ought to be—in the hands of the Executive and its agencies with the function of the judiciary confined to those rare cases presenting justiciable not operational questions.[86]

Additionally, some school districts interpreted Nixon's elimination of uniform standards as a sign of indecision and thus another opportunity for delay. Field research after the decision to drop the deadlines revealed "substantial evidence to suggest that the administration's vacillation has strengthened local defiance of the law."[87] In many instances school boards abandoned plans to desegregate believing that they would not have to obey the law. Obedient school officials were left out on a limb. Indeed, the guidelines had always contributed to this because they placed responsibility for progress on each school board. School officials are particularly vulnerable to local pressures, and many were harassed for obeying or trying to obey the law. In Alabama, George Wallace threatened to mobilize hostility against any school official who complied with the law. School officials were caught in a squeeze play; any decision they made brought criticism from one side or another.[88] The logical alternative would have been for strict guidelines that left little or no discretion and therefore, no room for criticism of local officials.

Enforcement has also suffered from political compromise. In many instances in which local HEW officers were able to overcome the obstacles to enforcement and place substantial pressure on school districts to comply with the law, counter pressures from the executive branch forced a retreat. The Southern Regional Council documented a pattern of resistance which amounted to appeals from local officials to their congressmen, who then gained special dispensation for their district from the White House. This furthered the impression that administration standards were flexible and "would bend in proportion to amounts of resistance and political pressure mustered against them."[89] Such policies facilitated resistance and demoralized field officers from HEW.

The administrative procedures established by HEW to enforce the guidelines also hamper progress because they contain considerable red tape. A good example is the purposely slow procedure used to terminate funds to noncompliant school districts. In the first stage HEW gives notice that it intends to institute formal enforcement proceedings and terminate a district's Federal funds. Next, a hearing is held before a Federal examiner who determines if the district is violating the law. If the examiner finds a violation, and this may be an extended affair, HEW can terminate funds unless the district appeals. In many instances HEW procrastinated before cutting off funds even when the appeal option was not exercised. Longer delays result if the district appeals to the five-man Review Authority appointed by the Secretary of Health, Education, and Welfare. In November of 1969 the Southern Regional Council found 26 cases pending before the board. "The average time lapse since the hearing examiner's decision was six months."[90] The council also found that even if the authority upheld the hearing examiner, HEW might have delayed in stopping funds. When the administrative process is this clumsy, any school can gain a year's delay by simply going through the appellate process.

A final flaw in enforcement was that until 1970 even those school districts which had their funds cut off by HEW were not brought to court by the Department of Justice if they continued to discriminate. Some districts were content to lose their funds and maintain segregated schools. Failure to swiftly prosecute these districts usually hurt black students the worst because integration was not achieved and loss of funds frequently meant the end of school lunch programs for children from low-income families.

Limitations of the Guidelines

Even if the guidelines had been enforced vigorously, progress would have been limited, because they were marred by numerous loopholes which school districts could use to pacify HEW and the Department of Justice without making any real efforts to desegregate. For example, one way HEW allowed school districts to show compliance was by submitting to a final court order. Experience has shown that too often court orders issued by district judges are far less stringent than HEW standards. Many schools retained their Federal funds by submitting to a court order that was far more permissive than HEW standards.[90]

Furthermore, many school districts that submitted to court orders refused to make any desegregation efforts. Some district judges did not care, and others who did have been reluctant to use their contempt powers against local officials under public pressure. The unwillingness of courts to use their contempt powers against law-breaking public officials has been an important factor in facilitating and encouraging defiance of the law.[92]

The most fatal flaw in the guidelines was the tolerance of freedom-of-choice plans which placed the burden of desegregation on black citizens. In *Brown II* the Supreme Court placed responsibility for desegregation on school boards, but through inaction most boards shifted the burden to blacks. Blacks whose children dared to cross the color line were frequently subjected to physical, mental, and economic intimidation. Freedom of choice turned out to be separate but equal by another name. Nonetheless, HEW was slow in mobilizing against the many districts in which freedom of choice obviously did not work. The Supreme Court tried to regulate freedom-of-choice plans by setting down standards for evaluation, but these efforts did not come until 1968. Even under the Court's standards a district would have to be given a period of time in which its plan could be evaluated, thus contributing to additional delay. Of course another reason freedom of choice did not produce more progress is that some blacks do not want to attend integrated schools. This has been especially true in the last few years.

Another problem with the guidelines is that until recently they did not allow HEW to review a number of decisions by school boards that have a potential impact on segregation. For example, school boards normally have a great deal of discretion in making a number of decisions which can limit or increase racial isolation. In drawing school attendance zones, boards can bring children together from mixed neighborhoods or segregate them. These decisions need to be constantly revised because of shifts in population which cause some schools to be underutilized while others are crowded. The board may decide to handle such situations by redistributing school children, expanding schools, or building new ones. Nationwide these decisions have frequently been made so as to perpetuate segregation. The building of Anza Elementary School in San Francisco in 1962 shows how both the determination of a school site and the size of a new school can perpetuate segregation.

Anza was built in a white area about eight blocks from the predominantly Negro Golden Gate Elementary School in the Fillmore area, a Negro residential neighborhood. At the time Anza was planned, Golden Gate was overcrowded and some of its students were being bused 15 blocks to the Pacific Heights School. But Anza was planned to accommodate only 540 students and opened as a nearly all-white school. Children from nearby Golden Gate continued to be bused to Pacific Heights.[93]

A second example, this one from the South, shows how dramatically these decisions can determine racial isolation. "In Houston, almost every school constructed after 1955 was located in racially homogeneous residential areas. Of the 56 Negro schools in Houston in 1965, for example, 49 were newly built or enlarged in Negro residential areas after 1955."[94]

Optional zones which allow students in one attendance area to choose another school have also been used to perpetuate racial concentration. For example, if a predominantly white school becomes overcrowded, white students may opt to attend a predominantly white school in another part of town, rather than attend a predominantly black school closer to their homes.[95] In many Southern cities and in several Northern ones (e.g., Cleveland and Milwaukee), busing has been used to keep the races segregated.[96] Often the coincidence of residential segregation and neighborhood schools obviate the need for busing to perpetuate segregation in both the North and the South.

Another problem is that the guidelines do not provide for adequate regulation of private schools. Many of the new private schools in the South are nothing more than racist sanctuaries, and the Nixon administration has taken no affirmative steps to dismantle them. Many of these schools have been granted tax-exempt status without having to establish that they operate on nonracial policies.

The final problem is that according to Nixon's latest stand the guidelines do not cover de facto segregation. As we have seen, a substantial reason for the lack of progress in school desegregation is the increasing concentration and isolation of black Americans in central cities all over America. Nixon's position that de facto segregation is not against the law, because it is the result of natural processes, is clearly based on fallacious reasoning. As we point out in Chapter Six, de facto segregation is the result of persistent racial discrimination, both public and private. Housing discrimination, income desparities, and dozens of other forms of white racism keep black citizens segregated and isolated. Until these conditions are alleviated, the goal of full integration will remain elusive.

Summary

This analysis has revealed many causes for the slow progress in school desegregation. Each of these factors can be traced to a weak commitment on the part of Congress and the executive branch to the complete dismantling of dual schools. For the better part of ten years after *Brown,* the Supreme Court had to pursue desegregation singlehandedly and cautiously because it had only token backing from the other branches of government.

When Congress did get involved with the school desegregation struggle in 1964, its commitment was still limited and largely symbolic. Crass violations of the law that had gone unpunished for ten years in the South not only continued, in large part, but were often facilitated by weak Federal policies. The guidelines established by the Johnson and Nixon administrations were designed to produce only gradual progress and contained loopholes easily exploited by recalcitrant officials. The commitment to even these weak policies was one of equivocation and compromise. Those who wanted to disobey the law were helped, and those who wanted to obey it were confused and frequently left unsupported. Enforcement efforts were hampered by the commitment of niggardly resources and personnel, administrative red tape and incompetence, and political compromise with justice. Without the leadership and constant prodding of the Supreme Court much less progress would have been achieved.

THE CONSEQUENCES OF AN INTEGRATED EDUCATION

The most obvious question about school integration is whether it is worth the effort. That is, is there evidence that black and white children and society in general can expect to gain any substantial benefits from integrated educational systems? Although research on this topic is not very plentiful, the evidence available indicates that the benefits are numerous. At the most fundamental level studies reveal that segregated schools retard black achievement and integrated schools enhance it. On average each year spent in a segregated school leaves the black student farther behind the typical white with the same number of years of education. For example, third-graders in Harlem who were a year behind the average New York City pupil in reading comprehension and word knowledge had fallen two grades behind three years later.[97] The average IQ scores of blacks drop 20 points in the course of a dozen years of public education.[98]

The Coleman report in 1966 found that integration into majority white schools was the most important school factor in improving the educational performance of black children.[99] Also a study of eight integrated cities in the North and South conducted by the New York Times in 1970 reported that fears that the progress of white children in integrated schools would suffer were baseless.[100] The study found that black students in these systems were making substantial gains in achievement and white performance remained high or improved. Additionally, substantial improvements in race relations had taken place in these schools.

If integrated schools lead to better-educated blacks, then an obvious benefit would be improved qualifications for skilled and professional jobs. Less obviously, integration may have implications for the amalgamation of blacks into the predominant middle-class culture, with possible payoffs in terms of the development of greater support for the political system. The reason to believe so is that schools play an important role in imparting civic knowledge and shaping the political values of students, and by manipulation of the school environment the outcome of this training can, to some extent, be influenced in a positive way. The assimilation of political knowledge and values (referred to hereafter as political socialization) of the average student usually succeeds in producing attitudes associated with good citizenship, i.e., medium to high political efficacy, some interest in politics, feelings of a duty to participate in politics at least to the extent of voting, and support for political institutions and leaders.[101]

Many children in segregated schools and disadvantaged homes, however, do not seem to develop these attitudes. Whereas the school serves as an ally of the family in the political socialization of most youngsters, it may operate alone and even against hostility (latent or overt) in low-income, apolitical families. Particularly with the pre-schooler, and decreasing with age, many attitudes are transferred from

parents.[102]   For example, the young child tends to identify with the
political party to which his parents profess allegiance.[103]   Further, the
child's orientation toward politics and the political system are initially
determined by parental attitudes.[104]   Ties between the parent and the
political world are tenuous or even nonexistent in many poor families.
It is therefore not surprising that lower-class children frequently display
little political interest.[105]

Furthermore, black youths are frequently more politically cynical
and less efficacious than their white peers.[106]   While there seems to be
no difference in the level of cynicism of white and black students in the
South,[107]   black subjects of a study conducted in a Northern city
manifested significantly less trust toward the government. Black
children in the fifth and sixth grades (an age at which most children
manifest highly positive political values)[108]   in Toledo were more
cynical about the political system than were whites in high school.[109]

With median black earnings and education still substantially below
the national average, there is little reason to hope that home influences
will counter these attitudes. In the short run reliance must be placed
upon the school to engender political support among these youths. This
will not be an easy task. In imparting knowledge about the political
system to blacks, schools tread a narrow path with yawning chasms on
either side.

On the positive side, studies show that high school civics courses
impart new knowledge to blacks more often than to whites, for whom
much of the information is redundant. Blacks who take civics courses
normally display greater political efficacy, political knowledge, and
civic tolerance than do blacks without such training.[110]   Schley Lyons
is led to conclude that the high school years are a more critical period
in the political socialization of slum children than they are for other
children.[111]   Evidence that the high school curriculum and experiences
can help structure the hazy political orientations which many lower-
class youth have upon entering high school makes it disheartening that
so many young blacks drop out. Improvement of the atmosphere and
quality of schools may reverse this trend. Such improvements are most
likely in integrated schools.

A negative consequence is that exposure to civics courses sometimes
leads to more bitter disillusionment. Some blacks who take civics
courses, particularly Southern blacks, become more cynical.[112]   Educa-

tion seems to produce greater awareness of the indignities suffered by blacks and the nation's past failures to proscribe discrimination. For Southern blacks civics courses also produce a slight decrease in civic tolerance. This decrease is also evident in lower-status blacks outside the South, where it is accompanied by a declining sense of efficacy.

Some research indicates that the positive aspects of socialization can be achieved by integrating slum children into schools with higher-status youngsters. Studies have found that poor children educated in classrooms with upper- and middle-class peers adopt the attitudes of the higher-class youth, while poor children not exposed to children of other classes mature with distinctively lower-class attitudes which are more extreme than those of their parents.[113] For example, Kenneth Langton in his study of Jamaican children found that poor youngsters educated with equally poor friends became increasingly estranged from middle-class values, while the poor who were educated with middle-class children were "re-socialized in the direction of higher class political norms."[114] Applying the Jamaican findings to the United States, the phenomenon of lower-class imitation suggests that ghetto children educated with higher-status youth will frequently adopt the mores, aspirations, and positive political orientations predominant among white youth.[115]

The obligation to integrate now assessed against some public schools is a step toward multiclass, biracial education. These efforts should have positive consequences for the political system. Simply integrating schools, however, even if resulting in better education, will probably produce little additional support for the system if blacks are not allowed to participate fully in the nation's decision-making processes.

NOTES

1. "Federal Enforcement of School Desegregation," *Report of the United States Commission on Civil Rights,* September 11 1969, p. 4. The U.S. Commission on Civil Rights, like the Dept. of Health, Education, and Welfare, defines a desegregated school as a majority-white integrated school.
2. Alexander v. Holmes, 396 U.S. 19 (1969).
3. *HEW News,* U.S. Department of Health, Education, and Welfare, June 18, 1971.
4. *The Status of School Desegregation in the South 1970,* A report by the American Friends Service Committee; Delta Ministry of the National

Council of Churches; Lawyers Committee for Civil Rights under Law; Lawyers Constitutional Defense Committee; NAACP Legal Defense and Educational Fund, Inc.; and the Washington Research Project.

5. Benjamin Muse, *Ten Years of Prelude: The Story of Integration Since the Supreme Court's 1954 Decision,* New York: Viking, 1964, p. 22

6. Ibid.

7. 347 U.S. 483.

8. Jack W. Peltason, *Fifty-Eight Lonely Men: Southern Federal Judges and School Desegregation,* New York: Harcourt, Brace & World, 1961, p. 15.

9. Ibid., pp. 17-18.

10. Muse, op. cit., p. 23.

11. Ibid., p. 24.

12. Ibid.

13. "Federal Enforcement of School Desegregation," p. 2.

14. Peltason, op. cit., p. 98.

15. Ibid., p. 96.

16. Muse, op. cit., pp. 152-153.

17. Peltason, op. cit., p. 42.

18. Watson v. City of Memphis, 373 U.S. 526 (1962).

19. 373 U.S. 526, 531.

20. Griffin v. County School Board, 377 U.S. 218 (1964).

21. Duval County Board of Public Instruction v. Braxton, 326 F.2nd 616 (1964).

22. Peltason, op. cit., passim.

23. See Samuel Krislov, *The Supreme Court in the Political Process,* New York: Macmillan, 1964, pp. 134-155.

24. This section draws heavily from Peltason, op. cit., passim.

25. Muse, op. cit., p. 27.

26. Ibid.

27. Peltason, op. cit., p. 16.

28. Ibid., p. 4.

29. "Federal Enforcement of School Desegregation," p. 43.

30. Ibid., pp. 39-46.

31. Ibid., p. 45.

32. Peltason, op. cit., p. 45.

33. Ibid., p. 46.

34. Ibid., p. 51.

35. Ibid.

36. Ibid.

37. Ibid., p. 55.

38. Ibid.

39. Ibid., p. 21.

40. "Federal Enforcement of School Desegregation," pp. 21–22.

41. See George R. Osborne, "The NAACP in Alabama," in C. Herman Pritchett and Alan F. Westin, eds., *The Thrid Branch of Government,* New York: Harcourt, Brace & World, 1963, pp. 149-203.

42. Robert L. Crain et al., *The Politics of School Desegregation,* Garden City N.Y. Doubleday, 1969.
43. Ibid., p. 127.
44. Ibid., p. 135.
45. *Revolution in Civil Rights,* Washington: Congressional Quarterly Service, 1968, p. 92.
46. Ibid., p. 93. It should be kept in mind that these figures only indicate how many black students were attending schools with whites, not how many were attending majority-white schools.
47. Ibid.
48. Ibid.
49. Ibid., p. 95.
50. Ibid., p. 97.
51. Ibid., p. 97.
52. Ibid.
53. Green v. County School Board 391 U.S. 430 (1968).
54. U.S. Commission on Civil Rights, *Racial Isolation in the Public Schools,* Washington: GPO, 1967, p. 7.
55. Ibid., pp. 3, 5.
56. Ibid., p. 8.
57. Ibid., p. 10.
58. *Revolution in Civil Rights,* p. 97.
59. Ibid.
60. U.S. Department of Health, Education, and Welfare, *Staff Report,* January 4, 1970, p. 1 (mimeographed).
61 Ibid.
62. *Charlotte Observer,* September 15, 1968. Quoted in Harold Baker, *The Federal Retreat in School Desegregation,* Atlanta: Southern Regional Council, 1969, p. 2.
63. Philip Converse et. al., "Continuity and Change in American Politics: Parties and Issues in the 1968 Election." *American Political Science Review,* 63, December 1969, pp. 1083-1105.
64. Baker, op. cit., p. 9.
65. "Federal Enforcement of School Desegregation," p. 7.
66. *Atlanta Journal,* October 2, 1969, p. 12-A.
67. Ibid.
68. 396 U.S. 19 (1969).
69. *Atlanta Journal,* February 18, 1970, p. 4-A.
70. *Atlanta Journal-Constitution,* March 8, 1970, p. 1.
71. *Atlanta Journal,* March 25, 1970, p. 1.
72. *HEW News,* U.S. Department of Health, Education, and Welfare, June 18, 1971.
73. *The Status of School Desegregation in the South 1970,* pp. 1-7.
74. Ibid., pp. 31-37. The study was carried out in 467 of the districts desegregating in the fall of 1970 (three quarters of all such districts).
75. Ibid., pp. 38-40.

76. Ibid., pp. 40-44.
77. Ibid., pp. 44-49.
78. Ibid., p. 46.
79. Ibid., p. 47.
80. Ibid., pp. 52-56.
81. Ibid., pp. 74-105.
82. Baker. op. cit., pp. 11-15.
83. "Federal Enforcement of School Desegregation," pp. 31-39.
84. Ibid., p. 35.
85. Ibid., p. 33.
86. Ibid., p. 35.
87. Baker, op. cit., p. 47.
88. An indication of the stress school officials have felt is reflected in some 200 resignations by school superintendents in the Deep South in a two-year period (1968-1970). See the *Atlanta Journal-Constitution,* September 7, 1970, p. 3-B.
89. *School Desegregation 1966: The Slow Undoing,* Atlanta: Southern Regional Council, 1966, p. 12.
90. Baker, op. cit., p. 27.
91. "Federal Enforcement of School Desegregation," p. 35.
92. Baker, op. cit., p. 27.
93. *Racial Isolation in the Public Schools,* pp. 46-47.
94. Ibid., p. 62.
95. Ibid., p. 52.
96. Ibid., pp. 56-69.
97. Kenneth Clark, *Dark Ghetto,* New York: Harper & Row, 1966, pp. 120-134. Also see James S. Coleman et al., *Equality of Educational Opportunity,* Office of Education, U.S. Department of Health, Education, and Welfare, Washington: GPO, 1966, p. 21. Another study found that lower-class blacks educated in all-black schools had achievement scores more than a year below those of lower-class blacks who attended predominantly white schools. *Racial Isolation in the Public Schools,* Vol. 1, p. 90. Banfield denies that integration is effective in improving the achievement level of black students, contending that it is class culture defined as an orientation toward the future rather than the present which is the significant factor. Edward C. Banfield *The Unheavenly City,* Boston: Little, Brown, 1970, p. 145.
98. Charles E. Silberman, *Crisis In Black and White,* New York: Vintage Books, 1964, p. 260.
99. Coleman, op. cit., p. 297.
100. "Small Cities Hail Full Integration," *New York Times,* October 18, 1970, p. 1.
101. David Easton and Jack Dennis, *Children in the Political System,* New York: McGraw-Hill, 1969; Robert D. Hess and Judith V. Torney, *The Development of Political Attitudes in Children,* Chicago: Aldine, 1967; David

Easton and Jack Dennis, "The Child's Acquisition of Regime Norms: Political Efficacy," *American Political Science Review,* 61, March 1967, pp. 25-38.

102. Herbert Hyman, *Political Socialization,* New York: Free Press, 1959, p. 69; Greenstein, *Children and Politics,,* New Haven: Yale University, 1965, p. 44. Some researchers, however, challenge the centrality accorded the family in socialization. See M. Kent Jennings and Richard G. Niemi, "The Transmission of Political Values From Parents to Child," *American Political Science Review,* 62, March 1968, p. 183.

103. Angus Campbell et al., *The American Voter: An Abridgement,* New York: Wiley, 1964, pp. 86-87.

104. Easton and Dennis, *Children in the Political System,* pp. 249-254.

105. Hess and Torney, op. cit., pp. 114-120.

106. Schley R. Lyons, "The Political Socialization of Ghetto Children: Efficacy and Cynicism," *The Journal of Politics,* 2, May 1970, pp. 288-304; Kenneth P. Langton and M. Kent Jennings, "Political Socialization and the High School Civics Curriculum in the United States," *American Political Science Review,* 62, September 1968, pp. 852-867; Edward S. Greenberg, "Children and Government: A Comparison across Racial Lines," *Midwest Journal of Political Science,* 14, May 1970, pp. 249-275; Harrell Rodgers and George Taylor, "The Policeman as an Agent of Regime Legitimation," *Midwest Journal of Political Science,* 15, February 12, 1971, pp. 72-86.

107. Rodgers and Taylor, op. cit.

108. Easton and Dennis, Children in the Political System, Hess and Torney, op. cit.; Greenstein, op. cit.

109. Lyons, op. cit., p. 297.

110. Langton and Jennings. op. cit., pp. 859-865; Greenberg, op. cit., pp. 294-275.

111. Lyons, op. cit., p. 303.

112. Langton and Jennings, op. cit., p. 865.

113. O. J. Harvey and Jeane Rutherford, "Status in the Informal Group: Influence and Influencibility at Different Age Levels," *Child Development,* 31, June 1960, pp. 377-385; H. H. Remmers and D. H. Radler, *The American Teenager, Indianapolis: Bobbs-Merrill, 1957, pp. 234-237.*

114. Kenneth P. Langton, "Peer Group and School and the Political Socialization Process," *American Political Science Review,* 61, September 1967, pp. 751-758.

115. Kenneth P. Langton, *Political Socialization,* New York: Oxford University, 1969, pp. 137-138; Brown v. Board of Education, 347 U.S. 483 (1954). A contrary argument holds that the school experience simply reinforces the pre-existent upwardly mobile orientations of those lower-class students who adopt the mores and aspirations of their middle-class peers. Children lacking this orientation, so the argument goes, will experience no change in attitudes as a result of classroom experiences. Banfield, op. cit., p. 141.

CHAPTER FIVE

Black Employment:

The Last Hired and the First Fired

For centuries black Americans have been relegated to the most menial jobs available in white society. Racial discrimination has kept blacks from being hired and promoted on an equal basis with whites, and it has kept many blacks from receiving the education and training necessary to get decent jobs. The effect of job discrimination has been more than economic. Traditionally a man is judged by others and himself by the job he holds. Too often, the jobs black Americans have been relegated to have been so demeaning and low in pay as to rob them of their sense of pride and even of their sense of masculinity.[1] In Kenneth Clark's well-known study of Harlem, a black resident expressed this loss by confessing that "a lot of times, when I'm working, I become despondent as hell and I feel like crying. I'm not a man, none of us are men!"[2] Similarly, Ralph Ellison reports that, significantly, in "Harlem the reply to the greeting 'How are you?' is very often, Oh, man, I'm nowhere."[3]

During the sixties the Federal government made the first real efforts to correct and compensate for discrimination in employment. The efforts have been insufficient to counteract past discrimination; and they have not been as effective or as vigorous as the laws passed would have allowed. Nonetheless some gains have been made. For example, the Department of Labor reports that employment of minorities in white-collar, craft, and operative occupations increased 67 percent between 1960 and 1968.[4] These percentages are deceptive because they include minorities other than blacks and because relatively small numerical increases convert to large percentage increases since the original employment figure was small. Somewhat more revealing are the results of a study reported by the U.S. Bureau of the Census in June 1970 which revealed that black Americans got 28 percent of the new craftsmen's and operators' openings that went to family men between 1960 and 1969.[5]

Such increases may represent more than tokenism, but they are still short of the advances required to bring the proportion of blacks employed in higher occupational categories up to their proportion of

TABLE 5-1   *Negro and other (nonwhite) races as a percentage of all workers in selected occupations, 1960 and 1969**

	1960	*1969*
Total, employed	11%	11%
Professional and technical	4	6
Medical and Other health	4	8
Teachers, except college	7	10
Managers, officials, and proprietors	2	3
Clerical	5	8
Sales	3	4
Craftsmen and foremen	5	7
Construction craftsmen	6	8
Machinists, jobsetters, and other metal craftsmen	4	6
Foremen	2	4
Operatives	12	14
Durable goods	10	14
Nondurable goods	9	14
Nonfarm laborers	27	24
Private household workers	46	44
Other service workers	20	19
Protective serivces	5	8
Waiters, cooks, and bartenders	15	14
Farmers and farm workers	16	11

Source: U.S. Department of Labor, Bureau of Labor Statistics.

Note: Annual average is shown for 1960, and January to November average for 1969.

the total population. In 1969, black Americans made up 11 percent of
the total population. As Table 5-1 shows, blacks still fall below this
percentage in almost all the more desirable occupations. Improvement
from 1960 to 1969 was steady, but not dramatic. In Table 5-2 Norval
Glenn has computed an index which shows

the percentage of nonwhites (or of whites) who would have to
change occupational categories to make the white and nonwhite

TABLE 5-2 *Ratio of actual expected proportion of employed nonwhite workers
to white workers in each occupation group, 1940, 1959, 1960, and
1968*

Occupational group	1940	1950	1960	1968
Professional, technical and kindred workers	0.36	0.40	0.49	0.59
Farmers and farm managers	1.31	1.22	0.78	0.52
Managers, officials, and proprietors, except farm	0.17	0.22	0.23	0.28
Clerical and kindred workers	*	0.29	0.46	0.67
Sales workers	*	0.18	0.23	0.30
Craftsmen, foremen, and kindred workers	0.27	0.38	0.49	0.60
Operatives and kindred workers	0.57	0.94	1.08	1.27
Private household	1.53	2.00	2.02	1.81
Farm laborers and foremen	2.57	2.28	2.46	2.08
Laborers, except farm and mine	2.06	2.56	2.59	2.00
Index of dissimilarity[†]	47.8	40.9	38.5	31.9

Source: From Norval D. Glenn "Changes in the Social and Economic Conditions
of Black Americans During the 1960s," in Norval D. Glenn and Charles M.
Bonjean, eds., *Blacks in the United States,* © 1969 by Chandler Publishing
Company. Reprinted by permission of the author and publisher.

Notes: The "expected" proportion is the proportion of all employed workers in
the occupational group. The ratios and indexes for 1940, 1950, and 1960 are computed from decennial census data gathered in April of those years. The 1968
figures are computed from data from a sample survey conducted in June. See
U.S. Department of Labor, Bureau of Labor Statistics, *Employment and Earnings
and Monthly Report on the Labor Force,* July 1968.

*In the 1940 census reports, clerical and sales workers are not separated. The
ratio for clerical, sales, and kindred workers for 1950 is .12.

†This index is the percentage of nonwhites (or of whites) who would have to
change occupational categories to make the white and nonwhite distributions
identical.

distribution identical. The index declined by 6.9 points from 1940 to 1950, by 2.4 points from 1950 to 1960, and 6.6 points from 1960 to 1968. If the index declines at the 1960-1968 rate until 1970, the total decrease for the decade will be 8.3—an unprecedented ten-year rise in the relative occupational standing of nonwhites in the United States.[6]

Still, at the present rate of progress it would take about 200 years for blacks to gain equality in employment.[7]

The limited effect of a few years of upgrading in employment has also been reflected in unemployment rates. In November of 1970 the unemployment rate for black Americans was 8.8 percent compared to 5.5 percent for whites.[8] In central cities, where black concentrations have been greatest, the situation is even worse. For example, in Cleveland's black ghetto, Hough, the unemployment rate was 15.6 percent in 1967.[9] Additionally, millions of black Americans are underemployed in unattractive, dead-end jobs without a chance for promotion or significant financial advancement. Many of these jobs are likely to be wiped out by automation, leaving blacks unemployed and untrained for better jobs. Glenn points out that at the lower-status occupational categories little progress has been made.

> For instance, the ratios for nonfarm laborers and private household workers were little higher in 1940 than in 1968. At the latter date, nonwhites still did more than four times their proportional share of private household work and twice their share of unskilled labor.[10]

The effects of job discrimination are also reflected in black family incomes. In 1969 the median income for white American families was $8,936.[11] Black median incomes represented only 60 percent of this—$5,400.[12] In 1969 the poverty line for a family of four was set at $3,721.[13] Of all black families, 28 percent fell below this level, compared to only 8 percent of all white families.[14] These grim figures nonetheless do represent a substantial improvement for black families. In 1960, 48 percent of all nonwhite families were below the poverty line.[15] Still, the figure of $3,721 is extremely low and a family earning this amount or even 20 to 30 percent more might continue to live in abject poverty.

Some of the discrepancy between black and white incomes results from blacks being paid less than whites to perform the same jobs. For example, in 1969 white blue-collar workers earned a median income of $7,452, compared to a $5,756 median for black blue-collar workers.[16] A number of factors other than current discrimination contribute to these discrepancies (i.e., skill rating and seniority), but racism does seem to play a role. Herman P. Miller reported that in 1959 blacks with four years of college "could expect to earn less over a lifetime than the white who did not go beyond the eight grade."[17] Miller estimates that in 1961 alone discrimination cost black Americans 16 billion dollars.[18]

A number of factors such as economic expansion and higher levels of educational attainment by blacks have contributed to improvements in black employment. An additional factor has been a number of efforts by the Federal government to alleviate job discrimination and to help train black Americans for better jobs. The measures include: 1) Executive orders by Presidents Kennedy, Johnson, and Nixon forbidding job discrimination by the Federal government; 2) Title VII of the Civil Rights Act of 1964 which prohibited discrimination in all phases of private employment; 3) Executive orders issued by Presidents Kennedy and Johnson forbidding discrimination by any employer executing contracts with the Federal government; and 4) a number of federally aided employment services designed to help minorities obtain jobs and training for better jobs. It will be the purpose of this chapter to examine these programs and policies and to evaluate their impact on equal employment. Emphasis will be centered on why more progress has not been made.

FEDERAL EMPLOYMENT

A critical factor in holding back progress in this area of civil rights has been a lack of strong commitment to achieving progress by the Federal government. The weakness of Federal commitment to equality in employment is reflected in the unimpressive fashion in which the Federal government has endeavored to put its own house in order. Starting with Truman's administration and extending through Johnson's, meager efforts were made to insure equality in Federal employment. Executive Order 10925 issued by President Kennedy extended the government's obligations from nondiscrimination to affirmative action directed at overcoming present and past discrimination. President Johnson (E. O. 11246) obligated the Civil Service Commission (CSC) to "supervise and provide leadership and guidance in the conduct of equal employment opportunity progress . . . within the executive departments and agencies."[19]

Despite these measures, discrimination in Federal employment continued unabated primarily because "CSC's role under E. O. 11246 was characterized more by passivity than by 'leadership'; more by neutrality than by 'guidance.'"[20] A 1967 study revealed that 15 percent of all Federal employees were black but almost all of them were concentrated in the lowest-paying jobs. Only 1.8 percent of the higher paying (GS 12 through 18) jobs were held by blacks.[21]

In 1969 President Nixon issued E. O. 11478 which greatly expanded the government's policy on minority employment and CSC's authority. CSC is charged with seeing that each department and agency: 1) create and maintain an affirmative program of equal employment; 2) obtain the best utilization of each employee; 3) provide opportunities for employees to improve their skills in order to obtain promotions; and 4) expand their recruitment activities in an effort to bring more minority members into Federal employment.

Under new leadership CSC reorganized, centralized, and strengthened its efforts to supervise the order. During 1970 CSC functioned more energetically and imaginatively to increase minority representation in Federal employment. Measures taken by CSC included:

a. Increased efforts to recruit more minority employees.
b. Continuing reappraisal of civil service examinations to weed out bias and to eliminate tests that tend to winnow out minority group applicants.
c. Revision of Federal merit procedures to reduce the possibility of deliberate or inadvertent discrimination and to facilitate more rapid promotions for minority group employees.
d. A requirement that all first-line supervisors undergo training to make them aware of and sensitive to equal opportunity problems.
e. Increased attention in CSC inspections to equal employment aspects of agency problems.
f. Revision of discrimination complaint procedures to facilitate resolution of problems on an informal basis.
g. Modernization of the system for collecting and maintaining

Federal employment data by race and ethnic origin, with recommendations for adoption by all Federal agencies.

h. Increased efforts to promote communications between Federal agencies and private groups and individuals concerning issues of equal employment opportunity.[22]

On paper these efforts are impressive but they have been in effect too short a period to have had much impact. In 1970 minorities still held very few of the better-paying Federal jobs (GS 14-15, 1.5 percent; GS 16-18, 1.2 percent).

PRIVATE EMPLOYMENT

Title VII of the Civil Rights Act of 1964 attempts to regulate job discrimination in private employment by making it unlawful

to fail or refuse to hire or discharge any individual, or otherwise to discriminate against any individual with respect to his compensation, terms, conditions, or privileges of employment, because of such individual's race, color, religion, sex, or national origin.[23]

For a number of reasons success under this law has been meager. As frequently happens in civil rights, the machinery created to enforce the law is weak. Title VII created the Equal Employment Opportunity Commission (EEOC) to supervise the behavior of employers, employment agencies, and unions. The commission is impotent to enforce, being limited to such informal means as conferences, conciliation, and persuasion. The commission has understandably been dubbed "a poor, enfeebled thing."[24]

If the EEOC cannot settle a complaint through informal means, its only recourse is to ask the Attorney General to bring suit in behalf of the government. The Attorney General can bring suits at his own discretion, but rarely has. If a citizen has exhausted state and EEOC procedures without satisfaction, he can file a suit on his own behalf in Federal court. Few citizens take this option because it entails a considerable financial commitment.

The authority of the commission is further limited by a provision in Title VII requiring EEOC to defer any complaints received from a state which has its own laws prohibiting discrimination in employment and an agency to enforce the laws. If the state is unable to complete action on the complaint in 60 days, EEOC may then enter the case. Since most states outside the South have their own laws and agencies, this deferral process often severely limits EEOC, even though most state agencies do not exercise their powers forcefully. Most state agencies define their powers narrowly and limit their investigations to those complaints brought to them.[25]

The commission also suffers the dual infirmities of being understaffed and poorly financed. The commission was originally designed to handle about 2,000 complaints a year. In its first year of full operation, 1966, the commission was inundated by 8,854 complaints. The capabilities of the staff were so outstripped that long delays and severe disappointments awaited citizens seeking relief under the law. The next year the commission made an effort to streamline its procedures, but the number of complaints increased to 13,435 causing continued delays.[26] By August 1970, the commission had received 52,085 complaints.[27] The backlog of cases has become so pronounced that it now takes the commission approximately two years to process a complaint.[28]

Even when the commission has been able to investigate complaints its efforts have met with only limited success. Through 1969, the commission was able to persuade less than half of the employers, agencies, and unions with whom it negotiated to pledge to end discrimination.[29] The commission does not follow up on pledges and the Department of Justice has infrequently lent support to EEOC work, so there is no assurance that any real change is taking place. By 1970 the Department of Justice had filed fewer than 100 suits against discriminating employers. The result is that many acts of blatant discrimination go uncorrected.

Even though EEOC has not been able to handle the complaints it has received, the number would probably increase dramatically if it were easier to file a complaint with the commission. The law stipulates that complaints must be filed in "writing under oath."[30] Any black fearing reprisal would be hesitant to take this action. One civil rights worker estimated that only 10 percent of the black citizens in his community would have enough courage to file a complaint under these circumstances.[31] About half of the race discrimination caseload of the commission has been generated by the NAACP and its Legal defense Fund. Civil rights groups, however, have generally found the commission to be of limited helpfulness; one civil rights official characterized EEOC as "at best a conciliation agency. Its major virtue has been that, however, awkward and clumsy, it provides a procedure for getting job discrimination cases into the Federal courts."[32]

Civil rights groups have been especially critical of the slowness of EEOC and of its meager enforcement powers. Many blacks who were encouraged by passage of the Civil Rights Act of 1964 had their hopes dashed when they filed complaints with EEOC and then waited a year without hearing from the commission. Others who were able to get EEOC to enter into negotiation on their behalf found that little could be done to correct their grievances. Such experiences have undoubtedly dissuaded other blacks from filing complaints. Even a former chairman of EEOC said: "We're out to kill an elephant with a fly gun."[33]

Two of the more difficult practices the EEOC has had to deal with have been the discriminatory applications of seniority systems and employment tests. Title VII provides that nondiscriminatory employment tests are legal. The line between discrimination and nondiscrimination is frequently hairbreadth and the commission has had difficulty making the distinction. In 1964 EEOC defined a nondiscriminatory employment test as

> a test which fairly measures the knowledge of skills required by the particular job or class of jobs which the applicant seeks, or which fairly affords the employer a chance to measure the applicant's ability to perform a particular job or class of jobs.[34]

Still, EEOC did not adopt any specific standard to determine if employers were abiding by the decision, and its staff is too small to do much investigation.

With the help of the Federal courts, EEOC has made some progress in the eradication of discriminatory seniority systems. As with employment tests, the 1964 act permits the use of seniority systems as long as they are nondiscriminatory. Prior to Title VII many black employees were routinely placed on separate seniority lists reserved for less desirable jobs. There is no doubt that such lists are now prohibited. The more controversial question has been what type of adjustment must be made for black employees who have been discriminated against over the years. In 1967 a district court upheld an EEOC ruling that the mere elimination of dual lists was not enough, and agreed that an adjustment would have to be made for past discrimination.[35] Since this decision, adjustments have usually been made on an ad hoc basis.

Labor unions have also been a difficult area for EEOC. About 20 percent of the complaints filed with EEOC have been against unions.[36] Many unions have been extremely slow in opening their membership to blacks or in making an effort to compensate for past discrimination. Upon receiving a complaint against a union EEOC usually tries to enlist the aid of its national headquarters in reaching a settlement. The National Labor Relations Board has allied itself with EEOC on a few occasions with good results. Still, labor unions remain largely segregated.

In summary, EEOC has not been terribly effective in enforcing Title VII. Given its anemic enforcement powers, limited jurisdiction, inadequate staff, and stingy financing—it is hard to believe that Congress ever expected the commission to perform successfully. The Civil Rights Act of 1964 was primarily symbolic, and Congress undoubtedly felt that it would have to move cautiously in this area in the first few years. New and more powerful legislation has been needed for some time but Congress has been vacillating, as its repeated refusal to authorize EEOC to issue cease and desist orders demonstrates.

STATE AND LOCAL EMPLOYMENT

Another limitation of Title VII that has affected progress is that state and local governments are exempt from its requirements. A study released by the U.S. Commission on Civil Rights in 1969 clearly reveals that this has been a mistake.[37] The commission found that many state and local governments have failed to assure equal job opportunities to minorities, and some actively engage in job discrimination. Since there are over 80,000 state and local governmental units, failure to achieve more progress at this level has cost black Americans many decent jobs. In the North blacks are represented in state and local employment in proportion to their number, but in the South they reach this proportion only in the most menial jobs.[38] In Louisiana, for example, where 31.7 percent of the population is black, only 3.5 percent of the nonmenial jobs were held by blacks in 1968.[39] In the North discrimination is practiced mostly where white-collar jobs are concerned. For example, in New York City blacks hold only 6.4 percent of the white-collar jobs; in Chicago, 5.8 percent; in Cleveland, 3.9 percent; and in Washington, D.C., 9.7 percent.[40] The least changed area of state and local government, both in the North and the South, is fire and police departments. Not only do nonwhites have a difficult time gaining such employment, but the Commission on Civil Rights uncovered a large number of instances in which black firemen and policemen had been subjected to discrimination and harassment by fellow workers.[41]

State and local governments practice many of the same discriminatory acts found in private industry. They 1) discriminate in hiring and promoting minority group members; 2) make no special effort to recruit minority group members; and 3) use methods of hiring and promoting which place minorities at a serious disadvantage. For example, written and oral examinations, which are frequently used to fill jobs, discriminate against the culturally deprived. Performance tests, which generally do not contain a built-in disadvantage for minorities, are rarely used. Standard education, experience, and character require-ments also frequently mitigate against minority group members. The result is that nonwhites are often evaluated on criteria unrelated to their ability or willingness to fill a position. A Texas official pointed out that "The jobs open are those requiring experienced people and minority group members just do not have the experience. It works sort [of] like the grandfather clause."[42] This is a good example of institu-tional racism. Bias is so ingrained in the rules and everyday practices of the system that few whites ever question or appreciate the role they play in subjugating minorities.

The Commission on Civil Rights found little evidence that state and local officials are reevaluating job requirements so as to increase oppor-tunities for minority group members. Most state and local officials felt that their only obligation was to refrain from actively discriminating against minorities. They did not recognize a need for positive corrective action such as recruitment and training of minorities.

Even though EEOC has no jurisdiction over state and local agents, there are Federal laws which forbid discrimination in state or local agencies which administer federally aided programs. The Federal Merit Standards law was amended in 1963 to prohibit discrimination based on race or national origin in any program aided by Federal monies. The law made all state and local agencies guilty of discrimination subject to fund or program withdrawal or a Federal court suit. The potential of the law is obvious, but the Office of State Merit Systems (OSMS) which is responsible for supervising the law has been lax in establishing guidelines. The first substantial application of the law came finally in 1968 when the Department of Justice brought suit against the state of Alabama over "systematic and unrelieved" discrimination in federally financed programs. Overall, the law has been used very little, and the potential it promises has not been realized.[43]

Another law which has the potential to affect black employment at the state and local level has also been virtually unused: the statute creating the Department of Housing and Urban Development (HUD) prohibits discrimination in employment by local agents using Federal funds for public housing and urban renewal.[44] In addition, local agents are required to take "affirmative action" to bring more minority members into the job market. HUD can enforce the law by withholding funds, instituting a Federal court suit, or taking over the project. Like other low-visibility nondiscrimination laws, this one has not been enforced in a systematic or vigorous manner, and its potential for getting blacks into the job market has not been realized.

In summary, state and local governments have done very little to change employment practices or attract minorities to government services, and in many cases are overtly discriminating against minorities. Federal laws have been passed which could alleviate this situation, but enforcement has been lackadaisical.

FEDERAL CONTRACTORS

In 1965 President Johnson issued Executive Order 11246 prohibiting discrimination by any employer receiving Federal funds. Johnson's order was the sixth issued by American Presidents on the topic, going back to 1941.[45] Johnson's order, which went beyond the scope of President Kennedy's, required Federal contractors to take "affirmative action" to employ minorities. Under E. O. 11246 a Federal contractor must:

1. State in all job advertising that he is an equal employment opportunity employer;
2. Give appropriate notice to the union with whom he has contracts;

3. Comply with all orders of the Secretary of Labor, including requirements for information and records and the inspection of books; and

4. Make reference to these commitments in all subcontracts and purchase orders "so that such provisions shall be binding on each subcontractor or vendor."[46]

In 1968 affirmative action was defined as obligating Federal contractors: "1) to perform an analysis of minority utilization of all job categories; 2) establish goals and timetables to correct deficiencies; and 3) develop data collection system and reporting plans documenting progress in achieving affirmative action goals."[47] Since the Federal government lets billions of dollars worth of contracts a year, the possibilities of the order are obvious. Unfortunately, its potential has not been realized.

It will come as no surprise that the major factor inhibiting progress has been the government's halfhearted compliance efforts. Until 1968, each Federal agency letting contracts was responsible for obtaining compliance. For example, the Department of Defense was responsible for seeing that each contract it let was put into the hands of a contractor who would abide by the order. There were 26 departments and agencies that had staffs responsible for this function. The result was that "The machinery for implementing Executive Order 11246. . . [was] dispersed and little known even within the Federal Government."[48]

The dispersion and unwieldiness of the enforcement process was only partially corrected in 1968 with the reduction of the number of compliance-enforcing agencies to 15, and assignment of responsibility for specific industries to particular agencies. Other problems continue. The staffs concerned with enforcing the order have always been too small. In 1968 it was estimated that only about 10 percent of all Federal contractors were inspected to see if they were abiding by the order.[49]

Coordination of the various departments and agencies responsible for enforcement is provided by an understaffed agency in the Department of Labor, the Office of Federal Contract Compliance (OFCC). Unlike the EEOC, the OFCC has enforcement powers that are potentially strong. In cases of violation, the OFCC or the contracting agency can cancel, terminate, or suspend any contract or portion thereof. Individual contractors can be debarred (blacklisted) from receiving future Federal contracts. These sanctions, however, have been used sparingly. The various agencies and the OFCC have been so reluctant to challenge discrimination that some of the credibility of the order has been eroded, and skepticism clouds the seriousness of the government's commitment.[50] One civil rights official summed up a growing sentiment when he characterized the Executive order as a "sleeping giant lying in the money it controls."[51]

Until 1968, Federal contract specialists mainly functioned to advise and counsel contractors, and some specialists reported to the Commission on Civil Rights that they were not always backed up when they wanted to crack down on foot-dragging contractors.[52] Moreover, before 1968 OFCC failed to define or enforce "affirmative action." Primarily, Federal contractors were expected to voluntarily comply with the order.

In 1968 and 1969 the first minimal efforts to enforce the law were made after the Federal courts gave the various enforcement agencies a prod forward by enforcing the requirements of both E. O. 11246 and Title VII.[53] Also, President Nixon showed some interest in employment during his first year of office and ordered the various agencies to press harder for compliance. Nixon seems to believe that progress in black employment will bring progress in all areas of civil rights, and at times he has demonstrated a willingness to push for change. As Nixon's Assistant Secretary of Labor for Wages and Labor Standards Arthur Fletcher has said: "this is the one side of the civil rights movement he [Nixon] understands best . . . Nixon is well aware that you can get only so much [out] of a voluntary approach."[54] Although Nixon has not effectively followed up on many of his early efforts in this area, there is less reluctance about pushing for affirmative action and enforcing the provisions of the Executive order under his administration. By 1970 no contracts had been terminated or canceled although some had been held up and a few contractors debarred.

Nixon has also stated support for city plans such as the highly publicized Philadelphia Plan. The focus of the city plans has been the construction industry and labor unions, with the goal being to force contractors to hire significantly more minority group members. In Philadelphia studies revealed that although the city's population was almost one third black, only 1.6 percent of the members of six key building trades were black.[55] Under the plan contractors were required to hire a certain percentage of minority employees in each of the six trades over a three-year period. The percentages ranged from 4 to 8 percent by the end of 1970, to 19 to 26 percent by 1973.[56] It is clear that these goals are not being met,[57] but OFCC has made some efforts to enforce the guidelines.[58] Several contractors were passed over in contract considerations because they failed to include plans for minority employment with their bids, and by spring 1969, 19 million dollars in construction contracts were being held up for reviews and adjustments in the affirmative action programs.[59]

The administration has been slow to move against discrimination in the construction industry in other cities. In 1969 blacks held only 0.8 percent of the jobs in the higher-paid mechanical trades.[60] In 1970, OFCC reported that it was prepared to establish Philadelphia-type plans in 91 additional cities unless minority employment in construction improved, but six months later no action had been taken. Voluntary plans which 13 cities were allowed to substitute for compulsory plans have been allowed to linger although they have been failures.[61]

In summary, Executive Order 11246 yielded very little in its first years of existence because of dispersed authority, negligible leadership, timid enforcement policies, and small staffs. Under the Nixon administration there have been some limited improvements but many old problems persist. OFCC is still very reluctant to apply sanctions to recalcitrant contractors, and the various enforcement agencies have not used sanctions at all. OFCC has also failed to encourage and provide guidelines for the application of sanctions by government agencies. Voluntarism, which has never worked, is still widely practiced, and monitoring of compliance efforts by the various agencies remains ineffective.

FEDERAL MANPOWER AND JOB-TRAINING PROGRAMS

Federal programs designed to help minorities overcome past discrimination which has robbed them of the education or training necessary to qualify for better jobs have proliferated in the last two decades. Theoretically, the U.S. Employment Service (USES) of the Department of Labor and its 2,000 affiliated state employment services provide coordination and leadership for the manpower programs.[62] In reality the state employment services—which are financed entirely by the Federal government— have been slow to replace discriminatory practices, and Congress has been forced to develop several programs outside of their jurisdiction. The state employment services are designed to administer various training programs of the Federal government and to provide job referral, counseling, and testing services. In many states, especially but not exclusively in the South, the employment services have exercised their functions in a discriminatory manner. Some units had segregated facilities as late as 1963.[63] Even when the employment services have not openly discriminated against blacks, they have been criticized for being employer-oriented and uninterested in affirmative action.

To provide the state employment services with some competition, Congress enacted the Concentrated Employment Program (CEP) in 1967 to provide employment assistance for the disadvantaged in a number of metropolitan areas. In 1969 there were 146 CEP units. Each unit tries to provide services such as job placement, work experience, education, and counseling. The program seems to be particularly effective in reaching blacks. In 1968, 81 percent of CEP's clients were black.[64]

In addition, Job Opportunities in the Business Sector (JOBS) was instituted in 1966 to help industry train minorities for skilled jobs. The government pays industry a unit price to train minorities, most of whom are CEP referrals. In 1969 the target number of trainees was 100,000 with an increase to 500,000 by 1971. The antipoverty agencies created by the Equal Opportunity Act in 1964 also perform many job-related functions.

With the passage of the Civil Rights Act of 1964 new pressure was put on the state employment services to change their policies. Title VI of the 1964 act prohibited discrimination in any program or activity receiving Federal financial assistance, specifically including the state employment services. The responsibility to avoid discrimination is not new for the employment services—such requirements date back to 1947. The 1964 act, however, provides machinery to enforce the ban, and officials of USES have taken a strong stand on enforcement of nondiscrimination laws. The 1964 act created the Office of Equal Opportunity (OEO) with the following responsibilities:

1. to exercise continuing civil rights oversight for the employment service system;
2. to investigate Title VI complaints for all manpower programs of the Labor Department; and
3. To conduct special equal opportunity reviews on request from departmental officials.[65]

Most of the time and efforts of OEO have been spent with the state employment services. The large number of state employment offices has meant that the small staff of OEO has been able to investigate only a small number of units; in 1967 only six percent of all offices were reviewed. Discriminatory practices were found in 75 to 80 percent of the offices investigated. The most typical discrimination found was undercoding—assigning minority applicants a lower skill rating than whites with similar education, job record, or experiences.[66] OEO also discovered that many units persist in serving employers who still refuse to hire minorities. Some units were also found to be providing better services to white than black clientele. OEO has had some success in correcting these policies and in getting the services to desegregate their own staffs. The Commission on Civil Rights recently reported that the services have begun to think of themselves as providing service equally to employee and employer.

Accompanying better employment services has been improved USES leadership since 1966. USES has stressed nondiscrimination and special attention for the disadvantaged. As part of its new emphasis, in 1966 USES instituted the Human Resources Development Program (HRD) to provide assistance and counseling to help minorities overcome such barriers to employment as lack of tools, clothing, transportation, and training.

In addition to these manpower programs attempts specifically designed as "job preparation" programs were instituted by the Federal government during the sixties. Many of the programs are under the authority of the Department of Labor, but other departments sometimes share responsibility for administering a program. Table 5-3 shows estimates of the number of individuals served by some of the major programs in 1968.

The Manpower Development and Training Act (MDTA) established a

TABLE 5-3 *Selected manpower programs*

Program	New obligational authority, fiscal 1968 est. (in millions of $)	Individuals served, fiscal 1968 est. (in thousands)	Date of enactment	Administering agency
Manpower Development and Training Act Institutional*	246	129	1962	Manpower administration, Dept. of Labor; Bureau of Adult and Vocational Education, Office of Education, Dept. of Health, Education, and Welfare
On-the-job	182	186	1962	Bureau of Work-Training Programs, Manpower administration, Dept. of Labor
Other MDTA	80	57		
Total	508	372		
Neighborhood Youth Corps	375	435	1964	Bureau of Work-Training Programs (delegate agency for Office of Economic Opportunity)
Job Corps	285	98	1964	Job Corps, Office of Economic Opportunity
New Careers (Nelson-Scheuer)	28	10	1965	Bureau of Work-Training Programs
Special Impact (Kennedy-Javits)	20	10	1966	
TOTAL	$1,216	925		

Source: *The Budget,* fiscal 1969
*Includes work experience and training program for welfare recipients, veterans, and others.

number of employment programs administered by the Labor Department and HEW. One of the largest is OJT, on-the-job training, which by 1968 had served 800,000 persons.[67] Between 1963 and 1968, 23 percent of those participating in OJT programs were black. During the same period 35 percent of the participants in all MDTA programs were black.[68]

The Neighborhood Youth Corps (NYC) was established in 1964 by the Economic Opportunity Act, and has been credited with being one of the most effective programs in attracting minority employees. NYC provides public service jobs to 14- to 22-year-old men and women from low-income families. The employees receive $1.30 an hour and upwards. From 1964 to 1968, 42 percent of those served by NYC were black.[69]

Earlier legislation, the National Apprenticeship Act of 1937, authorized the Federal government to oversee on-the-job and related instruction to train workers to become journeymen in various skilled crafts and trades. The Labor Department's Bureau of Apprenticeship and Training (BAT) registers apprenticeship programs, supplies them with technical aids, and extends limited Federal services. Since the government does not actually finance the programs, BAT's authority is limited (although unions are obligated to adhere to its directive by Title VII, discussed earlier). The apprenticeship program has been the center of considerable controversy because only a very small percentage of its trainees have been black. BAT has moved slowly, but recently has gone on record as supporting Nixon's city plans, which should facilitate minority entry into craft unions.

It is difficult to evaluate precisely how valuable these various programs have been in improving black employment because follow-up studies are rare. Two persistent charges have been made against them: 1) they have not actually served blacks and the hard-core poor; and 2) many blacks trained in the programs remain jobless. Indications are that the programs are now overcoming to some extent failures to aid those most in need.

The unavailability of jobs, however, remains a critical problem and seems to be getting worse. According to one study, employment rates for those who completed job training were only 13 to 23 percent more than for a control group of friends, and neighbors who received no training.[70] It is obvious that the programs were not meant to create jobs.[71] Some have characterized the government's willingness to provide training but not jobs as an interest in changing the man but not the system. As Harmon Minsky has pointed out, the priorities of the government do not always seem logical.

> Once tight full employment is achieved, the second step is to generate programs to upgrade workers. I am afraid that in the poverty campaign we have taken the second step without the first, and perhaps this is analogous to the great error-producing sin of infielders—throwing the ball before you have it.[72]

Another reason frequently cited for limited yield by the various job programs is that many disadvantaged persons have been unwilling to profit by them. Edward Banfield, for example, argues that the efforts of the programs have been wasted on many unskilled persons who have developed "habits or cultural characteristics incompatible with employment in steady, high-paying jobs."[73] Trainees have frequently proven unreliable, insubordinate, and even dishonest and destructive. On occasion the behavior of trainees has been bad enough to attract the attention of the national press. Banfield points out that "more than 40 percent of the (Job Corps) enrollees drop out or are discharged within three months of enrollment."[74] Undoubtedly Banfield identifies a serious problem which Federal programs have not been sophisticated enough to deal with, and it is easy to conclude that if disadvantaged persons do not accept help, they do not deserve attention. But it would be more logical to conclude that the government's programs have been too restrictive in scope. Slavery and enforced poverty do ugly things to people, and the obligation to correct harm done cannot be easily dismissed.[75]

IMPLICATIONS AND CONCLUSIONS

Despite some progress in the sixties in freeing blacks from job discrimination and in helping them acquire job skills, the problem of equal employment remains pervasive. Black employment by the Federal and state governments is still low and restricted primarily to the least attractive jobs. In the private sector conditions are not much improved. As the Commission on Civil Rights recently pointed out:

> Despite strong Federal contract requirements, the record of government contractors, heavily reliant on Federal contracts for their

livelihood, is no better than that of employers not subject to the requirements. And while there have been overall minority employment gains in the general private labor market, discrimination continues largely unabated six years after Congress ordained equal employment opportunity as organic law.[76]

More progress could have been achieved if compliance with laws affecting employment had been more widespread. Typically we have found problems with the laws designed to promote equal employment and with the enforcement efforts of the various agencies and departments responsible for employment policy. Title VII of the Civil Rights Act of 1964, for example, contains strong provisions against discrimination but impotent enforcement powers. Executive Order 11246 embodies strong prohibitions and potentially powerful enforcement tools, but enforcement efforts have been weak. Enforcement has also been hindered by a scarcity of personnel and resources in all compliance agencies. For the person who is discriminated against compliance has usually been much too difficult to attain. For example, the enforcement machinery provided by Title VII is so difficult to use that many blacks have been discouraged from seeking justice. Also, antidiscrimination laws have frequently been entrusted to offices that seemingly make no effort to enforce them. For example, the Office of State Merit Systems has dawdled in enforcing the Federal Merit Standards Act.

The basic barrier to compliance has been the timidity of Federal commitment. In the face of resistance agencies have frequently backed off and waited for voluntary compliance, which has never worked. Similarly, the various agencies have usually been reluctant to speed compliance by clarifying vague passages in laws or by establishing standards and guidelines for enforcing and maintaining compliance. Richard Nathan refers to this reluctance as an "unwillingness to come to grips with politically sensitive issues."[77] An example would be OFCC's failure to define and establish goals for the affirmative action provision of E. O. 11246 until 1968.

As we have noted previously, progress in certain areas of civil rights seems to be dependent in part, at least, on advancements in other areas. This appears to be particularly true of education and employment. Equal educational opportunities will do much to help blacks achieve equal employment, especially in professional fields. Indeed, one reason that blacks have not achieved more progress in employment is that qualified blacks are frequently not available to fill opening jobs. In academe, for example, black Ph.D.s are scarce in many fields.

Progress in employment is also critical if black Americans are to enjoy and expand progress in other areas of civil rights. For example, even if open housing laws were vigorously enforced their impact would still be limited if most blacks could not afford to buy a house. Once the earning power of substantial numbers of blacks goes up, however, conscientiously enforced open housing laws will allow many blacks who want to leave the ghetto and central city to do so. Moving to suburbia may dilute black voting power but it should bring other benefits, such as the reduction of de facto school desegregation.

Even more important, economic advancement will increase black political participation and influence, which should lead to a host of benefits which we have discussed in Chapter Two. Lastly, increasing the financial stake of the average black American in the system should have the effect of reducing black frustrations and alienation, which should enhance his support for the political system.

NOTES

1. See, for example, Thomas F. Pettigrew, *A Profile of the Negro American,* Princeton, N. J.: Van Nostrand, 1964. pp. 30-31; Charles E. Silberman, *Crisis in Black and White,* New York: Vintage Books, 1964, p. 245; Lee Rainwater and William L. Yancey, *The Moynihan Report and the Politics of Controversy,* Cambridge: M.I.T. Press, 1967; Elliot Liebow, *Tally's Corner,* Boston: Little, Brown, 1966, p. 54.

2. Kenneth B. Clark, *Dark Ghetto,* New York: Harper & Row, 1965, p. 1.

3. Ralph Ellison, *Shadow and Act,* New York: Random House, 1964, p. 300. Cited by Rupert Emerson and Martin Kilson, "The American Dilemma in a Changing World: The Rise of Africa and the Negro American " in Talcott Parsons and Kenneth B. Clark, eds., *The Negro American,* Boston: Houghton Mifflin, 1965, pp. 641-642.

4. *The Social and Economic Status of Negroes in the United States, 1969,* Joint Report of the U.S. Department of Labor and the U.S. Department of Commerce, Washington: GPO, 1970, p. 40.

5. "Negro Married Men Gain in Blue Collar Job Report," *Atlanta Constitution,* July 1, 1970, p. 5.

6. Norval D. Glenn, "Changes in the Social and Economic Conditions of Black Americans During the 1960s," in Norval D. Glenn and Charles M. Bonjean, eds., *Blacks in the United States,* San Francisco: Chandler, 1969, pp. 45-46.

7. See the calculations of Leonard Broom and Norval D. Glenn, "The Occupations and Income of Black Americans," in Glenn and Bonjean eds., *Blacks in the United States,* p. 24.

8. *Employment and Earning,* Report of U.S. Department of Labor, vol. 17, no. 6, December 1970, p. 2.

9. U.S. Department of Labor, *Equality of Opportunity in Man Power Programs,* Report of Activity under Title VI of the Civil Rights Act of 1964, Washington: GPO, 1968, p. 1.

10. Glenn, op. cit., p. 47

11. *The Social and Economic Status of Negroes . . .*, p. 15

12. Ibid., p. 14.

13. Ibid., p. 22.

14. Ibid.

15. Glenn, op. cit., p. 49.

16. "Negro Married Men Gain. . .," p. 5.

17. Herman P. Miller, *Rich Man, Poor Man,* New York: Thomas Y. Crowell, 1964, p. 155. See also Paul M. Siegel, "On the Cost of Being a Negro," *Sociological Inquiry,* 35, Winter 1965, pp. 41-57; and David Capolvitz *The Poor Pay More,* New York: Free Press, 1963.

18. Miller, op. cit., p. 104.

19. U.S. Commission on Civil Rights, *Federal Civil Rights Enforcement Effort,* Washington, GOP 1970, p. 64.

20. Ibid., p. 65.

21. Ibid., p. 70.

22. Ibid., pp. 1040-1041.

23. Richard P. Nathan, *Jobs and Civil Rights,* Report prepared for the U.S. Commission on Civil Rights, Washington: Brookings 1969, p. 13. Much of this chapter is drawn structurally and substantially from this report, which is the most comprehensive analysis of the government's intervention in employment.

24. Ibid., p. 14.

25. Albert W. Blumrosen, "Antidiscrimination Laws in Action in New Jersey: A Law-Sociology Study," *Rutgers Law Review,* 19 Winter 1965, pp. 214-226.

26. Nathan, op. cit., p. 11.

27. *Federal Civil Rights, Enforcement Effort,* p. 269.

28. Ibid., p. 283

29. Ibid., p. 387.

30. Nathan, op. cit., p. 47.

31. Ibid., p. 48.

32. Ibid., p. 45.

33. *Federal Civil Rights Enforcement Effort,* p. 342.

34. Nathan, op. cit., p. 59.
35. Quarles v. Phillip Morris, Inc., 270 F. Supp. 505 (E. D. Va. 1968). See also, *Heat and Frost Insulators* Local 53 v. Vogler, Civil No. 24865 (5th Cir., 1969); Dobbins v. Electrical Workers Local 212 Civil No. 6421 (S. D. Ohio. 1968).
36. Nathan, op. cit., p. 62.
37. *For all the People. . .By all the People,* Summary of a report on Equal Opportunity in State and Local Government by the U.S. Commission on Civil Rights, memo., pp. 1-39.
38. Ibid., p. 3.
39. Ibid.
40. Ibid., p. 5.
41. Ibid., p. 22.
42. Ibid., p. 6.
43. Ibid., pp. 25-26.
44. Ibid., pp. 26-27.
45. Nathan, op. cit., p. 86.
46. Ibid., p. 90.
47. *Federal Civil Rights Enforcement Effort,* pp. 191, 192.
48. Nathan, op. cit., p. 86.
49. Ibid., p. 144.
50. Ibid., pp. 91, 143.
51. Ibid., p. 141.
52. Ibid., p. 133.
53. See f. 35.
54. Bill Hughes, "Rights Weapon is Forged." *Atlanta Journal,* February 26, 1970, p. 6-A.
55. Bill Hughes, "U.S. Constructs Set Color Ratio of Work Force," *Atlanta Journal,* February 25, 1970, p. 1-A.
56. Ibid.
57. Elliot Carlson, "The Philadelphia Plan to Integrate Union Called Failure by Some," *Wall Street Journal,* December 3, 1970, p. 25.
58. *Federal Civil Rights Enforcement Effort,* pp. 216-250.
59. Hughes, "Rights Weapon is Forged," p. 6 A.
60. Hughes, Ibid., p. 7-A.
61. *Federal Civil Rights Enforcement Effort,* pp. 206-208.
62. Nathan, op. cit., p. 156.
63. Ibid., p. 159.
64. *Statistics on Manpower,* Supplement to the Manpower Report of the President, U.S. Department of Labor, March, 1969, p. 96.
65. Nathan, op. cit., p. 163.
66 Ibid.
67 *Statistics on Manpower,* p. 90.
68. Ibid., p. 93.
69. Ibid., p. 93.

70. Garth L. Mangun, *Constitutions and Costs of Manpower Development and Training,* Policy Papers in Human Resources and Industrial Relations, No. 5, Institute of Labor and Industrial Relations, University of Michigan and Wayne State University with the National Manpower Policy Task Force, Washington, December 1967, p. 15.
71. See Edward C. Banfield, *The Unheavenly City,* Boston: Little, Brown, 1970, pp. 88-113.
72. Harmon P. Minsky, "The Role of Employment Policy," in Margaret S. Gordon, ed., *Poverty in America,* San Francisco: Chandler, 1965, p. 200.
73. Banfield, op. cit., p. 105.
74. Ibid., pp. 110-111.
75. No one has dealt with this problem with more insight or eloquence than Liebow, *Tally's Corner* (passim).
76. *Federal Civil Rights Enforcement Effort,* p. 57.
77. Nathan, op. cit., p. 226.

CHAPTER SIX

Housing:
Situation Unchanged, Segregation as Usual

Racial equality in housing, like integration in education and employment, is a matter of national and not just regional concern. While blacks have, in recent years, made notable gains in the political, economic, and educational spheres, housing segregation has gone largely uncorrected. As the nation's black population has been lured from the rural Black Belt of the South to urban centers in search of work, the newly arrived have received something less than the key to the city. Black migrants have begun urban life in the same fashion as the ethnic groups which have preceded them. Lacking the talents needed by an urban society, blacks have entered the economic system at the lowest-skill and lowest-pay levels.

As the newest and poorest urbanites, blacks have been restricted to whatever housing has been available. Consequently they have tended to settle in the slums where crime, disease, and overcrowding are worst. By moving into the tenements and shanties cast off by earlier immigrants, blacks began the cycle experienced by all groups new to the city. But for blacks, the cycle embarked upon with hopes of a good job and a better life has not run its course. While other groups have been able to move out of the slums after a generation or two, this route has been closed to most blacks. For even when they were able—against long odds—to earn salaries sufficient to afford homes in better neighborhoods, racial prejudice usually blocked their escape. The immigrant could lose his accent or change his name and be accepted in nonethnic neighborhoods if he so desired. Blacks, indelibly marked by color, frequently remained trapped in the ghetto.

The work of Karl and Alma Taeuber well documents the universality of segregated housing patterns in this country. They conclude:

> In the urban United States there is a very high degree of segregation of the residences of whites and blacks. This is true for cities in all regions of the country and for all types of cities—large and small, industrial and commercial, metropolitan, and suburban. It is true whether there are hundreds of thousands of Negro residents, or only a few thousand. Residential segregation prevails regardless of the relative economic status of the white and Negro residents. It occurs regardless of the character of local laws and policies, and regardless of the extent of other forms of segregation or discrimination.[1]

As an example of what the Taeubers found, in 1960 housing in St. Louis, Omaha, and Milwaukee was almost as segregated as in Birmingham.[2] Hyman and Sheatsley in 1964 concluded that residential racial segregation was the aspect of discrimination on which white attitudes have mellowed the least.[3]

Circumscribing blacks' housing options has resulted not only in their being confined to the ghetto, but has contributed to much higher density rates than among whites. In Atlanta, for example, while blacks constitute half of the population, they occupy roughly 20 percent of the city's land area.[4] In the United States 25 percent of the blacks but only 8 percent of the whites live in overcrowded conditions.[5]

Along with overcrowding, the invisible walls of discrimination have created an artificially high demand for ghetto housing. It is estimated, for example, that Newark blacks pay, on the average, 10 percent more for their housing than do similarly situated whites.[6] In Chicago, the same quality shelter costs a black family $20.00 per month more than a white family would pay.[7] In Cleveland, where 91 percent of the blacks but only 33 percent of the whites occupy older dwellings (i.e., housing built prior to 1939), 34 percent of the blacks, compared to 9 percent of the whites, paid more than 35 percent of their income for shelter.[8]

Such then are some of the products of housing segregation. In the course of this chapter, we will discuss techniques of housing discrimination and legal responses to them. We will analyze the success of attempts to end discrimination and suggest reasons for the tenacity of racial practices in housing. Finally we will point out possible implications of open housing.

RACIAL WALLS

Black pressures for more and better quality housing are not new—they are as old as the ghettos themselves. The counterpressures of whites are of similar vintage. Whites have used the whole array of discriminatory techniques to keep their neighborhoods racially pure. Local laws requiring segregation have been passed. When these have failed public officials have applied laws, nondiscriminatory on their face, so as to exclude blacks. The efforts of public officials have been supplemented by many private citizens who, even in the presence of fair housing legislation, have refused to sell or rent to blacks. In addition to the sellers and landlords, builders, realtors, and mortgagors have been culprits in promoting ghettoization of blacks. When blacks have succeeded in entering white neighborhoods, they have sometimes been harassed.

An early technique to prevent racial change was the enactment of ordinances requiring residential segregation. Such attempts to freeze settlement patterns were held unconstitutional more than half a century ago.[9] City fathers, once barred from such overt propagation of racial separation, developed more subtle methods. For example, suburban communities have used their condemnation powers to perpetuate racial homogeneity. Once it is learned that blacks are building in a town, their land has been condemned for use as parks or for other public purposes. Work on houses being built for blacks has been stopped by building inspectors who find minor deviations from building codes, variances winked at in houses built for whites. Some such actions have been judged to be discriminatory by the courts.[10]

In addition to using the authority of the government to prevent integration, property owners in the past sought to prohibit it by mutual agreement. Residents have signed agreements, called restrictive covenants, forbidding anyone to sell to a black family. Restrictive covenants are no longer legally enforceable, but they are still found in some sales contracts. Before these clauses were judged unconstitutional, should one of the signers or a subsequent owner break the agreement, the other parties to the contract could sue the violator for damages in addition to voiding the sale. In a 1948 case, *Shelley* v. *Kraemer*,[11] the Supreme Court reasoned that the courts were being used to propagate discrimination and that this constituted state action since the courts are an arm of the state. State involvement in discrimination is, of course, a violation of the equal protection clause of the Fourteenth Amendment.

Shelley opened to blacks housing unwanted by whites. While these dwellings were often better than what had been available beforehand, the decision did not make accessible to blacks the gamut of residential developments. Whereas whites' housing choices were limited only by economic considerations, race remained the primary factor in determining where a black family would live. The housing opened to black settlement as a result of *Shelley* did not meet the needs of rapidly growing black urban populations; consequently, overcrowding and high rents continued to be the rule in the ghetto. In essence, then, all the court decision did was to remove legal barriers which might otherwise have prevented whites who desired to sell to blacks from doing so.

Except for disarming restrictive covenants, the Federal government for years stood aloof from the open housing controversy. In the best tradition of not rocking the boat, Federal authorities continued to tolerate informal discrimination. The Federal Housing Authority (FHA) continued to guarantee loans in segregated subdivisions, unless a builder was found to have violated a state antidiscrimination law. Indeed for two years after *Shelley* FHA continued to encourage the inclusion of restrictive covenants in sales contracts, having gone to the extent of providing a model one.[12] In another Federal program, various public housing authorities continued to use racist criteria "for many years after the courts had made it clear that such [actions were] in violation of the Constitution."[13]

At no time did Federal agencies assume the obligation of insuring that those benefiting from Federal housing programs were free of the taint of discrimination.[14] FHA's disinclination to be a pioneer is clearly shown in the following statement by one of its leading officials a decade ago:

> No further changes are presently contemplated in FHA policy or practice to impose an open-occupancy requirement in FHA-assisted housing without such a policy directive from either Congress or the Executive.[15]

The reluctance of civil servants to venture where courts, Congress, and the President feared to tread reflects a not incomprehensible fear of being rejected by the official policy makers in the face of determined opposition.

Prudence was reinforced by economic considerations. With it generally accepted that racial heterogeneity caused property values to drop precipitously, Federal mortgage guarantors (FHA and the Veterans administration—the VA) were reluctant to sponsor social change which might jeopardize the security of their loans in a neighborhood. Therefore, they were not overly supportive of state open housing laws. For example, between 1958 and 1960, FHA secured loans on thousands of homes in a New Jersey Levittown even while the developer stood accused of violating a state statute prohibiting housing discrimination.[16]

Not only was Federal financing used to perpetuate segregation, housing policy makers did not pay even lip service to the precept of separate but equal treatment. Only a tiny percentage of Federal loan guarantees found their way to black homeowners. During FHA's first quarter century 5.8 million dwelling units were constructed under its auspices. Of these, approximately 200,000 were for blacks and most of these were in segregated developments in the South.[17] Evidence such as this has prompted the Civil Rights Commission to the following accusation: "FHA was a major factor in the development of segregated housing patterns that exist today."[18]

The racial policies of FHA and other Federal agencies were echoed in the private sector by the nations's bankers, home builders, and realtors. These three partners in meeting America's housing needs were also prompted to practice discrimination by the belief that integration caused lower property values. Moreover, realtors and bankers were reluctant to help black families enter white neighborhoods for fear that they would be boycotted by whites.[19]

Since, regardless of builder and realtor preferences, integration would be impossible in the absence of mortgage money, it has been said that, "Banks dictate where Negroes can live."[20] Banks have often adhered to the following lending policies: 1) deny loans to blacks, 2) reject all loan applications in largely black areas, or 3) make loans to blacks but only under more exacting terms.[21] The frequent absence of mortgage money from sources tapped by whites has at times forced blacks to pay interest rates as high as 19 percent.[22]

For years realtors, too, have discriminated against blacks. Article 34 of the code of ethics of the National Association of Real Estate Boards provided that:

A realtor should never be instrumental in introducing into a neighborhood a character of property or occupancy, members of any race or nationality, or any individual whose presence will clearly be detrimental to property values in the neighborhood.[23]

While this was rewritten in 1950 to exclude reference to race, few realtors have amended their practices in response to the change, and some who have, have been expelled from the profession for selling to blacks in white neighborhoods.[24]

Although most realtors have been staunch protectors of the status quo, a few have made fortunes by blockbusting. i.e., introducing blacks into white areas. This scheme involves the rapid transformation of a residential neighborhood from all white to virtually all black. At its worst it is carried out in somewhat the following manner. A house will go on the market in a block of white-occupied, inexpensive, single-family residences. A realtor will sell the home to a black family, or perhaps show the dwelling to a black family, then place a "Sold" sign in the front yard and circulate the rumor that the purchaser is black. In the next phase, nearby whites are bombarded with telephone calls, letters, and door-to-door solicitations by real estate agents encouraging them to sell before the area goes all black. Blockbusters play on the whites' fears of racial isolation, economic loss, and physical harm. The landowner is warned that if he does not move now his may soon be the only white family in an area which will become increasingly unsafe. And since the influx of blacks will cause property values to decline, the realtor cautions, the owner had better sell immediately. As evidence that the neighborhood is deteriorating rapidly, some blockbusters have been known to hire blacks to roar through the area in noisy cars and to have black women with numerous children walk the sidewalks.[25] Except when neighborhood organizations geared to maintaining the area on an integrated basis spring to life, the blockbuster has usually had his way.

The blockbuster's elaborate plan for changing the complexion of a neighborhood is executed with an eye toward handsome profits. By

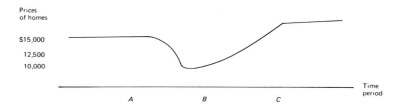

FIGURE 6-1   Price fluctuations in a neighborhood undergoing racial
transition. *A* = period before first blacks move into area. *B* = period of low prices
caused by panic selling once blacks buy in the area. *C* = period of price re-
covery after the market has absorbed houses hurriedly unloaded by frightened
whites.

frightening whites into stampeding deeper into suburbia, the realtor
creates a buyers' market. As the simple plotting in Figure 6-1 shows,
the realtor can buy the homes for substantially less than their fair
market value. However, this area which has lost its appeal for whites is
far superior to what blacks have been able to purchase in the ghetto.
Their demands for these newly available homes with green lawns in
areas with low crime rates and integrated schools permit realtors who
bought homes cheaply from whites to sell them dearly to blacks. This
points up a basic popular misconception about the impact of integration on property values. As Luigi Laurenti has shown, the odds against a
permanent price drop following black penetration are almost six to one.
After analyzing a number of neighborhoods before and after blacks
moved in, Laurenti found that prices went up 44 percent of the time,
held constant 41 percent of the time, and declined only 15 percent of
the time.[25] If the frightened whites had held on to their property until
after the scare selling, they could probably have sold without a loss and
perhaps even realized a higher return.

In transition neighborhoods realtors have profited not only from the
rise in the demand curve but also from the financing arrangements
worked out with black purchasers. With the typical sources of mortgage
money often unavailable to blacks moving into integrated neighborhoods, the void may be filled by the real estate firm which offers
installment land contracts.[27] Rising property prices plus interest and
finance charges often result in blacks having to pay 35 to 115 percent

more than what the fleeing whites sold their homes for.[28] The potential for profits in blockbusting is well summed up by one practitioner: "If anyone who is established in this business in Chicago doesn't earn $100,000 a year, he is loafing."[29] An average blockbuster can earn 100 percent profits in approximately two years.[30]

Even in the absence of blockbusting the prospect of a neighborhood remaining integrated for long is not good. Realtors often show homes in transitional areas only to blacks and advertise them only in the black press. Should a white ask to be shown a home in the area, he will be warned that the area is going all black in the near future. By their practices realtors make such prophesies self-fulfilling.[31] Selective practices such as these gradually transform the racial composition of a neighborhood until what is called the tipping point is reached and the remaining whites leave. Panic selling begins and the blockbuster once again reaps handsome profits.[32]

Neighborhood associations seeking to keep an area from going all black are thus confronted with two problems. They must forestall initial mass exodus, and if successful in that endeavor they must entice white families to buy some of the homes as they come on the market, to perpetuate racial balance. Such efforts rarely succeed. Even an attempt to use quotas to perpetuate a racial mix in New York City public housing was unsuccessful and finally abandoned.[33]

In the light of past experience in which neighborhoods became all black once the color line was broken, one wonders what likelihood there is for lasting housing integration. Is white flight from integrating neighborhoods a characteristic of only certain groups? Available evidence suggests not. Those most likely to leave are families with higher incomes who are renters and who are self-employed. It does not appear that people who deny being prejudiced are less likely to move out than are those who express their intentions to leave. Indeed the whites who remain differ from their neighbors who flee in only one regard: they are too poor to move.[34]

ATTACKING THE WALLS

Federal opposition to housing discrimination has been relatively slow compared to the actions of several cities and states. In December, 1967, there were 88 local and 21 state laws dealing with fair housing. The scope of these laws varies, but it was estimated that by the end of 1967 almost 60 percent of the American public lived under some kind of open housing statute.[35] Viewing these laws over time, a pattern becomes apparent. Earlier statutes dealt with property which was publicly owned. Next covered was housing financed by public money. Then came units operated by commercial realty firms, and finally some states banned discrimination from all but owner-occupied units. Thus there appears a trend to expand fair housing coverage from public to increasingly private property.[36]

State and local statutes vary both in scope of coverage and in enforcement provisions. The least formidable call for only a token penalty from offenders. A remedy with greater potential for corrective action provides for an injunction to prevent sale or rental of the property involved until the controversy has been resolved. This is far more effective than levying a fine on the offender long after the house has been sold to a white family. The strictest reprimand is found in city and state laws focusing on the activities of salesmen. Some laws dealing with blockbusting as well as discrimination call for the revocation of the real estate license of those guilty of discrimination.[37] No Federal authority has imposed a penalty so severe.

Although there are many state and local fair housing laws, they seem to have had limited influence, most being infrequently enforced. Lynn W. Eley, writing in 1968, concludes:

> Laws have not yet brought any fundamental change in realtor practices or housing patterns. Realtors have learned to comply with the laws at explicit, formal levels, and yet maintain substantially the same informal practices and patterns.[38]

During the first half of the sixties the confluence of Federal inaction, realtor opposition, and the spotty coverage of state and local laws produced a situation in which housing segregation became increasingly acute. In a dozen cities in which a census was conducted in the mid-sixties the proportion of blacks living in largely black census tracts had invariably increased.[39] In the most extreme case, Buffalo, New York, 69 percent of the blacks lived in census tracts which were at least 75 percent black. Six years earlier, in 1960, only 35 percent of the black populace had been as racially isolated. While Buffalo is exceptional, the pattern is unmistakable: racial segregation in housing is on the rise.

In fair housing as in other areas, when the Federal government finally declared itself in favor of equal treatment, it did so on a limited scope which was subsequently broadened. In November 1962, President Kennedy issued an Executive order ending discrimination in all property owned, sold, or leased by the Federal government. Also covered by this edict were residences with loans secured by the Federal government. It is estimated that approximately 18 percent of the nation's 58 million dwelling units were affected by the Kennedy proclamation.[40]

Neither public housing nor urban renewal projects were affected by the Kennedy order if the financing agreements had been consummated prior to November 20, 1962. While a subsequent section of the order authorized challenges to discrimination in projects predating the order, nothing was ever done.[41] It remained for Title VI of the Civil Rights Act of 1964 to extend nondiscrimination prohibitions to all public housing and urban renewal developments which still received annual Federal allotments.

Not until 1968 did Congress move against discrimination in housing which could not be linked in some way to Federal funding or management. The Open Housing Act of that year provided for a gradual expansion of the housing market subject to fair housing provisions. Phase one, immediately effective, was simply a reiteration of Kennedy's 1962 Executive order. Phase two, which became applicable on January 1, 1969, banned discrimination in apartments and single-family residences owned by realty companies and commercial landlords.[42] Mortgage lenders and realtors were also forbidden to practice racial discrimination. The third stage of the act, which took effect at the beginning of 1970, freed all transactions handled by realtors from racial discrimination including owner-occupied single-family residences. Sales or rentals carried out by an individual without the assistance of a realtor were covered only if the owner had expressed his intention to discriminate in advertising the dwelling. If the family suffering discrimination was impoverished, legal assistance could be made available at no cost. It was estimated that as of January 1969, 18 to 20 million units would be covered, and when the statute became fully effective 80 percent of the nation's housing would be theoretically open to Americans of any race.[43]

Ironically, no sooner had Congress come to the aid of prospective black homeowners, than the Supreme Court also took action in *Jones* v.

Mayer. Two months after passage of the Open Housing Act, the Court interpreted the long-dormant Civil Rights Act of 1866 as proscribing housing discrimination. The Court turned to the following section of the act: "All citizens of the United States shall have the same right . . . as is enjoyed by white citizens thereof to inherit, purchase, lease, sell, hold, and convey real and personal property." This language, said the Court, prohibited racial discrimination in all real estate.[44] *Jones* thus goes well beyond the 1968 legislation.

More recently the case has been made that commercial property owners have an obligation to do more than to simply abstain from overt racism. The question being litigated is: Must a landlord advertise his property so that blacks will be aware of its availability? The state of New Jersey in a suit filed under the state fair housing law argues that the landlord's failure to advertise so as to inform blacks of vacancies constitutes discrimination. Neither the intent of the owners nor the fact that there was token integration—35 black families among the development's 5,684—was considered to be an adequate defense by the prosecution.[45] A decision for the plaintiff in this case, if adopted and amplified by the Federal judiciary, could have far-reaching effects.

In addition to legal and legislative efforts at compliance, there have been attempts to promote open housing through the Federal fisc. For example, the Department of Housing and Urban Development (HUD) has bought tracts in middle-class suburbs of various cities. The land purchased will be developed with low-rent housing, enabling the poor, black and white, to join the middle class in suburbia.

A second facet of HUD efforts has been the impounding of funds for urban renewal, water and sewage plant development, etc., until communities agree to take steps toward honoring the terms of the Open Housing Act of 1968.[46] Exactly what behavior will be accepted as constituting compliance with the statute remains to be clearly defined. These attempts, if widespread and successful, may contribute significantly to the realization of nationwide fair housing.

The location of revenue-producing Federal facilities is another incentive which can be manipulated to promote the objective of fair housing. Thus far, the General Services Administration (GSA) has failed to implement a year-old policy statement urging that Federal installations not be placed where low-income housing is unavailable. Neither the GSA statement nor Executive Order 11512, dealing with the same topic, specifically mentions racial considerations. Nor has the Defense Department sought to insure that landlords near military bases comply with fair housing policy. Location of installations and the power of a base commander to declare areas "off limits" are as yet underutilized tools in promotion of Federal racial housing policies.[47]

WHY THE WALLS REMAIN UNSCALED

The 1968 law makes the bold statement that, "It is the policy of the United States to provide, within constitutional limitations, for fair housing throughout the United States." While we may be too close to the events to accurately interpret them, it seems that the actions taken to end housing discrimination have yet to greatly alter existing residential patterns. Housing continues to be the context in which interracial contact is least frequent.[48] The near-universal pattern has been one of white withdrawal in response to black overtures to integrated living. In other contexts whites have adapted their behavior to the influx of blacks. In this section we will speculate on the roles of white prejudice, government efforts, and some attitudes of the black community, in suggesting why so little change has occurred.

Attitudes of Whites

In his classic study of American race relations, Gunnar Myrdal discusses what he calls a rank order of discrimination,[49] meaning that whites do not find all types of biracial contact equally distasteful. Racial contact least acceptable to whites is miscegenation involving a black male and white female. The less the interracial activity impinges upon sex and status, the less objectionable whites find it. Of the aspects of integration discussed in this book, housing is perceived as having the greatest potential for leading to interracial marriages. The romance between boy and girl-next-door has been so often celebrated in song and soap opera that to many whites it has a ring of authenticity. Consequently, many fear that black neighbors will lead to a black son- or daughter-in-law. Whites who accept integrated schools, work forces, and public facilities fear that mixed neighborhoods will result in breaking the deepest of racial taboos.[50]

Aside from the horror of miscegenation, integrated housing is opposed because of the prevalence of a number of widely held stereotypes. For example, in 1966, 52 percent of a sample of whites thought blacks smelled differently than whites, 50 percent thought they were less moral, and 43 percent doubted that blacks were ambitious and hardworking.[51] These are not the qualities which one would hope for in a neighbor. And while one might also prefer that his fellow worker or his child's classmate not have these characteristics, their presence would be more tolerable in milieus other than next door. Thus for many whites the crux of the problem is that the potential for social contact is much greater in housing than when integration occurs in other realms. In line with the negative perceptions about black characteristics, half of the whites polled in 1966 did not want black neighbors.[52]

Some writers have suggested that fears of miscegenation and declining property values are not the only causes of white antipathy. They speculate that the arrival of blacks causes whites to suffer status anxiety. Especially among whites who have only recently attained the lower reaches of the middle class, integration raises the specter that they are being engulfed by the lower class from which they emerged.[53] Such fears are reinforced by the general assumption, promoted by blockbusters, that integration will undercut property values causing the white homeowner to lose a portion of his investment.

Bound up with much of this is the attitude expressed in the cliché that "a man's home is his castle." Many people who would accept government action in regulating other behavior contend that housing with its greater impact on the individual should be above government control.[54] The home, being one's most cherished and expensive possession, has an aura of individuality which is lacking in other items to which blacks seek equal access.

The strong antiblack bias held by many whites when it comes to housing robs civil rights protest of support. Curiously, more whites recognize that discrimination exists in housing (65 percent) than in education (40 percent) or in general (60 percent), yet the proportion of whites considering black protests justified is lower when the object is housing (49 percent) than when it is directed at unequal employment opportunities (59 percent) or segregated education (60 percent).[55] Whites know housing discrimination exists, yet their consciences do not cause them sufficient guilt to accept black neighbors.

Federal Efforts and Failings

With all these reasons for whites to oppose open housing—and to oppose it more vigorously than integration in other contexts—public policy has tended to tolerate discrimination. Even when discrimination has contravened written law, it has often gone unpunished as has already been discussed. Blanket Federal prohibitions in the area of shelter are quite new and like earlier state and local laws have yet to be implemented on a large scale.

In analyzing Federal efforts, It becomes evident that while some attempts have been made to achieve policy objectives, these have suffered from weaknesses inherent in the 1968 act, hesitancy on the part of enforcers, and an absence of data with which to determine the presence of discriminatory behavior.

Department of Housing and Urban Development On the positive side, HUD has processed various complaints of discrimination. In 1969 the department received almost 1,000 complaints. Final results of these are not available, but HUD had succeeded in 100 of the 176 attempts at conciliation, and 33 unsolved complaints were referred to the Department of Justice for prosecution. Three actions involving 22 complaints had been filed by the Department of Justice as of April 1970.[56]

FHA has also taken some steps against noncompliers. Between November 1962 and November 1968, FHA received 195 complaints alleging discrimination by builders or landlords who had received Federal money. Penalties assessed against the 86 found guilty of discrimination were relatively light; only 18 defendants were barred from participation in HUD programs, and 12 of these were later reinstated. The greatest black successes were 45 instances in which "the complainant actually acquire[d] the home or rental unit."[57]

The relatively small number of complaints processed suggests that Federal enforcement efforts have been less than they might have been. Indeed the complaints received may be only the tip of the iceberg of discrimination. Since HUD's arsenal is limited to "informal methods of conference, conciliation, and persuasion"[58] (it can neither issue cease and desist orders nor file suits), it seems likely that relatively few acts of discrimination will actually be resolved by the department. Requiring those suffering discrimination to trigger government action reduces the likelihood of policy change because potential complainants may be unaware of the available administrative remedies, or fearful to use them. Another drawback of enforcement through complaint processing is the delays while reviews are being conducted. The "complex and time-consuming complaint procedures are likely to stifle complaints."[59] Even if complaints are expeditiously processed, there is evidence that lower-income citizens shy away from instituting legal proceedings.[60] In summary, when blacks must assume the burden of filing complaints, less integration occurs than when an agency is responsible for seeking out and destroying vestiges of discrimination.[61]

Compliance has been further hampered by Title VIII of the 1968 act, which requires that HUD forward complaints to state or local agencies when remedies exist at these levels. In 1969, 74 complaints were passed on to 21 states, but with no attempt having been made to determine the disposition of the referrals.[62]

The Department of Housing and Urban Development is also a victim of a malady which seems to debilitate most Federal civil rights enforcers. The staff concerned with open housing is meager and the funding penurious.[63] We can speculate that much more might be accomplished if the office were being more kindly treated by the Bureau of the Budget.

While enforcers of the 1968 legislation are to some extent hamstrung, they have often failed to fully utilize the authority available. HUD has not attempted to marshal data to determine whether discrimination is practiced by banks, realtors, builders, or by those benefiting from Federal programs. This deficiency persists despite the Commission on Civil Rights' judgment that, "As in other areas of civil rights compliance, the collection of racial and ethnic data is crucial."[64] The appropriate figures would facilitate determination of whether a pattern or practice of discrimination existed and thereby provide the basis of private or Federal court actions.

At least a partial explanation for HUD's failure to maximize its powers to achieve compliance is the seeming uncertainty among policy makers as to their goals. Secretary of HUD George Romney who once spoke of "forced integration" has now become moderate and espouses "prevention of discrimination."[65] Accompanying the less sweeping goal is the apparent failure to clearly place responsibility for fair housing enforcement.[66] In the same vein HUD has not set goals for its housing program. Establishing integration objectives, as has been done in some areas of civil rights, would be a move toward requiring that affirmative action be taken to promote integration rather than relying on freedom of choice to end discrimination.

Department of Justice If there are to be any prosecutions stemming from the 1968 law, they are to be instituted by the attorney general. The Department of Justice is authorized to file suits when a "pattern or practice" of discrimination is alleged.[67] Because of limited manpower, litigation has been directed at "target cities" offering the greatest potential for affecting minority groups. The 13 attorneys in the housing section of the Department of Justice's Civil Rights Division filed 40 suits naming 120 defendants, through August 1970.[68]

Even if prosecution is undertaken, proving the existence of discrimination may be more difficult than demonstrating the presence of other types of civil rights impairment. Thus, the absence of blacks from voting rolls or schools in areas where a sizable segment of the population is black has come to be accepted as prima facie evidence of discrimination. However, courts have yet to assume that the absence of blacks from a subdivision or apartment complex evinces legally punishable prejudices held by the builder, realtor, mortgagor, or lessor. Unless such assumptions are made, integration in housing may rise as slowly as black registration and integrated schooling did prior to the latter half of the sixties. Indeed consideration of the rank order of discrimination of most whites leads to the conclusion that integrated housing will come even more slowly than other changes.

Anything less than tightly drawn standards and vigilant enforcement seems unlikely to overcome white resistance in the near future. To quote the Commission on Civil Rights:

> In an area where racial discrimination for decades has been operating industry practice and where residential segregation has become firmly entrenched, vigorous enforcement and creative administration of fair housing laws are necessary if the rights that are legally secured are to be achieved in fact.[69]

The Situation of Blacks

The underdeveloped state of housing law (underdeveloped in comparison with requirements in other spheres of civil rights), probably is indicative of more than white opposition, administrative hesitancy, and

congressional parsimony. Many blacks prefer to live in racially homogeneous neighborhoods. Interview data collected in 1964 in four cities,
as well as a nationwide urban sample, reveal that a majority of blacks
opt for all-black neighborhoods.[70] More recent surveys show, however,
that the proportion of blacks favoring interracial living has risen, until
now a majority of the blacks sampled in Detroit, Miami, and Bedford-
Stuyvesant want integrated living.[71] The newness of this goal for many
blacks coupled with the scarcity of blacks at the innovative stage of
housing policy[72] would seem to help account for the lack of progress
toward a strong open housing law.

The urgency of black demands for open housing may also be
reduced by the primacy of other needs. Thus while 80 percent of the
blacks in Bedford-Stuyvesant in 1967 favored integrated living, "integration received relatively low priority compared to the need for better
housing, employment, and education."[73] Black demands for more
vigorous pursuit of open housing goals may remain in abeyance until
more critical issues are resolved.

Finally, even stringent laws and constant enforcement, and changed
attitudes will be of limited success in effectuating biracial neighborhoods in the absence of substantial income gains by blacks. The
apartments, homes, and town houses which shelter the white American
middle class elude the financial reach of the vast majority of blacks.
Open housing requires a deep foundation of economic equality which
awaits full realization of fair employment laws and improvements in the
education offered black youngsters.

However, time alone will not erase racial separation. If blacks'
occupational statuses improve during the next century at the same rate
as between 1950 and 1960, the average segregation indices in Northern
cities will decline by only 15 points.[74]

IMPLICATIONS OF "CLOSED" HOUSING

The minimal progress toward open housing is related to the pace of
integration in other spheres. Racially homogeneous housing patterns
produce de facto school segregation. The unavailability of housing
restricts the employment opportunities accessible to blacks. With most
cities cursed with deteriorating public transportation systems, ghetto

blacks are often unable to reach vacant jobs in the industrial parks now ringing many cities.[75]

The impermeability of the housing market at times denies today's black adults good jobs and consigns their children to the marginal existence of those who miss out on education and drop out of school. Continuous integrated living would pay dividends to the entire polity by producing a better educated, better paid, and more productive population. These results could perhaps extinguish the smoldering coals of revolt which all too often recently have roared to inferno intensity.

Housing conditions were one of the most frequently cited causes of urban riots.[76] Open housing, by making available a larger pool of dwellings, would break the hold which slumlords have over blacks. The increased supply could cause rents in the slums to drop to a point more commensurate with the value received. The passing of exploitation in this manner combined with civil rights advances elsewhere should reduce black alienation and hostility.

Moreover, introduction of blacks into white communities can result in positive attitudinal changes in both races. Blacks who live in integrated, middle-class neighborhoods are less alienated than are their middle-income peers who remain in the ghetto. Blacks living outside the ghetto have a higher sense of political efficacy and in general express attitudes more closely paralleling those of whites than of ghetto blacks.[77]

Whites who remain in an area once it is integrated also have different attitudes than do their peers in homogeneous neighborhoods. When murder and rape do not become commonplace on the streets and when the black-owned homes do not deteriorate, whites appraise their new neighbors in a different light. They become more tolerant of having black neighbors than do whites in one-race areas.[78] The extent to which attitudes on having blacks as neighbors reshape other attitudes on biracialism is not yet known, but it would seem to be positive.

CONCLUSION

Progress in integrated living has great potential for promoting harmonious racial interaction. Biracial neighborhoods should produce less alienated blacks and less apprehensive whites. Black adults would benefit by having access to better jobs for themselves and better educations for their children.

With benefits—not just for blacks but for the nation—within reach, it may be that policies will be forthcoming to extend our reach until the goal of a truly integrated society is obtained. This could probably be done through Federal enforcement sufficient to demonstrate that white-only settlements will not be tolerated. To accomplish this, more men, more money, and more motivation on the part of the Federal government are needed. It may be necessary to establish goals or to require affirmative action on the part of the housing industry participants to achieve integration. Compliance with Federal law should become more widespread if it is demonstrated that those seeking to circumvent the law are caught and punished. Moreover panic selling should end when whites see that blacks can and do live in all neighborhoods and not just in fading ones on the periphery of the ghetto.

However, for the present this discussion is utopian. Prosecution is not widespread at the state or national level. The crucial players in the housing industry continue to evade the law at will. Whites remain unconvinced that integrated living is a permanent phenomenon and flee contact with blacks, moving further from the urban hub.

Advances in other areas did not come easily. If anything, the deeper white prejudices forebode that racism will be more difficult to dislodge in housing. So far there has been no Federal follow-up to the Open Housing Act of 1968. Experience leads us to conclude that early edicts may be largely symbolic, and that in the absence of renewed initiative few changes will be forthcoming.

NOTES

1. Karl E. Taeuber and Alma F. Taeuber, *Negroes in Cities,* Chicago: Aldine, 1965, pp. 35-36.
2. Ibid., pp. 32-34.
3. Herbert H. Hyman and Paul B. Sheatsley, "Attitudes toward Desegregation," *Scientific American,* July 1964, pp. 16-23.
4. Lorraine Bennett, "Housing Needs Attention," *Atlanta Journal,* September 8, 1969, p. 1-A.
5. *Report of the National Advisory Commission on Civil Disorders,* New York: Bantam, 1968, p. 470.
6. Ibid., p. 471.

7. Whitney Young, *To Be Equal,* New York: McGraw-Hill, 1964, pp. 144-145.
8. *Report of . . . Disorders,* pp. 470-471.
9. Buchanan v. Warley, 245 U.S. 60 (1917).
10. Several such instances are recounted in U.S. Commission on Civil Rights, *Housing, 1961,* Washington: GPO, 1961, pp. 132-137.
11. Shelley v. Kraemer, 334 U.S. 1 (1948).
12. *Housing, 1961,* p. 63.
13. U.S. Commission on Civil Rights, *Federal Civil Rights Enforcement Effort,* Washington: GPO, 1970, p. 470.
14. See *Housing, 1961,* pp. 62-68, for numerous examples of FHA foot-dragging.
15. Ibid., p. 65.
16. Ibid., pp. 64-65.
17. U.S. Commission on Civil Rights, *Report of the United States Commission on Civil Rights,* Washington: GPO, 1959, pp. 462-463. For additional data on the paucity of FHA homes going to blacks, see *Federal Civil Rights Enforcement Effort,* pp. 491-492.
18. *Federal Civil Rights Enforcement Effort,* p. 469.
19. For additional material on these points see Luigi Laurenti, *Property Values and Race,* Berkeley: University of California, 1960 pp. 16-22.
20. *Federal Civil Rights Enforcement Effort,* p. 512.
21. Ibid., pp. 512-513.
22. Louis L. Knowles and Kenneth Prewitt, eds., *Institutional Racism in America,* Englewood Cliffs, N.J.: Prentice-Hall, 1969 p. 28.
23. National Association of Real Estate Boards, *Code of Ethics,* adopted 1924.
24. Leonard Freedman, *Public Housing: The Politics of Poverty,* New York: Holt, 1969, p. 135.
25. Norris Vitchek, "Confessions of a Block Buster," *Saturday Evening Post,* July 14, 1962, pp. 15-19.
26. Laurenti, op. cit., pp. 51-52. More than half a century ago the Chicago Commission on Race Relations concluded that black settlement in a previously all-white neighborhood did not cause property values to decline. Discussed in Stokely Carmichael and Charles V. Hamilton *Black Power,* New York: Vintage Books, 1967, pp. 153-154.
27. With an installment land contract the buyer gets neither a warranty nor a mortgage deed. The seller retains full title until the property is paid for. Therefore, if at any time during the 10 to 20 years in which the buyer is making payments, he defaults, he has nothing. In case of a default, even one missed payment, the rights of the buyer terminate and the seller can resell or rent the property.
28. Daniel R. Mandelker, ed., *Managing Our Urban Environment,* Indianapolis: Bobbs-Merrill, 1966, p. 848.
29. Vitchek, op. cit., p. 18.
30. Knowles and Prewitt, op. cit., p. 27.
31. Eleanor Leacock et al., *Toward Integration in Suburban Housing: The Bridgeview Study,* New York: Anti-Defamation League of B'nai B'rith, 1965, pp. 32-33.

32. Howard Singer, "How to Beat the Blockbusters," *Saturday Evening Post,* March 23, 1968, pp. 50-55.

33. Freedman, op. cit., pp. 142-144.

34. Eleanor P. Wolf, "Racial Tensions in a Middle-Class Area," *Journal of Intergroup Relations,* 1, Summer 1960, pp. 75-81.

35. Lynn W. Eley and Thomas W. Casstevens, eds., *The Politics of Fair-Housing Legislation,* San Francisco: Chandler, 1968, p. xi.

36. This was the pattern in New Jersey where fair housing provisions were applied to public housing in 1950. Seven years later they were extended to publicly assisted housing and to privately financed housing (in apartments with more than two units and single family residence developments of more than nine homes) in 1961.

37. *Housing, 1961,* pp. 121-131.

38. Eley and Casstevens, op. cit., p. 15.

39. *Report of . . . Disorders,* p. 249.

40. *Housing, 1961,* pp. 62-65.

41. *Federal Civil Rights Enforcement Effort,* pp. 429 430

42. 'The second phase . . . extended coverage generally to private, nonfederally assisted housing except single family housing, and buildings containing no more than four housing units one of which is occupied by the owner." Ibid., p. 433. This interpretation seems geared to excluding the private homeowner and small-scale landlord, but covers most commercial operations.

43. Ibid., p. 434.

44. Jones v. Mayer, 392 U.S. 409 (1968).

45. Complainants' brief, Blair v. Knoll Manor, Inc., State of New Jersey, Department of Law and Public Safety, Division of Civil Rights, Docket Nos. H14R 1872-76, 1878-80, 1883-91, 1922-25.

46. Peter Braestrup, "Desegregated Housing—How?" *Atlanta Journal,* July 27, 1970, p. 7-B.

47. *Federal Civil Rights Enforcement Effort,* pp. 521-536.

48. Data from the 1968 S.R.C. Election Survey indicate that there is less interracial contact in housing than in education, employment shopping, or social interaction. The data were supplied in partially proofed form and the consortium bears no responsibility for either the analysis or interpretation presented here.

49. Gunnar Myrdal, *An American Dilemma,* New York: Harper, 1944, pp. 60-67.

50. Raymond E. Wolfinger and Fred I. Greenstein, "The Repeal of Fair Housing in California: An Analysis of Referendum Voting," *American Political Science Review,* 62, September 1968, p. 765.

51. William Brink and Louis Harris, *Black and White,* New York: Simon and Schuster, 1966, p. 136.

52. Ibid., pp. 136, 222.

53. Mandelker, op. cit., pp. 847-848.

54. In a 1963 Louis Harris Poll 91 percent of the whites polled favored Federal laws to insure blacks' voting rights. Support for equal employment legislation was 86 percent and for public accommodations, 74 percent. In contrast only

52 percent favored a national open housing law. In Hazel Erskine, "The Polls: Negro Housing," *Public Opinion Quarterly,* 31, Fall 1967, p. 484.

55. 1966 data, Brink and Harris, op. cit., pp. 136, 222. Less widespread white support for open housing may be important since, as Lipsky notes, relatively powerless groups often need the sympathy and backing of decision makers' reference groups if they are to achieve their objectives. Michael Lipsky, "Protest as a Political Resource," *American Political Science Review,* 62, December 1968, pp. 1144-1159.

56. *Federal Civil Rights Enforcement Effort,* pp. 448-452.

57 Ibid., p. 487.

58. Open Housing Act of 1968, Title VIII, sec. 808(e) (5).

59. *Federal Civil Rights Enforcement Effort,* p. 449. For example, in Chicago of 18 complaints on file in the Office of Equal Opportunities, half had been there at least 10 months (p. 486). In New Jersey, the state office handling discrimination complaints often took as long as half a year to process them. When it found for the complainant it offered no monetary recompense but simply ordered the realtor to offer the next available house or apartment to the wronged individual. If a developer had completed a subdivision, the complainant would not even have an opportunity to buy another house. For a discussion of these and other inadequacies of the New Jersey law see Alfred W. Blumrosen, "Antidiscrimination Laws in Action in New Jersey: A Law-Sociology Study," *Rutgers Law Review,* 19, Winter 1965, pp. 225-241; Leonard Zeitz, "Survey of Negro Attitudes toward Law," *Rutgers Law Review,* 19, pp. 288-315.

60. Zeitz found from interviewing a sample of black males in Newark that only 2 percent would file a complaint with the State's Division on Civil Rights if discriminated against. Use of the division's services was related to income and education. Zeitz, op. cit., pp. 295-306. In a broader context court usage is also associated positively with socioeconomic level. Herbert Jacob, *Debtors in Court: The Consumption of Government Services,* Chicago: Rand McNally, 1969, p. 20; Roger B. Hunting and Gloria Neuwirth, *Who Sues in New York City: A Study of Automobile Accident Cases,* New York: Columbia, 1962, pp. 11-12.

61. Blumrosen, op. cit., pp. 214-226.

62. *Federal Civil Rights Enforcement Effort,* pp. 453-454.

63. Ibid., p. 538.

64. Ibid., p. 520.

65. "Integration Force Denied by Romney," *Atlanta Journal,* January 7, 1971, p. 18-A.

66. *Federal Civil Rights Enforcement Effort,* p. 539.

67. Ibid., p. 435.

68. Ibid., pp. 493-496.

69. Ibid., p. 536.

70. For interview results drawn from Atlanta, Birmingham, Chicago, and New York, see Gary T. Marx, *Protest and Prejudice,* New York: Harper & Row,

1967, p. 176. Edward C. Banfield discusses this finding in *The Unheavenly City,* Boston: Little, Brown, 1970, pp. 78-82.

71. Marx, op. cit., p. 224.

72. Harold L. Wolman and Norman C. Thomas, "Black Interests, Black Groups, and Black Influence in the Federal Policy Process: The Cases of Housing and Education," *Journal of Politics,* 32, November 1970, p. 894.

73. Marx, op. cit., p. 224.

74. Taeuber and Taeuber, op. cit., pp. 94-95.

75. *Federal Civil Rights Enforcement Effort,* p. 521; Elliot Liebow, *Tally's Corner,* Boston: Little, Brown, 1967, p. 44.

76. *Report of. . .Disorders,* pp. 143-150. Housing conditions were cited as a cause of riots more frequently than anything other than police brutality and lack of job opportunities.

77. Bonnie Bullough, "Alienation in the Ghetto," *American Journal of Sociology,* 72, 1966-67, pp. 469-478.

78. Bernard Meer and Edward Freedman, "The Impact of Negro Neighbors on White Home Owners," *Social Forces,* 45, September 1966, pp. 11-19.

CHAPTER SEVEN

The Uneven Push from Washington

In the preceding chapters we have shown that greater changes have occurred in some areas of civil rights than in others. In the next two chapters we shall probe reasons for the uneven rate of progress. One major factor, the role assumed by the Federal government in promoting black civil rights, is the topic of this chapter. Another factor, to be discussed in Chapter Eight, is the willingness or refusal of state and local public officials, as well as private citizens, to bring their behavior into conformity with civil rights laws.

The Federal government has set the pace in the civil rights revolution. Rarely has state or local law set more demanding standards than those specified by Washington. In the South, but for Federal pressure, strict segregation would probably still be the rule. Outside the South some state and local governments have held the spotlight briefly in the struggle for equality, but once the Federal government became active they were relegated to supporting roles and bit parts. In Southern and Border states, Federal participation has been the catalyst producing the initial gains for blacks, while elsewhere it has frequently signaled the introduction of more stringent standards and new vigor in enforcement. The standards set by the Federal government for measuring equality affect progress because they determine the amount of integration needed to demonstrate the absence of discrimination.

Variations in Federal standards and possible explanations for these variations will be discussed in this chapter. First, we shall distinguish and define two standards of enforcement, freedom of choice and affirmative action, and show where each is being applied. Then we shall discuss why the same standard has not been applied in all areas of civil rights.

STANDARDS

Chronologically the earlier, and the less stringent, of the two standards used in deciding whether actionable discrimination has occurred is freedom of choice. While "freedom of choice" is commonly applied to a type of school desegregation plan, i.e., one permitting a child to attend any school in his district, we apply the term here to any standard which requires only that blacks be allowed equal access to a particular civil right. Freedom of choice places the burden for accomplishing integration on blacks who in the past have been discriminated against. If no one seeks to integrate a facility, it remains segregated.

The second standard, affirmative action, is more demanding. It has been adopted only after a freedom-of-choice approach has proven insufficient to bring about equal opportunity. It requires that steps be taken to end discrimination, shifting the burden of insuring equality from the person who has been discriminated against to the actor who in the past may have practiced discrimination. One definition is:

> An affirmative action program must go beyond mere nondiscrimination. It must be devised to overcome obstacles that impede equality of opportunity for minority group persons and should be governed by a plan of action tailor-made to the problems and needs of the installation.[1]

Elsewhere affirmative action has been characterized as "the accomplishment of full equality through the use of specific goals and within a specific—and prompt—time frame. . . ."[2]

Federal officials use the phrase "affirmative action" rather freely, applying it to a range of activities that at a minimum require little more than a symbolic commitment to equal opportunity. For example, the Civil Service Commission (CSC) refers to its attempts to recruit blacks for Federal employment as affirmative action, even though no objective, stated in number or proportion of blacks to be employed, has been set.[3] The Equal Employment Opportunity Commission (EEOC) applies the phrase to four services it provides: aid to state and local programs for equal employment, technical assistance to those seeking to comply with fair employment laws, efforts to propagandize equal employment efforts, and data collection.[4] The Office of Federal Contract Compliance (OFCC), while ostensibly conducting an affirmative action program, has yet to define the term.[5] Hedging on a definition has also characterized the so-called affirmative action program which the Federal Housing Administration is supposed to be implementing.[6]

In evaluating where affirmative action exists, we have relied upon criticisms directed at some of the above efforts by the Commission on Civil Rights.[7] For purposes of this chapter an affirmative action program is defined as one having the following components:

1. Some type of numerical standard or goal against which to evaluate compliance efforts.
2. The availability of data with which to appraise efforts at eliminating discrimination.
3. Monitoring of compliance actions on a continuing basis by Federal officials, rather than passive reliance upon complaints.
4. Location within a single governmental unit of both monitoring and sanctioning powers.

Affirmative action offers the potentiality of Federal authorities' initiation of challenges to discrimination when voluntary compliance is not forthcoming. Under freedom of choice the Federal government has helped prosecute cases only upon receipt of a complaint. In essence, affirmative action requires that steps be taken to accomplish integration; freedom of choice requires only that nothing overt be done to prevent desegregation.

To flesh out the standards adopted and to demonstrate how affirmative action differs from freedom of choice, we will discuss in some detail the criteria for an affirmative action program. Marshaling evidence from earlier chapters, we will also note some of the policy differences associated with the choice of which standard to apply. Careful study of Table 7-1 may also prove helpful in distinguishing which standard is applied in various areas.

TABLE 7-1 *Characteristics of Federal enforcement agencies in five areas of civil rights*

Agency and responsibility	Numerical standards	Monitoring	Corrective powers	Data	Standard applied
Civil Rights Division, Department of Justice (voting)	Set by Voting Rights Act of 1965	Continuous in counties covered by 1965 act, at both registration and elections	Federal officials can register voters and observe elections. Attorneys to prosecute discrimination	Available and current	Affirmative action
HEW (education)	Set by HEW pursuant to Civil Rights Act of 1964	Continuous where de jure segregation exists	HEW can impose fund cutoffs. Prosecutions must be referred to Department of Justice	Available but may be a few years old	Affirmative action where de jure segregation was practiced and in a few districts accused of de facto segregation
OFCC (private employment under Federal contract)	Established for Federal construction projects in a few cities	Exists in some industries in a few cities, elsewhere complaint-oriented	Unused, although available. No instances of contract termination or disbarment.	Estimates available for construction industry in some cities	Affirmative action in cities where a "hometown solution" has been required for Federal contractors, elsewhere freedom of choice

CSC (Federal employment)	Specifically rejected	Complaint-oriented	Authority to discipline supervisors guilty of discrimination remains unused. Corrective powers weak.	Available only for higher grades	Freedom of choice
EEOC (private employment not covered by OFCC)	None	Complaint-oriented	Authority limited to conferences, conciliation, and persuasion. When agency is unsuccessful it can refer cases to Justice, or private suits may be brought.	Generally unavailable	Freedom of choice
HUD (housing)	None	Some in public housing, generally complaint-oriented	Same as EEOC	Available for public housing. Plans to collect it for FHA are being formulated. Nonexistent for most of private housing industry, realtors, banks, etc.	Freedom of choice
None exists in public accommodations	—	—	—	—	Freedom of choice

Numerical Standards

Affirmative action is presently required by the Federal government in education, voting, and employment practices of some Federal contractors. In these areas evaluation of the adequacy of compliance has been made on the basis of the proportion of blacks exercising a particular right. A few examples will illustrate the policy outcomes associated with the affirmative action concept. Affirmative action has necessitated large-scale transfers of teachers and students to achieve racial balance in schools. Freedom of choice which was widely practiced prior to 1968 required only that blacks wishing to attend white schools not be stopped.

In the sphere of voting rights, Congress in 1965 established a numerical standard to determine when a presumption of discrimination is warranted. If less than half of a county's eligible electorate was registered or voted in 1964, Federal examiners might register those who were qualified. Federal observers might be on hand during elections in counties charged with discrimination to note any abridgements of the suffrage. A numerical standard has also been devised to measure the existence of racial discrimination in the construction industry in selected cities. Initiated in the Philadelphia Plan and programmed for extension to 91 cities has been a timetable for the employment of specific proportions of minority group workers in Federal construction projects.[8]

Standards for desegregation in public accommodations, housing, and other aspects of employment have been less exacting.[9] No attempts have been made to numerically define the existence of discrimination in these fields. Realtors, restaurateurs, innkeepers, and most employers (private and public) bear no obligation to see that some share of their clientele or workers are black. For example, landlords—even the Federal government—are not obligated to have some proportion of blacks in their dwellings. All that has been required is that outright discrimination be eliminated. Federal enforcement officers have not probed to determine whether overturning overtly discriminatory policies has produced changes in the treatment actually accorded blacks.[10]

The standard used colors perceptions about the amount of progress made. In education the goals of integrated faculties and student bodies have resulted in large numbers of school districts being judged noncompliant with the principle enunciated in *Brown* v. *Board of Education.*[11] Contrariwise, the lower hurdle of simply accepting blacks who choose to assert their rights makes it appear that compliance in public accommodations is almost universal. However, if it were Federal policy to test the willingness of restaurants, hotels, barbershops, and so forth to accept blacks, compliance might appear as low as in education.

Availability of Data

While all findings of discrimination require a showing that blacks have been denied the use of some facility or the exercise of some right because of their race, the data necessary to sustain a positive action program are more extensive than those needed where freedom of choice is tolerated. For affirmative action there must be reports showing the numbers or proportion of eligible blacks exercising a right in order to determine whether the compliance goals are being met. Thus, for example, authorization of the appointment of Federal officers to register blacks in counties in which less than 50 percent of those eligible were registered or voted in 1964 would be meaningless in the absence of registration statistics by race and county.

The Philadelphia Plan, which established objectives for the proportion of minority group workers to be employed on Federal construction job sites, is another example of how affirmative action would have been impossible in the absence of figures, in this case on the proportion of blacks in each of several unions. Nor could reassignments of faculty members in order to achieve the same ratio of black and white teachers throughout a system have been done, without data on the racial composition of the teaching staff at each school.

Where figures are missing on the proportion of blacks present in previously all-white or largely white facilities or jobs, freedom of choice has remained the rule. A recent report of the Commission on Civil Rights repeatedly cites the statistical void as a handicap in guaranteeing equal employment opportunities and policing the housing industry.[12] Thus even if HUD wanted to determine whether banks applied the same standards in evaluating loan applications of blacks and whites, the material has not been collected which would permit such judgments.

Continuous Monitoring

The third criterion for affirmative action, continuous monitoring, means that there are Federal officials who check whether the terms of antidiscrimination laws are being fulfilled. When these officials conclude that discrimination exists, they can set in motion corrective procedures. For example, when the attorney general's office finds a county in which discrimination is presumed to exist, he can abrogate the use of tests and devices requisite for registration and dispatch Federal examiners to register prospective voters.

When agents of the Federal government are not empowered to take steps *sua sponte* to correct discrimination, the burden of initiating remedial action falls upon those who think that they are being mistreated. Reliance upon the complaints of the abused reduces the likelihood of policy change because the poor are often hesitant to file a complaint or bring suit,[13] no doubt a concomitant of the reduced sense of efficacy typically found in the lower stratum of society. Thus blacks who suffer discrimination may be reluctant to file complaints even when aware that a complaint processing agency exists.[14] Additional obstacles to rectification include the failure of the wronged to recognize justiciable discrimination, to know where to seek relief, or to be able to pay the costs of justice.

Continuous monitoring is also conducive to efforts to apply uniform standards on a national or regional basis. Such efforts have, of course, been impaired because of an insufficient number of personnel employed in the Department of Justice's Civil Rights Division and HEW's Office of Enforcement Activities and Contract Compliance. Nonetheless despite small budgets and small staffs, these offices have acted against inequities which might have gone unchallenged had the agency had to await a complaint before taking action.

Additionally, monitoring, whether undertaken by an administrative office or a court, permits the constant assessment of feedback on the success of earlier orders.When progress remains elusive, the governmental unit can adjust its strategies to cope with the latest ploys of circumventers. In the absence of surveillance it might be necessary for a separate complaint to be filed to challenge each new avoidance technique.

Locus of Sanctioning Powers

Affirmative action is more likely to be required when monitoring and sanctioning powers are held by a single governmental unit than when they are divided. When both powers are combined in an agency or a court, the enforcer may act as the ramrod, coordinating enforcement efforts and pursuing policy objectives. Once the agency has a clear comprehension of its mandate it may be able to operate on its own momentum. When this stage is reached, as it seems to have been in voting rights, the agency may continue to pursue its policy goals even in the face of Presidential opposition. For example, the Nixon administration has sought to disengage itself from policy stands taken by the Democrats on voting by weakening the Voting Rights Act of 1965 when it came up for renewal. Nonetheless, the change in administrations, while perhaps impairing morale, has been accompanied by an increase in the proportion of Southern blacks registered to vote.[15] Thus there has been progress even though the enforcers and the Nixon administration have at times been at loggerheads, the former intent upon discharging their mandate while the latter pursued a "Southern strategy."

The willingness of civil servants entrusted with civil rights enforcement to perform their duties even when opposed by the Chief Executive is suggestive of the significance for policy realization of having agencies specifically responsible for particular programs. As J. Leiper Freeman has observed:

> The bureaus composed wholly or almost wholly of career personnel and possessed of the technology and the capacity to perform the tasks of the agency, are neither easily moved by the party in power nor overly embarrassed at urging their time-tested viewpoints upon "non-career" leaders in the Administration.[16]

Where freedom of choice is the rule, those responsible for evaluating progress in the elimination of discrimination often have no sanctioning powers. Thus while agencies now exist to process complaints alleging discrimination in private housing and employment, they are restricted to "conference, conciliation, and persuasion."[17] These agencies lack authority to issue cease and desist orders or to otherwise enforce their judgments. For their decisions to be implemented in the absence of voluntary compliance it is required that the Attorney General's office file suit and this is done only when a "pattern or practice of discrimination" is alleged. Relatively few unresolved complaints are forwarded to the Department of Justice and even fewer suits are filed. Figures on the disposition of complaints filed with the EEOC are insightful. Through fiscal 1969, EEOC received over 40,000 allegations of discrimination of which 60 percent were recommended for investigation. Of the complaints investigated, approximately 2,000 were not successfully resolved. Yet there were only 112 instances in which EEOC recommended that the Department of Justice become involved. The Attorney General acted on 12 of these recommendations.[18]

REASONS FOR DIFFERENCES IN STANDARDS

That different yardsticks have been used in measuring compliance has now been demonstrated. A less obvious matter is to account for the adoption of different standards. To this task we now devote our attention. Five factors which help explain why freedom of choice is used in some areas while a positive duty is assessed elsewhere will be discussed. The first two factors are the extent of white support and black demands for pro-civil rights laws. Also considered is whether enjoyment of a right is contingent upon prerequisites. Finally two items are discussed which involve value judgments by some policy makers and their reference groups that progress in certain aspects of civil rights may be particularly important. To elaborate, a few years ago some civil rights supporters thought voting rights was the key to improving the condition of blacks in other spheres. Also achievement of equal treatment in some aspects of civil rights, such as employment, has been thought to be instrumental in the development of support of the system. While we have no way of weighing the significance of each item for the President, Congress, or for any individual, it appears that each is significant to some decision makers.

Whose Ox Is Being Gored?

The persistence with which discrimination in registration and education has been challenged is partially due to these inequities' being, at least at first, seen as regional. Since race was not an obstacle to voting or school attendance in most of the country,[19] opposition to early antidiscrimination efforts in these spheres rarely was voiced outside of the South. The absence of extensive popular disapproval of Federal intervention to assure these rights was unquestionably a consideration in the establishment of Federal antidiscrimination standards.[20]

Many Northerners who approved of opening polling places to blacks and of outlawing de jure segregation retreated from equalitarianism as the impact of civil rights laws spread northward. Public hesitancy in condemning discriminatory practices which occur nationwide has led to foot-dragging by all branches of the Federal government in eradicating discrimination in de facto segregation, employment, and housing. It is not surprising that the most sensitive of the civil rights, and one abridged as frequently in the North as in the South, private housing,[21] was the thicket last entered by Congress and the area where change has been least.

That masses and elites alike should be more supportive of some civil rights than others is to be expected. Most if not all whites use some sort of rank ordering of acceptability in evaluating gains made by blacks. [22] An important criterion for many people in judging civil rights policy is the degree to which they are directly affected by the policy changes. Much more commitment to equality is needed to condemn de facto segregation in one's own school district than to speak against de jure segregation elsewhere. It is easier to support black demands for voting rights in the South than it is to encourage open housing in one's own neighborhood or to promote equal employment when the results may be black challenges for one's own job.[23]

Federal efforts to secure voting rights have been exclusively directed at the South; and since these impinge upon fewer whites than do changes in the other policy areas studied, they have been the most persistent. School desegregation, the effort in which Washington has been second most active, affected only Southern and Border states until the end of the sixties. So long as the confrontation was the South versus the rest of the nation, indignation over Southern parochialism and intractability was extensive. Polarization prompted Northern demands that the Federal government "go down there and show those rebels who's boss." Such attitudes have evaporated as the hand of Federal law has extended into the cities and suburbs of the North and

West. Indications are that in the face of declining popular support the Federal government will continue to tolerate freedom of choice in housing and employment.

Black Demands

Another consideration behind variations in Federal formulas for evaluating racial policies is that demands of civil rights groups and their prominent spokesmen have not been focused with equal intensity on all goals. We argue elsewhere in this book that change occurs only in response to political pressure, actual or perceived. An important ingredient in how equal opportunity is defined and what efforts are made to protect it is the force mustered by blacks in support of particular policies.

The greatest inroads on discrimination have followed paths blazed by black activists. Federal efforts on behalf of equal opportunity have been most substantial where involvement of the masses and the elite of the civil rights movement has been most extensive, continuous, and frequent. Voting and school desegregation, areas in which affirmative action has become most widely implemented, have histories marked by long and persistent litigation. Equal opportunity in these spheres has also been a goal of protests and demonstrations in numerous towns and cities. Civil rights organizations, e.g., the Southern Regional Council and the NAACP, have often helped finance court challenges to school and voting discrimination and sponsored registration drives.

The two-pronged (masses and elites) attacks have succeeded in making the objectives of school integration and voting rights visible to Federal decision makers and to their reference groups. The perseverance of discontented blacks prodded Congress and the courts to go beyond the promulgation of largely symbolic statutes and wrestle with the demanding task of effectuating large-scale change. In housing and employment, black pressure has been less voluminous and often sporadic, with the result that Federal policy makers have generally accepted programs which require nothing more than freedom of choice. More rigorous standards and constant supervision are unlikely to become a goal, much less a reality, in housing and many aspects of employment in the absence of a greater public outcry or more test cases.

Need for Prerequisites

The kind of prerequisites before a right can be enjoyed has also been significant in determining Federal standards, with affirmative action required when prerequisites are minimal. Registration and education can be distinguished from other civil rights in that their enjoyment is not contingent upon the possession of certain skills or economic conditions. Neither financial status nor ability, our laws now hold, can stand between a person and an education or the suffrage. To vote one need only be of age, sound mind, meet residency requirements, and not have been convicted of a felony. To attend an integrated school the only essential precondition is that one seek knowledge.

Rejection of race as a relevant consideration does not, however, remove standards of achievement as a hurdle to equal access to public accommodations, housing, and many jobs. Before an individual can dine at a good restaurant or engage lodging for the night, he must be able to pay the bill. Before moving to suburbia, he must demonstrate his ability to meet mortgage obligations. To acquire the money needed to enjoy either public accommodations or fair housing, a person needs a well-paid job. Jobs with livable salaries, however, are beyond the reach of those who do not possess some skill or talent which society values. Regardless of race, few people can obtain lucrative employment without first reaching a fairly high educational or training threshold.[24]

Two points can now be made. First, we have demonstrated the primacy of the need for a good education—a goal often linked with the instruction offered in white schools. Second, until blacks are trained to handle managerial and professional responsibilities, they will be excluded from financially rewarding jobs even in the absence of racial prejudice. These conditions make it unlikely that affirmative action will be required in other areas as it has been in voter registration and education.

It is one thing for the law to exclude race as a criterion, to set expectations for black participation in registration and education, and to monitor progress toward these goals. It is unlikely that similar rigor will be brought to housing or employment except for those aspects requiring little affluence or preparation. On the other hand, freedom of choice need not be the limit of Federal enforcement in housing and employment. If enforcement officers were to be armed with statistics on the performance of realtors, mortgagors, employers, unions, and employment agencies, it would permit determination of where standards of achievement leave off and where racism begins.[25]

Importance of the Right

Another reason for differences in standards is that some activists in the struggle for equality believe that gains in one area will open the way to advances elsewhere. Specifically, first access to the ballot box and later educational integration have been perceived by some as wedges opening the way to full-scale equality. If the discrimination limiting the suffrage could be eliminated, the argument ran, equal treatment would emerge in the other areas as politicians courted black voters with nondiscriminatory public policies. This was a popular assumption in the late fifties and early sixties;[26] yet even armed with the ballot, blacks were unable to prod state and local policy makers into assailing discrimination in other spheres. Thus, for example, blacks were denied housing in white neighborhoods and were relegated to the jobs spurned by the latest European immigrants in the North long after they were permitted to vote. And while Northern blacks were not uniformly barred from public accommodations or consigned to segregated schools, there is no indication that they escaped the fate of their Southern brothers because of electoral leverage. On the other hand, black voting in the South has led to some material gains, for instance, the distribution of various social services such as playgrounds and clinics to the ghetto. Status gains—equality of treatment in biracial settings—have not stemmed from increased black political participation.[27]

Instead of being accepted as proof that no simple solution to the problems of racism existed, the failure of an enlarged black electorate to be a panacea prompted search for a different remedy. During the latter half of the sixties the racial problem became merged with a national effort to reduce poverty. In both contexts better education was seen by some as the key to change. As a vestige of the separate but equal era, black schools have continued to turn out youth less well-educated than the products of white schools. It was assumed that the caliber of education offered black students would be improved by conducting the process in an integrated setting, and indeed, as we show in Chapter Four, black students tend to perform better in integrated than segregated classrooms.

It has been argued that until the education gap is closed, blacks cannot get well-paid jobs in the same proportions as whites, even in the absence of discrimination. Education and employment are related in two ways, an obvious one being the need for training preparatory to job holding. Recent research suggests an additional linkage. Many jobs are found through leads furnished by one's friends; blacks educated in integrated schools have more white friends throughout their lives and consequently learn about and acquire better-paying jobs.[28] Once blacks obtain rewarding employment, their higher salaries may enable them to gain access to other goods and services on an integrated basis.

For those policy makers who anticipate that gains in housing and employment will come automatically after blacks acquire good educations, the recent concentration of efforts in desegregating schools while there is no push in housing, employment, and public accommodations has a rationale.

System Benefits

Imposition of a positive duty to open schools and voting booths to blacks may indicate that some Federal policy makers are operating on the premise that progress in these areas has unique potential for providing system benefits. There is evidence that education and political participation are of especial importance in the political socialization process, i.e., imparting political values and knowledge. Extensive Federal efforts have been directed towards securing changes which may be crucial for ghetto blacks to be incorporated into the predominant middle-class culture.

As we point out in Chapter Four, schools occupy a central position in developing in poor children traits associated with system support and stability. Further, although evidence is mixed, some blacks educated in integrated schools may emerge not only more committed to the political system but also better prepared for the job market. Being financially able to enjoy the better things of life should also be important in reducing the incidence of hostility and anxiety among blacks.

However, the system benefits produced by school integration will be of short duration if blacks are not allowed to participate fully in the nation's decision-making processes. Unless the political system is penetrable for the new generation of politically concerned blacks, the sweet wine of interest may sour to the vinegar of alienation. Thus at a minimum the right to vote is significant for the development of positive political attitudes.

To elaborate, while voting is a minimal form of political involvement, it is an act undertaken by those who become more involved and aware politically. Nonvoting is generally associated with a lack of political information and low interest. Political involvement, even at a low level, has the potential to promote growing concern and participation. Over time a person can develop stronger partisan ties, and voting turnout tends to increase until past middle age. With heightened involvement may come the soldering of commitment to the system and a willingness to play by the rules,[29] if blacks see their votes translated into desired policy outputs and political outcomes.[30]

As briefly outlined here, and discussed in some detail in earlier chapters, Federal actions in the areas of education and suffrage may yield important societal benefits, not the least of which is higher support for the political system. Matters of such import have, not surprisingly, drawn considerable Federal attention with the result that affirmative action has been required to integrate schools and to promote black voting.

SUMMARY

A major reason for the uneven pace of civil rights progress has been that the Federal government has made fewer demands in some areas than in others. Affirmative action to integrate has been required in voting rights and school desegregation. Freedom of choice has been the rule in housing and public accommodations. Federal requirements guaranteeing equal employment opportunities have become more extensive, particularly among Federal contractors in a few cities, but have become neither as far-reaching nor as fruitful as the efforts on behalf of blacks challenging suffrage and education discrimination.

In this chapter we have tried to delineate the characteristics of two Federal enforcement standards, freedom of choice and affirmative action. Often drawing upon material from earlier chapters, we have demonstrated some of the policy consequences of using one standard rather than the other. Finally we have suggested five reasons which help explain why affirmative action has been imposed in some areas while freedom of choice is the standard applied elsewhere.

NOTES

1. Quoted in U.S. Commission on Civil Rights, *Federal Civil Rights Enforcement Effort,* Washington: GPO, 1970, p. 111.
2. Ibid., p. 184.
3. Ibid., pp. 113-115.
4. Ibid., pp. 352-369.
5. Ibid., pp. 159-162.
6. Ibid., p. 488.
7. Ibid., passim.
8. The Philadelphia Plan, relying on estimates that only 1.6 percent of the workers on Federal construction projects were black even though the city's population was a third black, stipulated that by 1970 six building trades were to have 4 to 8 percent minority workers. By 1973 the proportion of minority workers was to have risen to between 19 and 26 percent. Bill Hughes, "U.S. Contracts Set Color Ratio of Work Force," *Atlanta Journal,* February 25, 1970, p. 1-A.
9. *Federal Civil Rights Enforcement Effort,* passim.
10. Ibid., pp. 1037-1052.
11. As of August 1970, the Department of Justice had filed suits against 412 noncompliant school districts.
12. This complaint is repeatedly made in *Federal Civil Rights Enforcement Effort,* passim.
13. Leonard Zeitz, "Survey on Negro Attitudes toward Law," *Rutgers Law Review,* 19, Winter 1965, p. 306. Other scholars have found that lower-income people are less likely to file court suits. Roger B. Hunting and Gloria Neuwirth, *Who Sues in New York City: A Study of Automobile Accident Cases,* New York: Columbia, 1962, pp. 11-12; Herbert Jacob, *Debtors in Court: The Consumption of Government Services,* Chicago: Rand McNally, 1969, p. 20.
14. Of a New Jersey sample who reported some discrimination, 81 percent did nothing; only 2 percent filed a complaint with the Division of Civil Rights. Zeitz, op. cit., p. 295.
15. Under the Nixon administration, the proportion of voting-age blacks registered to vote has risen from 62 to 66 percent. (See Table 2-1.)
16. J. Leiper Freeman, *The Political Process: Executive Bureau-Legislative Committee Relations,* rev. ed., New York: Random House, 1966, p. 24.
17. Material in this paragraph, including some direct quotations, is taken from *Federal Civil Rights Enforcement Effort,* pp. 267-268, 448-449.
18. Ibid., pp. 316, 327, 340-341. Several factors account for the small number of prosecutions, among them the 18 to 24 months which elapse between EEOC hearings and the recommendation that a suit be filed.
19. Here we speak of de jure and not de facto segregation.
20. For example, as early as 1963 only one in ten Northern white parents voiced objections to sending their child to a school with some black children. A third of the parents had qualms about sending their children to schools with

equal numbers of blacks and whites. *Gallup Opinion Index,* Report No. 58, April 1970. In contrast, as late as 1968, 42 percent of a Gallup survey favored open housing legislation with 37 percent opposing and 21 percent expressing no opinion. Based on our discussion in Chapter Six, we may assume that some, if not many, of those favoring open housing legislation would nonetheless move from a neighborhood if blacks moved in.

21. Karl E. Taeuber and Alma F. Taeuber, *Negroes in Cities,* Chicago: Aldine, 1965, pp. 32-35.

22. The concept of a rank order of discrimination was suggested by Gunnar Myrdal, *An American Dilemma,* New York: Harper, 1944, pp. 60-61. More recently the concept has been used with empirical evidence of its presence. See Donald R. Matthews and James W. Prothro, *Negroes and the New Southern Politics,* New York: Harcourt, Brace & World, 1966, pp. 335-339.

23. Guaranteeing the right of blacks to vote has had near-universal white support for almost a decade. In 1963 Louis Harris found that in a sample of whites, 91 percent favored laws protecting black voting rights. Support for laws in other areas was lower: equal employment opportunities 86 percent; public accommodations desegregation 74 percent; open housing 52 percent. Hazel Erskine, "The Polls: Negro Housing," *Public Opinion Quarterly,* 31, Fall 1967, p. 484.

24. *Federal Civil Rights Enforcement Effort,* p. 82.

25. Ibid., pp. 1976, 1082, and passim.

26. Examples of this type of reasoning are cited in William R. Keech, *The Impact of Negro Voting: The Role of the Vote in the Quest for Equality*, Chicago: Rand McNally, 1968, p. 2, and later shown to be questionable.

27. Ibid., passim.

28. Robert L. Crain, "School Integration and Occupational Achievement of Negroes," *American Journal of Sociology,* 75, January 1970, pp. 593-606.

29. Lester Milbrath, *Political Participation,* Chicago: Rand McNally, 1965, pp. 5-38. Along similar lines, legislative support is very significantly related to level of education, a variable related to participation. G. R. Boynton, Samuel C. Patterson, Ronald D. Hedlund, "The Structure of Public Support for Legislative Institutions," *Midwest Journal of Political Science,* 12, May 1968, p. 170.

30. However, to the extent that political participation does not lead to improved conditions, it may be associated with greater system disaffection. David O. Sears, "Black Attitudes toward the Political System in the Aftermath of the Watts Insurrection," *Midwest Journal of Political Science,* 13, November 1969, p. 538.

CHAPTER EIGHT

Law and
Social Change:
A Cost-Benefit Interpretation

Our analysis of selected areas of civil rights policy has frequently yielded insights about the conditions under which law can be a viable means of attaining certain policy goals. The most obvious point emerging is that the mere passing of a law and the development of machinery to institute and enforce that law does not guarantee that meaningful change will occur.[1] The government can pass sweeping and celebrated mandates, such as the Fifteenth Amendment, with great pomp and self-congratulation, but this does not mean that the rights supposedly assured by the law will actually be extended to the people.

On the other hand, we have found that some laws are very effective agents of social change. For example, after passage of the 1965 Voting Rights Act black registration in the Southern states increased from 43 percent in 1964 to 66 percent in 1970.[2] Additionally, we found that a law sometimes brings about considerable change in some areas of the United States, but almost none in others. Similarly, even in the same region or area a law may have a different impact.

This chapter will attempt to isolate some of the factors which determine the various consequences of laws, and thus, their impact on civil rights policy. We shall raise some questions about the conditions under which laws will be obeyed and the conditions under which they will be met with disobedience or even revolt. We believe that such findings are best summarized in terms of a cost-benefit framework.* We begin therefore by defining compliance as the consequence of individual evaluations about the cost and rewards of alternative courses of behavior.

THE UTILITY OF COMPLIANCE

Laws are political decisions (collectively made or otherwise) which can be perceived in a variety of ways by members of the political system. If a law is deemed to benefit all, compliance will probably be the rule.[†] If it is considered to benefit none, it will probably not be obeyed. Typically, however, a law will be seen as a benefit by some, and as a burden by others. The important question is under what circumstances will those who perceive that they are harmed by a law still obey it? One answer is that the individual will maximize his utility by taking that action which entails the least personal cost and the greatest benefits.[3] Evaluations of factors such as the certainty and severity of punishment for deviation, and the value hierarchy of each individual will determine how the costs involved in each compliance situation are perceived. If the individual determines that he stands to suffer a greater loss from obedience than disobedience, he will break the law. If he judges that he will suffer the greater cost by disobedience, he will comply.

The cost-benefit calculus is based on the assumption that the average individual's approach to law is rational.[4] Even though a number of factors mitigate against perfect rationality (e.g. lack of information about the value, consequences, and number of alternatives), we believe that over a period of time the average citizen's behavior does reveal a pattern of rationality.[5]

Our survey of the impact of law on five areas of civil rights policy

*For those interested in formal theories of compliance we should make it clear that we make no attempt here to develop a cost-benefit model. The data do not lend themselves to rigorous analysis. We use cost-benefit concepts only as a structure to tie our findings together. Although cost-benefits oversimplify the dynamics of compliance somewhat, we believe that the efficacy of the theory is suggested by our findings and that the generation and testing of specific hypotheses might yield useful results. We hope to do this kind of analysis in a future project.

†It should be kept in mind that compliance refers to a whole range of responses including complete obedience with the letter and spirit of a law to formal and perfunctory obedience. We would like to thank Professor Kenneth Dolbeare for bringing this point to our attention.

provides evidence which handily supports the cost-benefit calculus. Repeatedly we noted that the efficacy of law, i.e., the ability of law to produce change is determined in large part by public acceptance. That is, the effectiveness of the civil rights laws has been determined considerably by whether the public and state and local officials evaluated them positively and decided they should be obeyed. Similarly, in the face of recalcitrance, compliance has improved as the cost of noncompliance has been raised.[6]

To find that individual evaluations about the law are important to its efficacy runs counter to some traditional assumptions about democracy and majority rule. According to the norms of democracy a citizen's personal agreement or disagreement with a law should not determine compliance once the law has been promulgated. Society, it is assumed, can function only when most citizens are in the main willing to abide by the rules. We are, it is often said, a nation of laws and not of men, meaning that all men must be willing to accept the restraints of society for the common good. A citizen who disagrees with a particular law has only one legitimate option: to work through the democratic processes to achieve change. Even advocates of civil disobedience frequently argue that anyone who violates the normal pattern of seeking change in law must be willing to accept the sanctions of society.

Law-abidingness then is seen as basic to society. Children are taught from their earliest years, both at home and in school, that a good citizen obeys the law. Studies show that young children firmly hold this belief.[7] Evidence also indicates that even as adults, the vast majority of citizens still believe in the importance of law-abidingness. For example, in one study a sample of adults was asked to react to the statement: "Even though one might strongly disagree with a state law—after it has been passed by the state legislature, one ought to obey it."[8] Only 3 percent of the total sample disagreed.

Despite these findings, we have seen that in the area of civil rights large numbers of citizens and officials do not always obey the law. Can we conclude that the breaking of civil rights laws is exceptional behavior? Obviously not. Common sense and personal experience tell us that every citizen disobeys the law occasionally. Studies show that almost all citizens (91 percent) admit they have broken laws that carried penalties severe enough to send them to jail.[9] What this means is that individual attitudes about law and law-abidingness do not provide a very accurate guide to behavior where specific laws are concerned.[10] Once we descend from the civics books' ideal of law-abidingness and focus on specific laws, the cost-benefit calculus is a much more accurate guide.

Evidence about individual compliance is strongly supportive of the cost-benefit calculus. For example, one study found that when the average citizen evaluates a specific legal problem, he does not use a general societal standard, such as a sense of justice or a concept of law-abidingness, to decide how the dispute should be resolved.[11] Instead the personal attitudes of the individual toward the law or the participants involved in the dispute determine the type of rule application he prefers. The individual, in other words, will favor a decision which maximizes his private utilities (i.e., the most benefits and the least cost). Similarly, if the average citizen is asked whether he thinks a schoolteacher who breaks the law by holding prayer in class should be punished, his decision will most often be based on whether he favors prayers in school. The fact that it is the "Supreme Law of the Land" that school prayers are illegal is less salient than the respondent's subjective evaluation of the situation. Under such circumstances the individual does not reject the norms of democracy; he simply does not see the connection between his abstract attitudes toward law-abidingness and his attitudes toward the application of legal rules in a specific situation. This is very much like the average citizens' attitudes toward individual rights. On the one hand, citizens will say they believe in freedom of speech, but not for communists, atheists, or people with whom they disagree or fear.[12] Converse found a similar lack of constraint in most citizens' attitudes toward political issues.[13] The average citizen, it would seem, does not have the cognitive skills necessary to develop a consistent philosophy toward law, democracy, or political issues; therefore his attitudes and behavior are not as congruent as one might assume.[14]

Our argument does not hold that citizens subject every law that affects them to the cost-benefit calculus. Many laws that the average citizen comes in contact with affect him in such an unimportant way that he merely complies automatically without consideration of the cost-benefits of his behavior. Under these circumstances the law falls into what Chester I. Barnard has called the "zone of indifference."[15] It is when the individual perceives that the law affects him in a meaningful way that he evaluates the utility of compliance.

Although most citizens are prone to be compliant even when they disagree with a law, most employ the cost-benefit calculus at one time or another and decide against obedience. Two types of lawbreaking seem to result. It is safe to say that most citizens engage in a type of lawbreaking that might be called "rule exception," in which they break (make exceptions to) laws they generally support because an immediate benefit of noncompliance is perceived which outweighs the anticipated cost of compliance. For example, most citizens support traffic laws that they occasionally, or even frequently, break. Such behavior is rationalized with familiar excuses: "I was in a hurry," or "There was hardly any traffic." A more dramatic form of lawbreaking might be called "rule rejection," in which the individual breaks the law because he disagrees with it or he questions the right of the government to make such a law. Rule rejection is the type of noncompliance that has occurred so frequently in the area of civil rights. Sanctions play an important role in keeping rule rejection and rule exception from getting out of hand.[16]

Having established our conceptual framework, we turn now to an evaluation of the factors which determine the cost-benefits of civil rights laws and thus their outcome.

THE POLITICAL CONTEXT

Since individual attitudes and behavior are normally shaped by the traditions and mores of the society one lives in, the social, economic, and political characteristics of an environment have a tremendous impact on the success of a law. Dolbeare has found, in fact, that these factors are often more important than the substance of a law in determining what policy changes will take place.[17] Naturally rule rejection and rule exception are facilitated by public approval. A law that runs strongly against the mores of a particular environment has little chance of effecting change unless it is enforced very rigorously. An unpopular law (e.g., prohibition or civil rights laws in some regions) or a law that regulates a type of deviant behavior that many citizens engage in frequently or occasionally (liquor, gambling, or game laws)[18] is very difficult to enforce, the reason being that when the public or one's peers sanction disobedience, the cost of lawbreaking decreases dramatically. The punishment for breaking the law is not decreased; but if the social disapproval associated with an act of lawbreaking is low, the likelihood that the sanction will be invoked is lessened.[19] Thus, in some parts of the country even murder has gone unpunished. Also, under conditions of social approval, even if the lawbreaker is punished, the social stigma associated with the punishment is decreased. In fact, punishment may even enhance one's prestige (e.g., even though George Wallace lost the confrontation with Federal marshals at the University of Alabama, he won the undying loyalty of much of the electorate in the Deep South). When an act of lawbreaking is strongly condemned by society, the cost of disobedience is high both in terms of public (and possibly personal) disapproval and the chances of being punished. In such cases, lawbreaking occurs more rarely.

Frequently we have found local and state officials obligated to uphold civil rights laws with which they and their constituents have disagreed. Reflecting on the subjective orientation of individuals toward law, it is not difficult to understand why many of these officials would choose to violate or ignore the law. The fact that they ostensibly believe in the democratic system does not deter them from noncompliance. When the law violates personal beliefs or cultural mores, the perceived cost of compliance rises. Under these circumstances officials may feel justified in—even obligated to—disobeying the law.

The South, which has remained a subsystem of the United States, naturally finds itself frequently at odds with national laws. Since the South has long prided itself on a refusal to subordinate local practices to national norms, noncomplinace with a number of Federal laws has been more frequent in the South.[20]

Several studies have measured the association between certain social, economic, and political factors and compliance in one civil rights area, school desegregation. These studies provide insight into how social, economic, and political factors affect the cost-benefit calculus. For example, in a study of 55 cities located in the North and South, Dye was able to isolate a number of factors which seemed to affect the perceived cost of school desegregation and, thus, the progress achieved.[21] One of the most important determinants of school desegregation was percentage of black population. The higher the percentage of blacks in the population, the more intense was segregation, especially in the North.[22] This may be interpreted to mean that the larger the number of blacks in a given population, the greater threat they seem to pose for the white population. The more threatened the white population feels, the higher the assumed cost of compliance.

In the North desegregation proceeded best in those cities where the population had less reason to view integration as a high cost, i.e., those with high educational and occupational levels. In the South these status characteristics are not related to progress.[23] A large ethnic population in a city is related to desegregation, especially in the South.[24] The influx of ethnic groups has the tendency of diluting the white Anglo-Saxon population, which is most opposed to integration in the South.[25]

In the North the factors which seem to be most important in determining levels of desegregation are the environmental factors discussed above. In the South levels of desegregation were best predicted by political variables. For example, cities with a mayoral form of government were less segregated than those with council-manager governments.[26] The mayoral form of government allows citizens more access to decision makers and thus allows them to apply more pressure for change, making maintenance of segregation more costly. Similarly, Southern cities with partisan elections were less segregated than those with nonpartisan elections.[27] Also, appointed school boards and school boards elected at large instead of by wards were more often located in cities with higher levels of segregation.[28] In sum, the more "political" the environment, the less segregated the city was, because more pressure could be put on decision makers, raising the cost of noncompliance. Additionally, in a more "political" environment pro-civil rights powers have a better chance of becoming decision makers.

Several other studies have dealt with desegregation in strictly Southern counties.[29] The most comprehensive of these was carried out by John Robey, who studied the association between a number of social and political characteristics and integration in 872 Southern counties. Robey found only two variables associated with progress in school desegregation: "Public school desegregation is most easily attainable in those counties which do not have a large Negro population and which rejected George Wallace's bid for the presidency in 1968."[30]

These studies give us some indication (admittedly crude) of the types of social, economic, and political factors related to compliance with a specific law. The environment also plays a role in shaping attitudes that cannot be measured by these aggregate data but which have important consequences for compliance. We turn now to a couple of these topics.

Perception of the Legitimacy of Law As a Cost Factor

An important factor in determining whether an individual will comply with a specific law is his evaluation of the legitimacy of the law. If the individual rejects the legitimacy of the law, the psychic cost of disobedience is lowered considerably.[31] Legitimacy is related to whether the individual has a positive attitude toward the agent of the law and whether he believes that the agent had the authority to make the law. This evaluation may vary with the subject matter of the law (even when the same agent is involved) and is closely linked to the individual's agreement or disagreement with specific laws. For example, Southerners who reject the right of the Supreme Court to make certain decisions concerning civil rights may be more than willing to uphold its right to make powerful decisions in other areas.

Perceptions of the legitimacy of a law are closely related to the prevailing traditions and mores of a community or region. For example, Murphy and Tanenhaus found that Southerners are much more critical of the United States Supreme Court than are citizens in other parts of the nation.[32] They also found that the public's support for the Court is based, to a large extent, on its agreement with the Court's decisions.[33] Individuals who disagree with the civil rights decisions of the Court are then more likely to reject these laws as being illegitimate and, as a consequence, find the psychic cost of breaking the law to be lower.

The origin of a law can play an important role in conditioning perceptions of legitimacy. The Supreme Court is the most vulnerable branch of the national government when questions of legitimacy are raised because, as surveys show, the public's support for the Court has been moderate to low in recent years[34] and because the public does not perceive the Court as a policy-making agency. The public expects policy to be produced by popularly elected officials such as the Chief Executive or Congress. Consequently, there is less doubt about the legitimacy of a law if Congress or the President is the agent. For example, Congress would have been a much better agent of the policy initiated in the *Brown* decision. In the school desegregation cases the Court was making policy. Public awareness of this fact frequently lead to rejection of the legitimacy of the decisions. Hogan has observed that: "Supreme Court legislation has a great limitation—its effective authority is limited to doing those things which society is ready to do."[35] Wasby concurs, adding that "if the Supreme Court is 'ahead of the times' in its decisions, noncompliance bulks large, but if the Court is 'behind the times' (but not too far), reactions to its decisions will be positive, and they will be both applauded and accepted."[36]

Decision Makers

If the cultural context is the most important determinant of the outcome of a law, decision makers (elites) are the most critical ingredient of this context. Only a handful of studies have been conducted by political scientists on compliance, but they all agree that state and local decision makers exert the most important influence in the compliance equation.[37] Additionally, these studies indicate that the attitudes of the decision makers' constituents may influence how they react, but the most important determinant of their behavior is their own cognitive attitudes. In the area of race relations decision makers usually seem to be able to obey Federal laws if they want to. If local citizens are extremely hostile, the decision makers may have to pave the way for compliance, but this is usually possible.

Undoubtedly civil rights is novel in terms of the amount and intensity of public feelings on the topic.[38] Occasionally the public may be so violently opposed to compliance that decision makers cannot but wait for tempers to cool. In most cases where the public has become violent, however, it has taken its cues from the political leaders. As Dolbeare and Hammond point out, "clearly, compliance rates are linked to the words and action of state officials."[39] The ability of decision makers to set the tone and pace of compliance is revealed by the fact that the least compliance has occurred in those areas in which state and local leaders have been most vocal in their opposition. Let us look at an example. School desegregation has been a topic of intense debate in the South. In the Border states (e.g., Tennessee, Kentucky,

Virginia, Texas, and Oklahoma) some progress in desegregation was achieved in the years immediately following *Brown*. In the Deep South states (e.g., Georgia, Mississippi, Louisiana, and Alabama) progress did not begin for many years. In terms of social, economic, and political factors the two areas have much in common. Why then was there so much difference in progress? Officials in the Deep South states would have us believe that the difference resulted from more intense problems in their areas. This may be true in some parts of the Deep South, but it is clearly not the prime factor. The major difference is that many decision makers in the Border states accepted responsibility for seeing that the law was obeyed, while in many areas of the Deep South officials were still holding out. Clearly environmental hostility in the latter region generates some of this reluctance, but equally intense problems were overcome in several of the Border states. Mississippi and Alabama, which have had the most outspoken racist governors in the country, have progressed at a slower pace than Georgia, which had two moderate governors before Lester Maddox took office. As a result of Orville Faubus' reign, Arkansas has progressed more slowly than other Border states. The point is that when decision makers work toward achieving compliance they can produce results, especially when they have 15 years to do the job. When decision makers criticize and defy the law they free, and indeed cast a mantle of legitimacy upon, the most violent and recalcitrant elements in society.

We shall consider some of the factors which determine whether decision makers will consider compliance a benefit or a cost.

Disagreement with the law An obvious factor is that many decision makers have honestly disagreed with the civil rights laws and have believed that they would be letting themselves and their constituents down by complying. This is not surprising since decision makers usually have more intense political preferences than average citizens.[40] To many decision makers, being on the side of law and order has not been as important as defending what they believe to be the integrity of their state or community. In most instances, of course, racial prejudice has been the motivating factor behind disagreement with the law. Inherited fears about slave revolts and black political takeovers have motivated responses in other instances. Also, stereotypes linking blacks with violence, drunkenness, and immorality have played a negative role.

Demagogism Many decision makers saw personal benefit to be gained by defying the law. The race issue gave many public officials and would-be officials a means of elevating themselves by playing on the fears and hostilities of the public, e.g., Wallace's campaign in the 1968 presidential race.

Fear of conflict Many decision makers avoided enforcement of the law for fear that one of the costs of compliance would be serious conflict in their state or community.[41] These leaders probably realized that if they wanted to pave the way for compliance they could, but the path of least resistance was to simply avoid the issue at no risk to their image. In many cases local officials would have had a difficult time enforcing the law without serious conflict in situations in which their state leaders were opposed to the law. As Crain et al. pointed out, to obey the law local officials frequently "must take considerable risk, . . . must be willing to alienate the 'rednecks', to run the danger of social . . . or even physical attack."[42] Also since citizens opposed to the law were usually more vocal and more organized than citizens in favor of the law, no action resulted in the least conflict.

The need to be liked and to maintain existing relationships Many decision makers feared that if they defended or implemented the law, they would be shunned by their friends and neighbors. This was a serious cost, one weighing upon even some Southern judges. On the other hand, defiance of the law usually enhanced a decision maker's prestige with the local populace. The need to be liked and accepted is a powerful motivating force in most people,[43] and it is not surprising that many decision makers proved vulnerable.

The need to conform Similarly, studies show that the need to conform to local patterns and mores is extremely strong.[44] It is the rare person who transcends his culture, for the costs are heavy. To enforce the law or work toward achievement of compliance would be an act of considerable courage in many communities.

The need to be correct Most individuals likewise have a strong need to be correct.[45] To admit that one has been wrong entails certain personal costs. Public recanting does not come easily. Once decision makers decided not to obey a law or decided that a law was invalid, they resisted ever obeying such a law because this would be an admission that their earlier behavior was wrong. Dolbeare and Hammond in a study of compliance with the Court's prayer decisions found that decision makers in their study evinced this need. "Having once committed themselves to inaction, they apparently generated cognitive and perceptual screens against dissonance or role strain."[46]

IF PUSH COMES TO SHOVE: THE ROLE OF COERCION

If decision makers or the public will not comply with the law and the government must take measures to force compliance, a number of factors determine the cost-benefits of compliance and thus the success of the government's efforts. We will examine these factors in terms of: 1) the government's commitment, 2) the nature of the policy involved, and 3) the substance and mechanics of the law.

Before such an analysis we might note some of the pros and cons of using force to gain compliance. On the negative side it is clear than when the government has to force compliance with civil rights laws, extensive delays are in the offing. The first delay takes place while the government provides enough time for voluntary compliance. If voluntary compliance does not take place, a series of negotiations between Federal, state, and local officials occurs, followed either by attempts to enforce the law or another period of grace in which reluctant officials are given another chance to comply voluntarily. This round may produce little progress because officials may still refuse to comply voluntarily or because the law may be too weak to produce much change. More time may then be consumed while the government debates and passes a new law. This series of adventures and misadventures has been most obvious in the areas of voting rights, school desegregation, and employment. All of these activities require a large number of personnel, considerable finances, and a great deal of time.

Fear of other negative consequences has frequently been behind the government's failure to vigorously enforce civil rights laws. The government's reticence seems to be based on two things: 1) a belief that results will be more satisfactory if state and local officials recognize the legitimacy of the law by complying voluntarily; and 2) a fear that forcing large numbers of individuals to obey the law may have negative consequences. For example, unrelieved force may alienate large groups of citizens from the party in office or even from the political system.[47] The Supreme Court is as reluctant as Congress and the executive branch to coerce compliance with its decisions. The Court realizes that its authority is derived from the public (or at least elites)[48] and that this authority cannot be based on coercion alone.[49] Consequently the Court, like the other branches of the Federal government, usually tries patiently to persuade recalcitrant officials to comply with the law by emphasizing the legitimacy of the law and the obligation to comply.[50]

Another negative consequence of coercion is that it may not work. In many instances even rather vigorous attempts to force compliance by public officers have not been successful because it is almost impossible to write laws without loopholes through which determined decision makers can escape. Hundreds of evasive actions can typically be used to flaunt the law. In many instances truly exceptional creativity produced new ways of avoiding the law. One need only consider the efforts made by white Southerners to keep black Americans from exercising the franchise to understand this point. An acceptance of the rules of the game by all the parties involved is extremely important for the law to function.

Regardless of the disadvantages of coercion, it is critical to the cost-benefit equation. Even when citizens agree with specific laws and support the rules of the game, coercion is necessary to insure compliance. As Malcolm Freeley has pointed out, "the coercive provisions of law are . . . the 'cost factors' in the calculus of decisions affecting behavior governed by legal rules."[51] If the law is to be effective, there are conditions when coercion must be used. In civil rights policy the government has generally overlooked the functional nature of coercion, and this has greatly impeded progress. We might consider some of the conditions under which force is functional. First, the use of sanctions can show that the government is serious about its responsibility for achieving a certain policy. Second, if the government is steadfast in its position and demonstrates a determination to see the law enforced, the cost of compliance may be lowered for some decision makers. For example, if decision makers under considerable pressure from constituents not to obey the law are faced with penalties for noncompliance, they can obey the law and defer local sanctions by saying they had no choice. This works best if the alternatives for resistance are cut off and a consistent policy is applied to all communities. Local decision makers are put on the spot if their community goes further in obeying the law than neighboring communities. In many instances the government has failed to give local officials the support needed.

Additionally, it is well known that once an individual is influenced to go partway toward a goal, it is easier to get him to go all the way. By taking action toward a goal, the individual has accepted, in part, its legitimacy. This is referred to by social psychologists as the "foot-in-the-door technique."[52] If the government had forced officials to make a good faith start toward obeying the civil rights laws earlier, progress would have been much more dramatic. Similarly, when the government passes a law which calls for some benefit to be allocated to black Americans, and this law is successfully ignored or defied, it is harder to gain compliance later. The lesson is simple: if the government allows any part of the public to flaunt a law, a subsequent decision to enforce the law is more difficult to achieve. This has happened repeatedly in civil rights. The government continuously set up standards and regulations and then failed to enforce them. This failure led recalcitrant whites to believe that such laws could be safely ignored. Once decision makers decided they could ignore the law, the cost of changing their position and obeying the law went up drastically and continued to increase every time they successfully evaded new efforts at enforcement.

The Commitment of the National Government

The strength of the government's commitment to achieving compliance in a given policy area is very important in determining the costs of noncompliance. There should be no mistake that if the government wants compliance with its civil rights policy it can achieve it—possibly not immediately but certainly through persistent efforts. A law that is completely anachronistic (e.g., hanging horse thieves) or one opposed by a large part of the citizenry throughout the nation (e.g., Prohibition) might well be impossible to enforce. Polls, however, show that only a small percentage of the American public still favors strict segregation.[53] Recalcitrant groups can hold out for substantial periods, but ultimately the law can be enforced if the government makes the cost of resistance high.

The national government's commitment to gaining compliance with civil rights laws has typically been neither strong nor consistent. It has normally moved into areas of civil rights gingerly, even timidly. Early efforts, which are usually symbolic, recognize certain rights, develop limited machinery for enforcement, and provide rather weak penalties for noncompliance which are but laxly levied. If the law only calls for an end to discrimination, considerable voluntary compliance may take place. If, however, the law calls for some positive effort to overcome discrimination, compliance is much lower. Attention is usually centered on those individuals, communities, or states which will not obey the law at all. This has been the signal for new efforts to enforce the law which normally fail because the law is not strong enough to conquer a determined foe. A new law is now passed which is more encompassing and powerful. The cycle may be repeated; every time the government has to go back to the well, the law becomes more forceful, and more compliance is achieved.

The government's efforts to insure the right of all Americans to vote is a good example of this process. When the Fifteenth Amendment, the 1957, 1960, and 1964 civil rights acts, and several Supreme Court decisions proved unsuccessful in extending the franchise to all black Americans, the government redoubled its efforts with the 1965 act. The result was a takeover of some traditional functions of the states. In some areas Federal officials registered black voters, protected their right to vote, and verified the ballot count. This is an example of the government going all the way to insure compliance.

The government's commitment in the area of employment and housing has been very limited. In the area of school desegregation the government's commitment has been inconsistent and never very strong. Since the government has always tried to win the civil rights struggle with limited personnel and finances, its priorities determine in large part how much incursion the law will attain. Once the right of all Americans to vote was judged top priority, the government made sure the right was extended. This is, of course, simply another way of saying that the better organized, equipped, and persistent are efforts toward compliance, the more success is obtained in the face of resistance.

Differences in Policy Areas

Progress in civil rights has differed considerably in the various policy areas studied. Compliance has been more thorough in public accommodations and voting rights than in housing, school desegregation, and employment. The differences in progress are directly related to the cost-benefits of compliance. In the area of voting rights the government has made the cost of noncompliance very high. Compliance with public accommodations requirements contained a benefit to those responsible for implementing the law. The cost of noncompliance has increased in school desegregation and employment, and as the cost has risen compliance has been more widespread. Only in the area of housing has the cost of noncompliance remained very low, with progress minimal.

The function of the cost-benefit calculus becomes clearer if we compare progress in two policy areas, voting rights and public accommodations. Two reasons seem to explain why compliance with public accommodations has been considered by many to contain only a marginal cost. First, businessmen have been primarily responsible for desegregating public accommodations, and where profit is concerned the conscience is more easily rested. Businessmen have always appreciated the profit to be made from black citizens. Even in the Deep South businessmen usually coveted black patronage so long as it did not alienate white customers. If the business involved personal mingling of the races, special efforts were made to reduce contact. Many eating establishments had separate takeout counters or gave service from a rear door. Only the few businesses that could not achieve this state of separateness, e.g., taxi services, wholly excluded black patrons. Once the law was unambiguous and businessmen could claim to see no way out, they were usually willing or even happy to obey the law.

Second, the cost of compliance was lowered by the fact that most people did not feel as strongly about maintaining racial segregation in this area. The difference in the public's attitude related to the amount and type of contact between the races and the public's perception of the importance of this victory for black Americans. In the area of public accommodations the amount of contact is minimal, impersonal, and transient. In the contrary situations, such as schools, employment, and housing, white hostility goes up measurably. Also, the blacks that whites encounter in areas of public accommodations are more likely to be middle or upper-middle class. As such they do not conform to the stereotyped black (half Stepin Fetchit and half Sporting Life)[54] who conjures up the most fear and hostility in whites.

The cost of compliance with voting rights was, despite the foregoing, considered to be very high by many Southerners. The right to vote increased contact between the races very little but was perceived to be an important victory with potential status and material benefits—a victory that could spell the end of dominant white rule in parts of the South.

The various policy areas differ also in terms of how hard it is to raise the cost of noncompliance in an effort to gain compliance. We turn to a number of these factors.

First, it is more difficult to detect disobedience in some areas than others, which influences efforts to increase the cost of noncompliance. Feedback, in other words, is better in some areas than others. Failure to serve a black or refusal to allow him to vote or enroll in a school is much easier to detect than refusal to sell a house or employ an individual because of race. Employers can simply say that the applicant did not have the right qualifications. A homeowner is more restricted but he can simply refuse to honor appointments or stall a black potential buyer until he has found a white buyer. In many instances the difficulty of detection is based on whether an official or a private act is involved. It is much harder to regulate private discrimination (e.g., housing and employment) than official discrimination.

Second, if compliance necessitates changes in public behavior and attitudes, rather than simply official compliance, the law is harder to enforce.[55] Extension of voting rights, like reapportionment, necessitated only action by public officials. A major difference in these two areas, however, is that the constituents (especially in the South) are concerned about black voting but largely indifferent to the size of their state senate district.[56] Public acceptance can be important even when only official compliance is required because of fear of public hostility, both real and potential. In all areas of civil rights, public acceptance of the law is important, and this has slowed compliance. In several areas (e.g., employment and housing) progress is dependent on changes in private behavior.

Third, it is harder to raise the cost of noncompliance where there are larger numbers of decision makers to be supervised. Imagine the number of school boards in the South, and it will be obvious how difficult it is to force all these individuals to obey the law. On the other hand, in an area like reapportionment the Supreme Court could hold a handful of individuals in each state responsible for seeing that its decisions were obeyed. In civil rights the number of individuals who have to cooperate with the law is usually vast. Even within civil rights, however, there are some obvious differences. Voting registrars are much less numerous than private employers or individual homeowners and landlords.

Finally, the ability of authorities to raise the cost of noncompliance is also conditioned by the visibility of those individuals responsible for implementing a decision.[57] It is easier to supervise a highly visible decision maker such as the attorney general of a state than school board members, and the latter are more visible than private employers. Individuals responsible for implementing civil rights are usually low in visibility.

The Substance and Mechanics of a Law

The substance and mechanics of a law are important in determing whether obeying it will be considered a cost or a benefit and whether the government can raise the cost for noncompliance to unattractive levels. Important here are at least seven factors.

1. Dolbeare and Hammond have pointed out that the amount of change called for by a law affects public perceptions about the cost of compliance.[58] They argue that an incremental change *usually* entails less cost than a drastic one. This would seem to be especially true in civil rights. Many times an incremental approach, say in school desegregation or employment, has allowed whites to adjust to new situations.

   An equally important point discussed earlier, however, should be recalled, i.e., too much incrementalism can be extremely bad. For the law to be effective, the time allowed for adjustment must be controlled very carefully with the deadline fixed and with enforcement perceived as swift and sure. In civil rights excessive delays have often encouraged obstinate whites to believe that the law could be circumvented. The point, then, is that the law should allow only limited and legitimate delays; evasion should be swiftly and consistently penalized.

2. The way a law is written makes a considerable difference in individual calculations about the cost-benefits of compliance.[59] For example, if a law is too ambiguous or contains loopholes, the cost of noncompliance is lowered greatly. As noted earlier, most civil

rights laws have in their early stages been ambiguous and weak. The *Brown* decision is a good example. Calling for desegregation "with all deliberate speed" is too indefinite to bring about meaningful change. Ambiguity always lends itself to individualized perceptions, and naturally an individual will interpret the law in a way that is most favorable to him (i.e., the most benefit and the least costs). Civil rights laws have frequently been so ambiguous as to be ludicrous. If traffic laws only required drivers to act "in a safe manner" one can imagine how many interpretations there would be—one for every driver. In civil rights, efforts have frequently been made to regulate recalcitrant officials with similarly broad language, which the courts and Congress refuse to define more precisely. For example, government agencies have been extremely reluctant to define the requirement that employers executing Federal contracts take "affirmative action" to insure equality in employment. It is easy to doubt the seriousness of the government's efforts under these circumstances.

Vague laws have frequently allowed officials to claim that they were obedient when in fact they had changed their behavior very little. Ironically, some foot-dragging decision makers have claimed that they could not obey the law because they could not understand what it required.

Law is most effective when it carefully defines the type and amount of compliance required and cuts off all unacceptable alternatives. If the law allows too many options, disobedient officials will surely take the alternative that produces the least change. For example, in the area of school desegregation obstructionist school boards are allowed to continue receiving funds if they take any of a number of actions. Experience showed that submitting to a final court order produced the least change, so school boards naturally chose this alternative that did not produce desirable levels of compliance. Such evasive routes should be terminated. In sum, the clearer the legal standard, the greater is the movement toward compliance. Progress in the area of school desegregation, for example, increased dramatically when HEW laid down specific administrative standards for determining compliance.[60] When public officials were left to determine for themselves what action should be taken, change was minimal.

3. The law is more effective if it is clear than an offender will be punished for his disobedience. Just as a law cannot be effective if it rests solely on punishment, a law that can be broken with impunity will be frequently ignored. Many times public officials have failed to act in accord with civil rights law because they knew that there would be no punishment for defiance. The government's threats of sanction frequently lacked credibility. Studies have found that the certainty of punishment for noncompliance is at least as important as formal sanctions in deterring deviance.[61] Probably the whole pace of the civil rights effort would have been accelerated if a few public officials had received jail sentences for defying the law. School board members have been some of the most guilty. Every school board member takes an oath to uphold the United States Constitution, yet thousands have disobeyed the law for considerable periods of time with impunity. Several governors have obstructed the law and have suffered no sanction. Civil rights leaders who have violated racially motivated laws know the insides of jails well.

Not only must sanctions be employed for noncompliance, but these sanctions must be stringent enough to make noncompliance unappealing. Studies by social psychologists have revealed that in a compliance situation sanctions are of no value unless they are credible and severe enough to outweigh the benefits of noncompliance.[62] If the cost-benefits of a law are equally balanced, individuals who disagree with the law may decide against compliance for the reward of defying authority.[63] Sanctions have infrequently been levied against those who trample upon the civil rights of blacks and, when assessed, penalties have been comparatively mild.

4. The law is more successful when it centers responsibility for compliance on specific individuals or agencies.[64] If the law does not specify who shall be held accountable for insuring its execution, the cost of noncompliance will be reduced since the law will most likely not be enforced. For example, in most states no one is answerable for carrying out open housing laws.

5. Similarly, the cost of noncompliance can be raised if a specific agent or agency is created to enforce the law.[65] Civil rights laws in three areas surveyed provided such agencies, but they are badly

understaffed and underfinanced. Thus, in 1968 HEW tried to supervise school desegregation with only 48 enforcement officers. This is typical of other government agencies.

6. The cost of noncompliance is also affected by the availability of remedies for gaining compliance. In the areas of civil rights surveyed, it has been extremely difficult for black Americans to force obdurate whites to obey the law. Enforcement has been difficult in terms of money, time, and courage. Usually black citizens could not obtain justice except by hiring an attorney, if they could find one brave enough to represent them. This process required too much on the part of those whose rights have been so long discriminated against.

In recent years the government has improved the means of gaining compliance, usually by authorizing the attorney general to institute suits on behalf of citizens. Voting rights and school desegregation remedies have been improved considerably; but housing and employment remedies are still not viable. Even where the remedies have been made more accessible, the amount of time that may lapse before any action is taken can be extremely discouraging to those seeking relief. In the area of employment as much as a year may pass before a complainant even hears from the Equal Employment Opportunity Commission, and then the commission does not always have the power or the personnel to see that an obvious act of bias is corrected. The law quite simply has had limited impact in many instances because it has been too difficult for complainants to seek its protection and because too often the law has had no teeth.

7. The availability of remedies and the ability to make the cost of noncompliance high is also related to the power of the agent who originally formulated a civil rights law. For example, the Supreme Court has proved to be a less effective agent of civil rights policy on a day-to-day basis than the other branches of the national government.[66] This is true for a number of reasons. Both Congress and the executive have more resources and personnel to implement their decisions. Congress can appropriate money and hire the personnel it needs. The President can, and has, used the Army and National Guard to back up his decisions. The Supreme Court has limited resources, limited personnel, and only enforce-

ment powers—the injunction and comtempt proceedings—that it
has obviously considered too drastic for frequent use. Additionally, the Court lacks subordinates to carry out its decisions
who can be supervised as easily as those employed by Congress
and the President. The Supreme Court most frequently has to
rely on district judges to implement its orders. It is well known
that district judges do not always follow the Court's decisions.[67]
The Supreme Court can overrule district courts, but the process is
slow and expensive.

Courts, in general, are also less effective agents of change
because they function very slowly. The adversary process is by
design slow and deliberative. Since court dockets are usually
overcrowded, considerable delay usually occurs even before a
court can consider a case. Also cases handed down by the court
are frequently limited to the specific situation before the court,
thus no uniform standards are produced. Congress and the Executive are much better equipped to produce uniform standards.

SUMMARY AND CONCLUSIONS

We have defined compliance as the consequence of individual evaluations about the cost-benefits of alternative courses of behavior. The
evidence supporting the subjectivity of individual law-abidingness and
the cost-benefit calculus is substantial. By analyzing the impact of law
on five areas of civil rights we have been able to isolate a large number
of factors which determine the cost-benefits of various laws and,
consequently, their policy impact.

An obvious conclusion is that law "is better understood as a catalyst
of change rather than a singular effector of change."[68] To paraphrase
James Levine, the ability of law to produce social change is probabilis-
tic, contingent, and sequential. If a law is enacted it is probable that
certain changes will follow;[69] but the degree of change is contingent on
certain circumstances prevailing.[70] Law, in other words, is no talisman.
It is not self-executing. The cost-benefit calculus provides insight into
the factors that will determine the amount of change a law will produce
and reveals that the probabilities of each law are different.

Law is sequential to the extent that it must precede certain desired changes, but because a large number of factors influence progress, the time lag is not obvious. The gap between cause and effect may, in fact, be considerable.[71] Additionally, a number of factors other than the law may have an effect on change in a particular area (i.e., urbanization on school desegregation, economic expansion on black employment), which means that the cause and effect relationship between law and change is very difficult to identify.

DISCUSSION

The area of race relations probably reflects better than most the strengths and weaknesses of law as an agent of social change. Civil rights laws have frequently failed to produce all the changes that have been anticipated, but their overall impact has been significant. The progress achieved is more impressive when it is recalled that the government's commitment to progress in civil rights has normally been faltering and inconsistent and that one branch of the national government (the Supreme Court) was able to kindle the whole movement. As Franklin and Harr have said: "Probably there has never been anything like it before: A court leading a country and its leaders into awareness of a fundamental social problem and a determination to do something about it."[72] Probably in no other country in the world is the judicial system sufficiently powerful or respected to perform such an extraordinary role.[73]

Many have cast doubt on the ability of law to produce meaningful social change. Eisenhower expressed this sentiment when he defended his position on civil rights by saying that "you can't change men's hearts with laws." Similarly, William Graham Sumner argued many years before that "stateways cannot change folkways."[74] What Sumner argued, and Eisenhower echoed, was that law is restricted to the regulation of individual behavior and that it cannot be used to alter deep-rooted attitudes. Laws could force blacks and whites to attend the same schools, but they could not reduce racial prejudice. If law could do no more than this, its long-range effects would indeed be limited. The public could merely comply with the law without identifying with it or internalizing it as part of their value structure.[75] Under such circumstances obedience would probably be limited to situations of surveillance.

It is obviously true that in many instances white Americans have merely responded to civil rights laws with grudging acceptance and have not assimilated or applied the spirit of the law. This has undoubtedly impeded progress. But more often than not the evidence is clear that law can and does change deep-rooted attitudes. Studies of the effects of desegregation in situation such as "Armed Forces Units, housing projects, and employment situations, indicate that change required by law has lessened prejudice."[76] Similarly, William Muir found that the Supreme Court's decisions on school religion had a substantial effect on the attitudes of school personnel.[77] Even in the South new patterns of behavior required by law have helped produce significantly more tolerant attitudes toward black Americans. As Jack Greenberg points out, the ability of law to affect attitudes is strong enough to work both ways. In *"The Strange Career of Jim Crow,* C. Vann Woodward has demonstrated the great extent to which social patterns of segregation were created by law and not the other way around."[78]

Law, thus, is a sensitive agent of social change. The norms of democracy will normally lead citizens to believe that the law defines what is right and proper. As Gordon Allport points out: "Laws in line with one's conscience are likely to be obeyed; when not obeyed they still establish an ethical norm that holds before the individual an image of what his conduct should be."[79] When a law is passed democratic norms and the coercive powers of the state will insure considerable compliance. In establishing the boundaries of acceptable behavior, law creates new behavior patterns which frequently produce new attitudes.[80] Law not only regulates, then, it educates and inculcates; it changes the values of society.

Muir discusses the conditions under which law can produce attitude change: "Attitude change involves the individual's incentive to excise old attitudes, trustworthy associates who aid the individual to adapt, the intellectual tools to confine psychological repercussions to a minimum, and a social enviornment sufficiently compatible to permit new attitudes to develop."[81] Muir's analysis highlights how extensive changes in the South and many other areas will have to be before prejudice is truly erased from even a minority of the population. Political leaders, the mass media, schools, and religious institutions will all have to pull in the same direction if meaningful progress is to be obtained.

NOTES

1. This is a well-known finding. See for example: Gordon M. Patric, "The Impact of a Court Decision: Aftermath of the McCollum Case." *Journal of Public Law*, 6, Fall 1957, pp. 455-463; Frank Sorauf, *"Zorach v. Clauson:* The Impact of a Supreme Court Decision," *American Political Science Review*, 53, September 1959, pp. 777-791; Robert H. Birkby, "The Supreme Court and the Bible Belt: Tennessee Reaction to the 'Schempp' Decision," *Midwest Journal of Political Science*, 10, August 1966, pp. 304-315; Ellis Katz, "Patterns of Compliance with the Schempp Decision," *Journal of Public Law*, 14, Fall 1965, pp. 396-408; H. Frank Way, "Survey Research on Judicial Decisions: The Prayer and Bible Reading Case," *Western Political Quarterly*, 21, June 1968, pp. 187-205; Donald R. Reich, "The Impact of Judicial Decision-Making: The School Prayer Cases," Paper presented at the 1967 meeting of the Midwest Conference of Political Science, West LaFayette, Indiana; and Kenneth M. Dolbeare and Phillip E. Hammond, "Inertia in Midway: Supreme Court Decisions and Local Responses," *Journal of Legal Education*, forthcoming.

2. U.S. Commission on Civil Rights, *Political Participation*, Washington: GPO, 1968, pp. 12-13.

3. A considerable literature on utility theory is concerned with both individual compliance and collective decisions. See James S. Coleman, "Foundations for a Theory of Collective Decisions," *American Journal of Sociology*, 71, May 1966, pp. 615-627; James Buchanan and Gordon Tullock, *The Calculus of Consent: The Logical Foundation of Constitutional Democracy*, Ann Arbor: University of Michigan, 1962.

4. See William H. Riker, *The Theory of Political Coalitions*, New Haven: Yale University, 1962; William H. Riker and Peter Ordeshook, "A Theory of the Calculus of Voting," *American Political Science Review*, 62, March 1968, pp. 25-42; William H. Riker and William Zavoina, "Rational Behavior in Politics: Evidence from a Three Person Game," *American Political Science Review*, 64, March 1970, pp. 48-60; Anthony Downs, *Inside Bureaucracy*, Boston: Little, Brown, 1967; and Gordon Tullock, *The Politics of Bureaucracy*, Washington: Public Affairs Press, 1965.

5. Herbert A. Simon, *Administrative Behavior*, New York: Free Press, 1957, pp. 80-81.

6. See, W. J. Chambliss, *Crime and the Legal Process*, New York: McGraw-Hill, 1969, passim; William J. Bowers, "Normative Constraints on Deviant Behavior in the College Context," *Sociometry*, 31, Winter 1968, pp. 370-385; and Richard G. Salem and William J. Bowers, "Severity of Formal Sanctions as a Deterrent to Deviant Behavior," *Law and Society*, 5, August 1970, pp. 21-40. The role of sanctions in the cost-benefits calculus will be discussed in more detail at a later stage in the chapter.

7. Robert D. Hess and Judith V. Torney, *The Development of Political Attitudes in Children*, Chicago: Aldine, 1967, p. 215; Richard E. Dawson and

Kenneth Prewitt, *Political Socialization,* Boston: Little, Brown, 1969, p. 211; and Richard M. Merelman, "The Development of Political Ideology: A Framework for the Analysis of Political Socialization," *American Political Science Review,* 63, September 1969, pp. 750-767.

8. G. R. Boynton, Samuel C. Patterson, and Ronald D. Hedlund, "The Structure of Public Support for Legislative Institutions," *Midwest Journal of Political Science,* 12, May 1968, p. 173.

9. *The Challenge of Crime in a Free Society* Washington: GPO, 1967, p. v.

10. See Richard D. Schwartz and Sonya Orleans, "On Legal Sanctions," *University of Chicago Law Review,* 34, Winter 1967, pp. 274-300; Harrell R. Rodgers, Jr., *Community Conflict, Public Opinion and the Law,* Columbus, Ohio: Charles E. Merrill Books, 1969, pp. 111-115; Harrell R. Rodgers, Jr. and Roger Hanson, "The Application of Legal Rules: Data Testing a Rational Model Analogue," (memo); and Harrell R. Rodgers, Jr. and George Taylor, "Pre-Adult Attitudes toward Legal Compliance," *Social Science Quarterly,* 51, December 1970, pp. 537-551.

11. Rodgers, *Community Conflict, Public Opinion. . .,* pp. 111-115.

12. James W. Prothro and Charles M. Grigg, "Fundamental Principles of Democracy," *Journal of Politics,* 22, May 1961, pp. 276-294.

13. Philip Converse, "Belief System in Mass Publics," in David Apter, ed., *Ideology and Discontent,* New York: Free Press, 1964, pp. 206-261.

14. Social scientists are not at all sure what the relationship is between attitudes and behavior. James T. Tedeschi et al. have recently pointed out that "unfortunately, after thousands of experiments have been performed and scores of theories have been developed, little evidence has been produced to prove that attitudes mediate behavior in any direct fashion." "Power, Influence, and Behavioral Compliance," *Law and Society Review,* 4, May 1970, p. 521.

15. Chester I. Barnard, *The Functions of the Executive,* Cambridge, Mass.: Harvard, 1938, pp. 167-170.

16. Malcolm Freeley, "Coercion and Compliance: A New Look at an Old Problem," *Law and Society Review,* 4, May 1970, pp. 505-519.

17. Kenneth M. Dolbeare, "The Supreme Court and the States: From Abstract Doctrine to Local Behavioral Conformity," in Theodore L. Becker, ed., *The Impact of Supreme Court Decisions,* New York: Oxford University, 1969, pp. 206-213.

18. See Harry Kalven, Jr. and Hans Zeisel, *The American Jury,* Boston: Little, Brown, 1966, pp. 286-297.

19. See Salem and Bowers, op. cit., p. 26.

20. For example, the South in general has been less compliant with the Supreme Court's decision concerning school religion. See Way, op. cit., pp. 189-205.

21. Thomas R. Dye, "Urban School Segregation: A Comparative Analysis," *Urban Affairs Quarterly,* 4, December 1968, pp. 141-165. It should be kept in mind that the desegregation problems of urban and rural areas are somewhat different, both in the North and South, and Dye's study is limited only to urban areas.

22. Dye, op. cit., p. 151. Similarly, Kenneth N. Vines reports that the larger the concentration of black citizens in a Federal judicial district, the fewer the number of decisions favorable to blacks handed down by the courts. See "Federal District Judges and Race Relations Cases in the South," *Journal of Politics,* 26, May 1964, pp. 337-357.

23. Dye, op. cit., p. 155.

24. Ibid., p. 156.

25. Ibid., pp. 156-157.

26. Ibid., p. 161.

27. Ibid.

28. Ibid., pp. 161-162.

29. John Robey, "The Politics of School Desegregation: A Comparative Analysis of Policy Outcomes in Southern Counties," unpublished Ph.D. dissertation, University of Georgia, 1970; Donald R. Matthews and James W. Prothro, "Stateways Versus Folkways: Critical Factor in Southern Reactions to *Brown* v. *Board of Education"* in Gottfield Dietz, ed., *Essays on the American Constitution,* Englewood Cliffs, N.J.: Prentice-Hall, 1964, pp. 139-156; and A. Stephen Stephen, "Integration and Sparse Negro Populations," *School and Society,* 81, April 1955, pp. 133-135.

30. Robey, op. cit., p. II.

31. For a discussion of the importance of legitimacy see: Walter F. Murphy and Joseph Tanenhaus, "Public Opinion and the United States Supreme Court: Mapping of Some Prerequisites for Court Legitimation of Regime Changes," *Law and Society Review,* 2, May 1969, pp. 357-384.

32. Ibid., p. 372.

33. Ibid., p. 373.

34. Ibid., p. 370; Kenneth M. Dolbeare, "The Public Views the Supreme Court," in Herbert Jacob, ed., *Law, Politics,and the Federal Courts,* Boston: Little, Brown, 1967, pp. 194-212; Kenneth M. Dolbeare and Phillip E. Hammond, "The Political Party Basis of Attitudes toward the Supreme Court," *Public Opinion Quarterly,* 32, Spring 1968, pp. 16-30.

35. Harry Hogan, "The Supreme Court and Natural Law," *American Bar Association Journal,* 54, June 1968, p. 573.

36. Stephen L. Wasby, *The Impact of the United States Supreme Court: Some Perspectives,* Homewood, Ill.: Dorsey, 1970, p. 49.

37. The literature on this point is surveyed in Dolbeare and Hammond, "Inertia in Midway . . . ," pp. 3-4.

38. See Warren E. Miller and Donald E. Stokes, "Constituency Influence in Congress," *American Political Science Review,* 57, March 1963, pp. 45-46.

39. Dolbeare and Hammond, "Inertia in Midway . . . ," p. 8.

40. Herbert McCloskey, "Consensus and Ideology in American Politics," *American Political Science Review,* 58, June 1964, pp. 361-382.

41. Dolbeare and Hammond, "Inertia in Midway . . . ," p. 16.

42. Robert L. Crain et al., *The Politics of School Desegregation,* Garden City, N.Y.: Doubleday, 1969, pp. 3-9.

43. Charles A. Kiesler and Sara B. Kiesler, *Conformity,* Cambridge, Mass.: Addison-Wesley, 1969, pp. 42-44.
44. Ibid., pp. 24-34.
45. Ibid., pp. 44-45.
46. Dolbeare and Hammond, "Inertia in Midway . . . ," p. 18.
47. See Richard D. Schwartz, "Sanctions and Compliance," presented at the American Sociological Association Meeting, San Francisco, 1969; and Salem and Bowers, op. cit., p. 36.
48. As Dolbeare and Hammond pointed out, "The Supreme Court is chiefly an object of leadership attention and concern . . . ," "Inertia in Midway . . . ," p. 5.
49. See Samuel Krislov, *The Supreme Court in the Political Process,* New York: Macmillan, 1965, pp. 134-155.
50. Ibid.
51. Freeley, op. cit., p. 517. For a discussion of the need for coercion to insure compliance even among groups in which it is perceived that all members will receive benefits see Mancur Olson, *The Logic of Collective Action,* New York: Schocken Books, 1968, passim.
52. Kiesler and Kiesler, op. cit., p. 55.
53. The Survey Research Center at the University of Michigan reports that in 1968 only 14 percent of the public favored segregation.
54. Charles E. Silberman, *Crisis in Black and White,* New York: Vintage Books, 1964, p. 8.
55. Dolbeare and Hammond, "Inertia in Midway . . . ," p. 24.
56. Murphy and Tanenhaus, op. cit., p. 362.
57. Dolbeare and Hammond, "Inertia in Midway . . . ," p. 24.
58. Ibid., p. 23.
59. See Murray Edelman, "The Language of Law," in Herbert Jacob, ed., op. cit., pp. 39-49.
60. *Federal Enforcement of School Desegregation,* Washington: U.S. Commission on Civil Rights, 1969, p. 31.
61. J. Horai and James T. Tedeschi, "The Effects of Credibility and Magnitude of Punishment on Compliance to Threats," *Journal of Personality and Social Psychology,* 12, June 1969, pp. 164-169; and Salem and Bowers, op. cit., passim.
62. James T. Tedeschi, "A Theory of Social Influence within Dyads," Presented at the Sixteenth International Congress of Applied Psychology, Amsterdam, 1968.
63. Once sanctions become severe enough to make noncompliance unattractive, increasing their severity does not seem to increase the deterrant power of the law. For example, studies indicate that the use of capital punishment as a sanction does not deter certain acts any better than life imprisonment. For a review of this literature see Salem and Bowers, op. cit., passim. Obviously certain types of deviant personalities may not be concerned with sanctions at all, but we are concerned here with the average individual.

64. Dolbeare and Hammond, "Inertia in Midway . . . ," p. 24.

65. Ibid.

66. See U.S. v. Jefferson County Bd. of Educ., Civil No. 23345, 5th Cir., December 29, 1966, pp. 10-11.

67. See, *Federal Enforcement of School Desegregation,* pp. 39-46; Jack W. Peltason, *Fifty-Eight Lonely Men: Southern Federal Judges and School Desegregation,* New York: Harcourt, Brace & World, 1961, passim.

68. James P. Levine, "Methodological Concerns in Studying Supreme Court Efficacy," *Law and Society,* 4, May 1970, p. 592.

69. Ibid., p. 589.

70. Ibid.

71. Ibid., p. 590.

72. John Hope Franklin and Isidore Harr, *The Negro in Twentieth Century America,* New York: Vintage Books, 1967, p. 484.

73. See Joseph Tanenhaus, "Judicial Review," *International Encyclopedia of the Social Sciences,* 8, 1968, pp. 303-306.

74. William Graham Sumner, *Folkways,* Boston: Ginn, 1906.

75. For a discussion of the various types of compliance see Chester A. Insko, *Theories and Attitude Change,* New York: Appleton Century Crofts, 1967, pp. 337-344.

76. Jack Greenberg, *Race Relations and American Law,* New York: Columbia, 1959, p. 26.

77. William K. Muir, Jr., *Prayer In the Public Schools: Law and Attitude Change,* University of Chicago, 1967.

78. Greenberg, op. cit., p. 5.

79. Gordon Allport, *The Nature of Prejudice,* Cambridge, Mass.: Addison-Wesley, 1954, chap. 29. Quoted in Greenberg, op. cit., p. 26.

80. See the discussion by Greenberg, op. cit., pp. 1-30.

81. Muir, op. cit., p. 122.

CHAPTER NINE

Incrementalism:
An American Dilemma?

The last decade and half has been a period of meaningful progress toward the goal of racial equality in America. In every area of civil rights there are signs of slow, painful progress. However, two points should also be clear: 1) the change that has resulted is basically inadequate; and 2) progress has been very difficult to produce and very slow in coming. We have examined a multitude of factors that have held up progress in civil rights, and they can all be traced to a central impediment: the members of Congress and the executive branch have not acted with the forthrightness, strength, or consistency necessary to produce more dramatic change. The obvious question is why not? In attempting to formulate an answer we shall speculate briefly on a more fundamental question: what implications can be drawn from this analysis about the ability of the American political system to respond to the needs and maintain the support of the American people?

Fundamentally the major reason for the inadequate response of Congress and the executive branch to civil rights is that these branches of government normally take no actions they do not have to take and respond incrementally when they do act. Incremental policy is characterized by "Continually building out from the current situation, step-by-step, and by small degrees."[1] As we have seen throughout this book, Congress and the executive branch have taken actions in civil rights only in response to serious pressure or outright crisis. The reason, as Harold Fleming points out, is that "no administration, however wisely or humanely led, is likely to initiate far-reaching action in the face of public indifference, to say nothing of hostility."[2] This is equally true of the Congress. Even when Congress or the executive has taken stands against discrimination, the earliest responses have normally been too weak to produce much change and have had a largely symbolic value, establishing the legitimacy of a particular goal. If repeated efforts are made to deal with a problem, remedies become increasingly strong and encompassing and change becomes more comprehensive. In no area of civil rights has Congress passed laws calling for dramatic change until one or more weaker acts have been passed. Thus all civil rights laws are incremental, although some are more comprehensive. Only crisis can normally greatly speed the incremental process.

Progress in voting rights provides a good example of this process. In the face of overwhelming evidence that black Americans were being denied access to the ballot in the South, Congress took no steps to remedy the problem (in the twentieth century) until seriously pressured, and then responded with two weak civil rights acts (1957 and 1960) that resulted in relatively few additional blacks being registered to vote. Only a growing crisis forced the members of Congress into a more adequate response. In reaction to mounting demonstratons and sporadic violence, the Civil Rights Act of 1964, which contained stronger provisions for protecting voting rights, was passed. When events in Selma, Alabama, and elsewhere revealed that this act failed to protect prospective black voters from discrimination or satiate black demands, the Voting Rights Act of 1965 broadened Federal involvement dramatically and brought some immediate progress.

Even crisis-stimulated policy may be weak and ineffectual if standards in an area have not evolved past the earliest symbolic stages. For example, the Open Housing Act of 1968, passed in response to the assassination of Martin Luther King, was too feeble to produce much change. On the other hand, by 1965 the preliminary stages in Federal voting rights protection had been completed and the next incremental step was a powerful law.

If we grant that progress in civil rights results only from pressure and that it has come by bits and pieces rather than by leaps and bounds, our next consideration should be why incrementalism prevails. The reasons are numerous, and an in-depth analysis is beyond the scope of this study; but several considerations can be identified. The most obvious is that the members of Congress and the executive branch have not been united in a strong commitment to dramatic progress.

Even when a majority of Congress has been committed to stronger stands on racial problems, however, the structure, rules, and traditions of the national government favor opponents of innovation. This pro-status quo bias stems from such factors as the checks and balances and separation of powers built into the Federal system. Similarly, the House Rules Committee, the Senate filibuster, and the seniority system all impinge upon policy making, being among the points at which compromises must be made and obstacles surmounted. Since civil rights is an emotional issue and because many of the more powerful congressmen are Southerners (due to the seniority rule), change tends to be particularly elusive in this area. The ability of small numbers of individuals to frustrate the will of the majority has frequently extracted a tragic cost in civil rights. Often a congressional minority has succeeded in delaying or even blocking civil rights bills and at times has so emasculated legislation enacted as to render it ineffectual.[3]

Some other reasons for incrementalism are related to the relationship between the rulers and the ruled in the American political process. Few political analysts today would challenge the statement that "Elites, not masses, govern America."[4] Some have argued that incrementalism results because elites hesitate to make any substantial policy changes which might threaten their position in the system. The self-preservation instinct dictates that limited rather than revolutionary change be the general rule.[5]

Elites can normally pursue policy objectives largely at the pace and in the manner they please because they are relatively free of systematic public demands.[6] The reason is that most citizens are ill-informed and passive about the political system and make few policy demands.[7] This is somewhat less true in the area of civil rights than in other areas (e.g., welfare or international relations);[8] but, with the exception of Southern congressmen, most elites are not highly constrained by their constituents even in this area. As Dye and Zeigler point out,

> public policy does not reflect demands of the people so much as it
> reflects interests and values of elites. Changes and innovations in
> public policy come about as a result of redefinitions by elites of
> their own values.[9]

None of this should be construed to mean that decision makers
necessarily act irresponsibly or against the public interest; they may be
very public-regarding.[10] But the evidence is clear that elites in America
normally have great discretion in the policy goals they pursue, and
unless considerable pressure is brought they may ignore policy issues or
take whatever positions they please. During periods of crisis elites may
lose this discretion and be forced to enact certain policies. Civil rights is
an area that generates crisis periodically, so elites are sometimes compelled to take actions to relieve the stress. An obvious conclusion is that
without crisis even less progress would have been achieved in civil
rights.

The considerable independence of elites is revealed, in part, by the
frequent inability of civil rights activists to secure more favorable outputs. Even vigorous efforts by civil rights activists have frequently not
produced desired policies, because elites, drawn primarily from the
upper socioeconomic strata, are not equally receptive to the demands
of all groups.[11] Elites are more receptive to those with power and those
who represent established values in society.

A number of other factors, however, also help explain why blacks
have not been more effective in mobilizing Federal muscle on behalf of
equal opportunity. A study by Wolman and Thomas reveals that even
though access to public officials seems to be open, blacks have not fully
exploited these opportunities because they generally lack the resources
to make systematic contacts with officials, and often lack the political
savvy and bargaining skills necessary to elicit Federal participation in
promoting black aspirations.[12] Wolman and Thomas found, for
example, that civil rights groups have had little contact with or influence over congressional leaders and administrative officials involved
in housing and education.[13] The focus of black demands seems to have
been local instead of national; and those black demands made at the
national level are frequently emotional rather than strategic, which
reduces their impact.[14] The important point (and the tragic one) is that
unless peaceful demands are made to the "right" place, by the "right"
people, in the "right" way, nothing gets done.

THE IMPLICATIONS OF CONGRESSIONAL AND EXECUTIVE RESPONSE TO CIVIL RIGHTS

In a system where decision makers respond to social problems only under pressure and then typically react incrementally, great unmet needs may be long unperceived and unalleviated. Absence of strife in the system need not be indicative that public wants are being satisfied. It may simply mean that the disadvantaged lack the inclination, resources, or skills necessary to publicize their demands, or that they are being suppressed.[15] Blacks, for example, have obviously been abused for centuries, but have not been in a position to articlate demands to decision makers. In the past blacks may have been relatively quiescent because they had little sense of relative deprivation, had no hope of achieving improvements, or they accepted as just and immutable a pattern that provided for white supremacy.

Though new black awareness and pride have led to the displacement of quiet suffering by strident demands, a conculsion of our analysis, and several others,[16] is that relatively powerless groups, such as civil rights activists, can obtain favorable policies only through social conflict. Petitioning or quiet bargaining is unlikely to net benefits.[17] If low-level plying of decision makers is not a realistic avenue for civil rights groups, the range of productive tactics lies between peaceful demonstrations and insurrection.

If likelihood of acceptance of demands were proportionate to the level of pressure applied, riots would be a more successful technique than peaceful civil disobedience. Such does not always seem to be the case. Nonviolent protest, expecially when countered by a brutal backlash, may bring the injustice protested to the attention of elites, and may evoke sympathy for blacks. Moreover, policy makers, once awakened to the existence of an injustice, may become more sensitive to support among their reference group for the protesters, thereby arriving at a willingness to implement reforms. Passage of the 1964 and 1965 civil rights acts was seemingly facilitated by the violence directed at peaceful protesters in Birmingham and Selma, respectively.

Organized protest activities conducted in hopes of achieving a specific goal are what Lewis Coser would classify as realistic conflict.[18] Spontaneous actions, such as rioting, seem unlikely means of prodding Congress into working for specific civil rights objectives. Because of the unstructured and ad hoc nature of riots, blacks and whites have had different perceptions about the causes and cures of major urban eruptions. A number of studies have found that blacks viewed the major causes of big-city riots to be socioeconomic problems such as discrimination, deprivation, and unemployment.[19] Blacks feel that riots can be ended by alleviating ghetto conditions and discrimination.[20] Whites, however, primarily blame the riots on outside agitators, looters, and other undesirables and feel they can be stopped by more rigorous law enforcement.[21] Congressmen more, closely approximate whites than blacks in assessing causes and palliatives for urban disorders. In a *Congressional Quarterly* survey, only a small number of congressmen (5 percent) felt that the riots were caused by black resentment toward congressional inaction or restrictions on the Great Society program.[22] Most frequently congressmen believed the riots were caused by black irresponsibility, outside agitators, and failures by political institutions other than the Federal government. To prevent future riots most congressmen favored harsher penalties for rioters, larger and better-paid police forces, more emphasis on traditional church and family values, and undefined responses by state and local officials. The majority of congressmen surveyed clearly indicated a desire to avoid substantial social reform.[23]

Thus while urban riots may have permitted some blacks to vent their hostilities, they generally constituted what Coser calls unrealistic conflict.[24] They seem to polarize the races while not accurately communicating black demands. To the extent that urban rioting may have been a causal factor in passing of national civil rights or welfare legislation, the response is best thought of as shots in the dark designed to stop disorders but not to alleviate their causes. It is little wonder that such unsystematic efforts have frequently produced little progress.

The exception to what we have said about riots is that they may be effective means of gaining the attention of local officials. Especially in smaller cities where there is no history of violent protest, an outbreak of violence may quickly produce concessions that negotiations have failed to acquire. Repeated disturbances in the same city seem to reduce their impact even on local decision makers. Unfortunately, local officials cannot normally allocate the funds necessary to deal with serious ghetto problems, but they may be able to undertake useful community activities to alleviate racial problems.

While rioting is seemingly a demand technique marginally successful in terms of achieving specific goals from Congress, it is generally appraised as being useful by blacks. For example, Gary Marx found that an average of 50 percent of the blacks surveyed in five cities North and South believed that riots "do some good because they make whites pay attention to the problems of Negroes."[25] Similarly, in a study of Detroit Aberbach and Walker found that blacks are increasingly losing trust in the American system and that "these expressions of distrust . . . are accompanied by a militant racial ideology and an expressed willingness to resort to almost any means necessary to achieve their goals."[26]

When violence is perceived as a viable means of making demands, and when only crisis is judged capable of eliciting response to racial deprivation, surely therewith is contained a tragic cost and the potential for great instability. While we cannot dismiss the possibility that some participate in riots "for fun and profit,"[27] the fact that numerous blacks perceive rioting as offering policy payoffs indicates not only the frustration prevalent in the ghetto but also disenchantment with peaceful means of expressing grievances. After lying dormant for years black expectations have risen at an accelerated pace. Policy stands which provide largely symbolic benefits, even if initially hailed as victories, soon prove inadequate to satisfy growing appetites. Indeed new laws and decisions often kindle overly optimistic expectations. Discovery of the chasm between reality and anticipation may be instrumental in fueling the frustrations which have burned many cities in recent years.

The implications for future racial progress are ominous. Anything but piecemeal change will have to be gained by confrontation because neither Congress nor the Nixon administration seems committed to working toward social and economic justice for black Americans. Continued delays in civil rights not only deny millions of blacks rights long overdue, but also can easily lead to more violence, increased alienation on both sides, and loss of support for the system by many Americans. This seems to be especially true because substantial numbers of blacks do not seem to be reticent about using violence, and because progress in civil rights seems to be decelerating and polarization worsening.[28] Congress and the executive branch have the means of improving their perception of and response to demands. The effort and the need are long overdue.

NOTES

1. Charles E. Lindblom, "The Science of Muddling Through," *Public Administration Review* 19, Spring 1959, p. 80. See also Martin Meyerson and Edward C. Banfield, *Politics, Planning and the Public Interest,* New York: Free Press, 1955; Thomas R. Dye, *Politics, Economics, and the Public,* Chicago: Rand McNally, 1966; and Ira Sharkansky, *Public Administration,* Chicago: Markham, 1970.

2. Harold C. Fleming, "The Federal Executive and Civil Rights: 1961-1965," in Talcott Parsons and Kenneth B. Clark, eds., *The Negro American,* Boston: Houghton Mifflin, 1965, p. 397.

3. Howard E. Schuman, "Senate Rules and the Civil Rights Bill: A Case Study," *American Political Science Review,* 51, December 1957, pp. 955-975.

4. Thomas R. Dye and L. Harmon Zeigler, *The Irony of Democracy,* Belmont, Calif.: Wadsworth, 1970, p. 1. The discussion of elites which follows is based on the first chapter of this work. The term elite, as used here, simply refers to those who have power.

5. Ibid., p. 6.

6. John Wahlke, "Public Policy and Representative Government: The Roll of the Represented," prepared for the Seventh World Congress of the International Political Science Association, Brussels, Belgium, September 1967; Dye and Zeigler, op. cit., p. 5; and Warren E. Miller and Donald E. Stokes, "Constituency Influence in Congress," *The American Political Science Review,* 57, March 1963, pp. 45-56.

7. Wahlke, op. cit.; Dye and Zeigler, op. cit.; Miller and Stokes, op. cit.

8. Miller and Stokes, op. cit.

9. Dye and Zeigler, op. cit., p. 5.

10. See James Q. Wilson and Edward C. Banfield, "Public Regardingness as a Value Premise in Voting Behavior," *American Political Science Review,* 58, December 1964, pp. 876-887.

11. E. E. Schattschneider, *The Semi-Sovereign People,* New York: Holt, 1960, p. 3.

12. Harold L. Wolman and Norman C. Thomas, "Black Interest, Black Groups, and Black Influence in the Federal Policy Process: The Cases of Housing and Education," *Journal of Politics,* 32, November 1970, p. 894.

13. Ibid., pp. 883-886.

14. Ibid., p. 893.

15. Jack L. Walker, "A Critique of the Elite Theory of Democracy," *American Political Science Review,* 60, June 1966, p. 291.

16. Lewis Killian and Charles Grigg, *Racial Crisis in America: Leadership in Conflict,* Englewood Cliffs, N.J.: Prentice-Hall, 1964; Michael Lipsky, "Protest as a Political Resource," *American Political Science Review,* 62, December 1968, pp. 1144-1158.

17. Lipsky, op. cit., pp. 1144-1159.

18. Lewis. Coser, *The Functions of Social Conflict,* New York: Free Press, 1956, p. 49.
19. Joe R. Feagin and Paul B. Sheatsley, "Ghetto Resident Appraisals of a Riot," *Public Opinion Quarterly,* 32, Fall 1968, p. 354; T. M. Tomlinson and David O. Sears, *Negro Attitudes toward the Riot,* Los Angeles: UCLA Institute of Government and Public Affairs, 1967, p. 13; Angus Campbell and Howard Schuman, "Racial Attitudes in Fifteen American Cities," in *Supplemental Studies for the National Advisory Commission on Civil Disorders,* Washington: GPO, 1968, pp. 47-48; Nathan S. Caplan and Jeffrey M. Paige, "A Study of Ghetto Rioters," *Scientific American,* 219, August 1968, p. 21; and Harlan Hahn and Joe R. Feagin, "Rank-And-File versus Congressional Perceptions of Ghetto Riots," *Social Science Quarterly,* 51, September 1970, pp. 362-365.
20. Hahn and Feagin, op. cit., pp. 368-370.
21. Ibid., pp. 364-365.
22. *Congressional Quarterly Weekly Report,* no. 36, Sept. 8, 1967, p. 1738. This data was reanalyzed by Hahn and Feagin, op. cit., p. 367.
23. Hahn and Feagin, op. cit., p. 372.
24. Coser, op. cit., p. 45.
25. Gary T. Marx, *Protest and Prejudice,* New York: Harper & Row, 1969, p. 32.
26. Joel D. Aberbach and Jack L. Walker, "Political Trust and Racial Ideology," *American Political Science Review,* 64, December 1970, p. 1204.
27. Edward C. Banfield, *The Unheavenly City,* Boston: Little, Brown, 1970, pp. 185-209.
28. See the discussion in Kenneth M. Dolbeare and Murray J. Edelman, *American Politics,* Lexington, Mass.: Heath, 1971, pp. 407-414.

Court Cases Cited

Alexander v. Holmes, 90, 91, 92

Blair v. Knoll Manor, Inc., 159*n.*
Brown v. Board of Education (I)
(1954), 2-4, 12*n.*, 67*n.*, 70, 71,
72, 74, 104, 169, 199
Brown v. Board of Education (II)
(1955), 2-3, 12*n.*, 70, 102
Buchanan v. Warley, 158*n.*
Burton v. Wilmington Parking Authority, 68*n.*

Civil Rights Cases, 59, 62, 67*n.*

Daniel v. Paul, 68*n.*
Dobbins v. Electrical Workers Local 212, 136*n.*
Duval County Board of Public Instruction v. Braxton, 74

Evans v. Newton, 67*n.*

Garner v. Louisiana, 67*n.*, 68*n.*
Gaston County v. United States,
52*n.*
Green v. County School Board, 83
Griffin v. County School Board,
73

Harper v. Virginia State Board of
Elections, 53*n.*
Heart of Atlanta Motel v. United
States, 68*n.*
Heat and Frost Insulators Local
53 v. Vogler, 136*n.*

Jones v. Mayer, 148-149, 159*n.*

Katzenbach v. McClung, 68*n.*

Index